CLASS C

CLASS C

ROBISON

Otis & Orion, L.L.C.

CONTENTS

CONTENTS

CLASS C

Class C is a work of fiction loosely based on my time growing up in southeastern Montana. I never lost a teammate or sister while a high school basketball player, but watched far too many teams go through this during my time in school. Real town locations and public high schools are referenced in this book to keep it grounded in reality in southeastern Montana, but all characters and incidents are from my own imagination or are used fictitiously. Due to my line of work at the time of publishing, I have also made the decision to not publicly identify any places of postsecondary education referenced. While I drew from a plethora of people I grew up around to create these characters, any similarities between characters or incidents are not intended to depict any one person.

First paperback edition December 2022
Otis & Orion, L.L.C.

For my parents

The car still smelled like her. That was the first thing Kennedy noticed when she sat in the driver's seat of her sister's car. Nearly two years had passed since Jessica's death, yet somehow her perfume was as strong as if she had just gotten into the vehicle herself.

Kennedy hadn't planned on coming out and getting into the driver's seat of her sister's car on this day, one of the hardest days she thought she would experience since learning of her sister's death, but she hadn't been able to bring herself to get into her own vehicle until she had performed the sacred tradition, the one her sister had never gotten to do herself. Slowly, she pulled the strings apart on the top of the tassel, making a loop big enough to slip over the rearview mirror. She adjusted the strings, a combination of silver, black, and, a last-minute change to the lineup of class colors, hot pink, until they looked alright. She sat back and stared at the bedazzled "13" that glittered in the dim light of her family's shop, then down at her own class tassel that lay across her lap.

Her class had chosen its class colors the year before in hopes of buying graduation gowns for a cheaper amount and keeping more money for the class's senior trip. Their tassels and robes had appeared months earlier than every other classes, and they were enacting the tradition long before those before them had. Kennedy's tassel hung from her wrist at the moment, a maroon, dark blue, and silver combination. In a few minutes, she would go out to her car and hang it from her own rearview mirror, like her two classmates would likely be doing right now as well.

But first, Jessica was getting her tassel put up.

Kennedy adjusted the tassel again and sighed. It felt wrong to be doing this, but she knew it would feel more wrong had she not taken the time to do it. Jessica was the older sister, the one who was supposed to be doing these traditions first. But now, Kennedy was entering an unknown territory, where her path of life was beginning to advance and pass her sister's.

She reached out and pulled the tassels one last time before pushing the door open and slipping out of the car. She shut the door, the hinges sticking and squeaking as she did so. Jessica's car had been having engine problems the week before her death, and she had parked it in the shop so her dad could see if he could figure out the issue; she had begged him to fix the screeching sound that happened every time the driver's side door opened as well. It was weird to have the car here, still in decent condition, and not have Jessica here.

Kennedy ran her hand down the driver's side of the vehicle. She had once thought this car would be hers when her sister went to college, but the idea of driving it was too painful. Instead, it had been sitting here, taking up space.

Jessica had been driving one of her father's old work trucks when she had rolled into the ditch the night she passed. He was letting her drive it until they fixed her car—it was making a bit of a runny clicking noise, and her mother preferred her driving the larger vehicle on the snowy roads anyhow: she thought it would be "safer." Her mother's sobs when she saw the mangled, twisted vehicle still haunted Kennedy.

All five of the kids had grown up driving the curves that led to their house twenty or so minutes from town. While the town kids were learning to drive at fourteen and fifteen, the Helland siblings had been driving stick shifts up and down the county roads since elementary school. They all knew the roads between their fields and feedlots like the backs of their own hands; perhaps that is what made Jessica's death so hard to comprehend.

"Kennedy?"

She jumped at the sound of her name and tore herself away from her thoughts. Her father was standing at the door to the shop, the early morning light highlighting his silhouette.

"Hey, Dad."

Her father stepped into the dimly lit building, pulling the door shut behind him. "What are you doing, pumpkin?"

She smiled weakly. "Nothing."

Her father made his way across the shop slowly, his boots thudding lightly against the cement. His tall, wiry form never seemed to fit the deep voice that would come from within him when he spoke.

"Nothing, huh?" Silence enveloped the two. "Pretty big day for you to being nothing, the first day of school and all."

He bent down to the little, green car and peered through the uncovered window. Kennedy stood still, watching him study the new mirror decoration. He slowly rose and looked at his second-born daughter and nodded slowly at her. Kennedy gave him another weak smile before reaching over to the thick cloth that normal covered the vehicle and pulling it back over to cover the driver's side of the car.

"I better get going; don't want to be late," she answered.

Her father nodded slowly and then deliberately extended his arm out. Kennedy leaned into his side hug, resting her head into his chest for a moment, before pulling away.

"Love you," she said as she began to make her way across the shop to the closed door. Silence echoed back at her for a moment until her father's deep "Have a good day, honey. Love you, too" hit her just as she got to the door. She pulled it open and then found herself hesitating. She turned around for a last glance and saw that her father was looking at her as well. She raised her hand in a small wave, and her father echoed the gesture as she finally turned away and shut the door fully.

The shop was located just yards away from the family house that was surrounded by hundreds of flowers and a yard so green it seemed almost unreal. Even though the nearest neighbors were miles away, Kennedy's mother took great pride in making sure their yard and house was always neatly kept because "you never knew who was going to stop by"; her husband liked to joke this was a remnant of her days living in town as the mayor's daughter. The yard was always green in the spring and summer, and all the walkways were clear of snow in the winter months. The house, originally an old hospital for the deep countryside, had several renovations added to it over the years, but the country charm remained. Normally the family used the side door off the kitchen, but Kennedy was trying to avoid seeing her mother, Kathy, before she slipped away to class and knew her mother would be in the kitchen.

The thick, wooden door swung open quietly, and Kennedy snuck through the living room. Five pictures hung on the main wall of each of the children along with an oversized family portrait and wall art declaring family "the most important thing in our lives." The family picture was from Hunter's senior year in the fall, making it four years old. The pictures of the kids, though, varied in age. The two oldest brothers, Kris and Hunter, had the senior pictures their mother had liked the most hung in their nice frames up on the wall. Kennedy and the youngest, Jackson, had their school pictures from the most recent school year up. Jessica's was a different story. She and their mother had gone around for weeks trying to decide what senior photo should be displayed for the rest of eternity on the dark blue wall in the middle of the home. Jess had liked a serious-faced, somber image while their mother had wanted a smiling one that Jessica hated. The two ended up ordering both in the correct size from the photographer to fit the frame, only to have Kathy make the final decision over what image would be put up after Jessica's death. The smiling image that Jessica had hated now looked out over the family every time they gathered in the living room and the somber one was hanging next to her room.

The first time Kennedy had seen the new image up, she had stared at it for several minutes before her mother appeared behind her. Kennedy turned to her mother, furious that she had put this image up knowing how much Jessica hated it. The tears were already hot in her eyes when she whipped around at the sound of approaching footsteps and found her mother standing there, tears of her own gleaming in the lighting from above.

"I just want to remember her smiling," she said, choking back tears.

Kennedy's blood was boiling. "She wouldn't be smiling if she saw what you did!" she snapped, before rushing out of the house and leaving on one of the four-wheelers. The two didn't speak for several days after that.

Kennedy's relationship with her mother had always been a little strained, but especially so since her sister's death. Her mother and sister, despite their bickering, had always been very close, their voices easily coming together when speaking. Kennedy, meanwhile, preferred her father's quiet demeanor and silent observations about life. Kathy always seemed a little hurt that she and Kennedy weren't as close as she was with her other daughter, and since Jessica's death, Kathy had made it her goal to develop a closer relationship with Kennedy, which was often overwhelming to her younger daughter, especially since she had closed herself off from so many after her sister's death.

Kennedy snuck through the living room and to the staircase. She cursed herself for not bringing her bag and practice clothing downstairs the night before so that she could just slip out the door and head to town early; last year she had to take Jackson, the youngest Helland sibling, to town and wait for him after practice as well, making her schedule more predictable for her mother to be in the kitchen with breakfast or waiting at the door for her youngest children to get home after practice. This year, though, freedom was all hers and she could come and go as she pleased for the most part, especially after shooting off a text letting her parents know a general time frame that she would be leaving or arriving.

She was halfway up the stairs when her mother called out to her. "Kennedy, is that you?"

Kennedy froze, halfway up the staircase. "Yeah, Mom."

"Oh good," she answered. "Jackson didn't have morning lifting today and I made you both breakfast. You can still eat quick before you have to leave."

Kennedy turned back to look at the foot of the stairs, where her mother stood, looking hopefully up at her daughter.

"Thanks, but I can't. I promised Grace I would pick her up before school."

"Oh," her mother's face immediately fell. "Well, before you go," she said, brightening again, "we need to take our annual first day of school pictures."

Kennedy groaned. "Please, Mom, I really need to get going…"

"It will just take a second," Kathy snapped. She paused for a moment and composed herself. "Go get your stuff and then meet Jackson and me outside."

"Fine," Kennedy snapped back. So much for getting to cruise Main Street with Grace for more than a loop or two, she thought as she pounded up the rest of the stairs and stormed into her room.

Kennedy grabbed her bags from the floor at the foot of the bed and threw them onto her shoulders. She took a look into her mirror by the door. There was a photo of her and her sister taped up in the corner. Kennedy glanced at it.

She had been taller than Jess for years—the two barely even looked related, with her wavy brown hair and pale skin contrasting her older sister's tanned skin and bright blonde hair. The photo was from the summer before she passed away but it seemed like it could have been taken yesterday. They had gone to town to float the irrigation ditch with their friends and were both in cut off shirts and shorts. The only thing that really resembled each other was their bright freckles and green eyes, which you couldn't even see in the photo because of their large sunglasses.

She readjusted the bags on her shoulders and snuck out of her room and downstairs and back out the front door to the flower garden in the yard.

Jackson was already out there, his mop of hair sticking up in several different directions; Kennedy guessed her mother would comment on it in just a few seconds. Their father had joined the party as well, and Kennedy was surprised to see Kris, her oldest brother, was also in the front yard. He lived a about a mile up the road and came by regularly, but it still surprised Kennedy that he had appeared for this occasion.

Immediately, Kathy started directing Kennedy and Jackson as to where to stand. Just like Kennedy had guessed, she told Jackson to fix his hair and repeatedly told Kennedy to stop slouching as she chased the two around the yard with her phone. After a few torturous minutes, her husband finally stepped in and called out, "Kathy, they need to get to school."

"Just one more!" she called back and snapped three more photos before Kris said, "Mom, seriously."

She threw her arms around her youngest children. "Have such a good day, guys." Kennedy froze as she was pulled into the bear hug and then quickly pulled away while Jackson remained for a second more. She nodded at her father and brother as her mother tried once again to smooth out Jackson's hair and began walking to the driveway, where her own car sat. She tossed her things into the backseat and pulled out of the yard before Jackson had even made it to his pickup, her parents and older brother waving her goodbye as she began the trip to town.

Allen Davidson was already worried about the upcoming basketball season, even on the first day of school and four months before the season officially started. Dwindling numbers had limited the team's success the year before, and the current enrollment numbers for the girls in the high school weren't looking good either. Even his own children were no longer on the pine with his younger daughter, MacKenzie, graduating the year prior. He felt in his heart that his own days on the brown metal bleachers in the gym were winding down.

Allen was sitting in his office, tucked into the boys' locker room, in the last minutes before the bell would ring and he would need to go out to the gym for the morning remarks and then to his classroom to begin teaching. He had coached girls' basketball in Hysham for over twenty years, since he was roped into the position his first year of teaching, and this was the first year he was truly panicked about filling a roster during the season. Administrators had already started discussing what was going to happen the next year for sports and a co-op with nearby Custer seemed imminent.

Allen looked over his list of potential players again. Two exchange students had been enrolled in the school, and he had lightly penciled their names, Anna and Julia, under the nine names he had already listed. He stared at the options. Three eighth graders, the two exchange students (and who knew if they had even touched a ball before), two freshman, two sophomores, and two seniors.

He looked at the two senior names. Grace Larkin was a solid player, and he knew that she would be on the floor when practice officially started in November. The other name, Kennedy Helland, was a long shot.

Allen had been one of the first to learn about Jessica's death that fateful morning, nearly two years ago. He remembered reaching for his phone as it rang just hours after the bus got home from an away game, confused as to who would be calling at that time. Scott Helland's name had flashed across the screen, and Allen had immediately felt his heart stop. The two had been friends for years, and Allen had known the minute he saw the name that early that something had happened.

"Scott?" Allen had said. His wife, Marty, had begun to stir beside him, and she rolled over to face her husband, resting her hand lightly on his arm.

"Who is it?" she murmured quietly.

Allen hadn't answered as his friend quietly spoke through the phone to him. "Oh, my God," he said, his voice beginning to shake. Immediately, Marty gripped his arm. "Allen?"

"I'll be there soon," he said, his voice cracking on the last word. He put his phone down on the bedside table once again.

"Allen?" his wife repeated again. "What's happening honey?"

He didn't answer for a minute as he tried to compose himself. "You need to wake up Mac," he finally answered.

"Honey," his wife began.

"Just go get her," her husband answered, his heart pounding in his chest. "She needs to hear this from me before the news spreads."

"Tell me what is going on," Marty had said, her fingers now twisting his shirt.

Silence answered her again, but she waited. Finally, Allen had said the words that changed the lives of the town forever.

"Jessica Helland was killed in a car wreck."

Marty gasped and her hand hit her mouth. Immediately, the tears began falling. "Oh, my God. How? When? You just saw her."

"I know," Allen answered. "We need to tell MacKenzie now. I'm sure Scott has already called others. and Anthony will probably tell his girls as soon as he can, or Denise will—"

"What are we supposed to tell her?" Marty asked as she began to sob. "Oh my God, Kathy. I need to call Kathy."

"Not now," Allen had snapped at his wife the tone of his voice surprising even himself. He sat up in bed and hung his feet of the edge before putting his head in his hands, collecting himself before answering again. "We can't call now." He slowly moved from his position and reached out for his phone. "I need to call Mary-Ann. She needs to be in the loop." Marty reached out and touched his back lightly. He didn't move.

"I don't know what to say to her," she whispered, thinking of her daughter sleeping peacefully in her room, her boxer, Izzy, likely curled at the foot of the bed.

"Just go get her, please," her husband had answered. "We need to tell her."

The emotions from that night were still raw inside Allen. They had brought MacKenzie into the living room, the lights on full blast. He didn't remember what he said to her exactly, just that he was crying while she looked on with sleepy confusion. First, she had denied it, arguing that he didn't know what he was talking about, that they had just been texting before MacKenzie had fallen asleep. Then she was angry, her disbelief bouncing around the walls as she insisted they give her phone, which Marty had slyly grabbed before waking her, back so she could prove that she was right. And then finally the realization that it was nearly 5:30 a.m. and that her parents were not playing some sick joke on her. Her sobs and shrieks of "No" still bounced around his heart sometimes when the memory of that night would seize up inside of him. That day and the days that would follow were his most challenging of his career and he knew it, but the dilemma he was facing now brought back the feelings that he faced and the conversation he knew he needed to have with the other senior girl in this year's graduating class. Kennedy would be in his government class the second to last period of the day. It was time for the two of them to have a chat.

Grace waited outside her house impatiently for Kennedy's car to turn the corner. She only lived two blocks from the school, and her parents wouldn't let her take their car in the morning, even for a cruise. So, she depended on Kennedy to allow her to enjoy the tradition of "cruising Main" most days and nights.

She checked her phone again. Kennedy had sent a text about fifteen minutes ago, which meant that she should be arriving any moment. Normally, Grace was the one running late in the morning and Kennedy was waiting outside for her to come rolling out, half awake and blurry eyed. Grace wondered why she had gotten such a late start in the morning—probably something to do with her mom. Grace had known Kennedy since kindergarten and knew everything about the strained relationship between the two. Sometimes, Grace wondered if they would ever repair the broken bond; she had a better relationship with her stepmother than those two had. She tried to just be a listening ear when Kennedy felt the need to go off on the struggles the two had.

The silver car slowly came around the corner, and Kennedy waved as she pulled up in front of the house on the corner. Grace darted out and flung the door open, shoving her backpack onto the ground and she swung into the front seat. "What took you so long?"

"Mom stuff," Kennedy answered as she pulled forward. She glanced at her friend. "Seatbelt."

"Oh, come on, we're just in town," Grace complained. Kennedy slammed on the brakes and whipped her head to the side to look at Grace, her brow furrowing.

Grace sighed. "Fine, I'm sorry." She glanced at the auxiliary cord plugged into the radio and gestured at it as Kennedy began to drive again. "May I?"

Kennedy often drove in silence, which drove Grace crazy. She always needed background sounds to get anything done; if it was too quiet, she couldn't concentrate on anything. Kennedy, meanwhile, seemed to thrive in the silence. The combination of introverted and extroverted personalities and the mutual respect the two usually had for each other was probably what allowed their friendship to last for so long.

Grace hooked her phone up to the car speakers and immediately the volleyball playlist the two had spent hours creating began filling the speakers.

The two went through the "loop," as the most typical town-cruising path was usually called, with their windows rolled down, waving at the other students who were also driving along the pothole-ridden roads. The crumbling streets were often the brunt of a joke between the town people, with the running joke being the sober drivers swerved to miss the gaps in the road and the drunks drove straight through them. Year after year, it seemed like the same divots in the road would appear and disguise themselves as puddles, no matter how often they were filled; the novice drivers of the community and visitors would often hit these at full speed, and a sickening scraping sound usually followed as the bottom of their cars dragged along the ground.

Grace sang along to the soundtrack of their senior year, her voice floating out of the window; Kennedy kept her eyes on the road and her hands on the wheel, only lifting two fingers to wave at their fellow students and those out in their front yards in the early August morning. Their drive wasn't as long as it normally was because of Kennedy's late start, and before the two girls knew it, they needed to pull into the half-oval parking lot next to the only public school in the county.

Grace pulled the cord out of her phone and sighed as she opened the door of the vehicle. "Do we have to go back?"

Kennedy got out and reached into the backseat to pull out her own bags. "Wouldn't you rather get it over with?"

"I'd rather skip this part and just hit up college," Grace answered. "New town, new people..." she looked back at Kennedy and wiggled her eyebrows. "...New boys."

"Shut up," Kennedy said, turning bright red.

Grace sighed and rolled her eyes. "Someday you'll start dating, Kenna. And then you'll get it." Kennedy blushed but did not respond. Grace was always the one of the two to go on dates, dragging Kenna along for her to meet her latest's friends. She had also found Kennedy a date to every dance they had ever gone to.

The two walked up to the huddle of girls on the volleyball team. Twelve girls were out for the season, and there was enough to suit a varsity and a junior varsity for the first time in several years. Volleyball had been the sport of choice in the school for the last couple of years, following a back-to-back state run, and all the girls in the high school participated in the sport, unlike basketball, which Grace knew was going to be hurting for numbers this year following the graduation of four players last year. She was trying not to think about it at the moment, though Coach Davidson had already mentioned to her that it might be a rough season if she didn't recruit some of the others to play.

She already knew that by "some of the others" he meant Kennedy, and she was struggling to figure out how to bring up the request to her friend.

The girls snapped a few pictures of their group as the morning bell rang, and slowly the student population gathered outside moved into the gym.

Greg Johnson was retiring at the end of the year. He had put over forty years in at the district, and the school board was driving him up the wall. Only his wife knew that this would be his last year, and he was trying to keep it under wraps for the time being, which meant that the first day of school was business as usual. The first bell had just rung, and he stood up from behind his desk, shuffling his notes for the morning assembly, the only one that would be held in the gym. The knock came at his door and he looked up to see Allen Davidson peering through the windows to the side.

"Come in," Greg said. "What can I do you for, Allen?" he asked as the history teacher opened the door.

"Morning, sir," Allen said. "Just checking to see what the numbers looked like today for enrollment."

Greg looked up from his notes. "Didn't we just go over this yesterday, Allen?"

Allen nodded slowly and shrugged, sticking his hands in his pockets. "Just trying to make a game plan."

The principal sighed. "Honestly, Allen, the first day of practice is still months away. Don't let this worry you too much."

The basketball coach looked at his boss and longtime colleague, who had since become a friend. "I know. It's just not like anything we've had to experience before, having this low of numbers."

"I'm afraid it will likely not be the only time we face it if we don't come to an agreement about a cooperative," Greg answered. He made his way to the door, and Allen followed him into the front office. "I won't lie," he said as the two began walking to the gym, "this will likely be the last year of us being Pirates. The board wants to save some money, and I can't keep fighting this if we can't keep the numbers up."

Allen felt his heart sink. "Which is why it is so important to me that we have a successful season this year," he answered. The two were now at the door to the gym. He glanced up to the "Beware all ye who enter here" sign that was made in a shop class long ago and marked the entrance to the gym.

Greg clapped the slightly younger man on the back. "It'll all work out. Don't fret yet."

He moved onto the gym floor and the students, buzzing in the bleachers, immediately quieted. Allen slipped in after him and lined against the south wall with the other staff members. He scanned the audience. Kennedy was sitting in the top corner of the bleachers, Grace next to her.

There was an option that he hoped would work out already present in the room. It was time for Kennedy to get back into the paint.

Kennedy hadn't touched a basketball since her sister's death. At least not in public. Not even Grace knew about the ball she kept tucked under her bed, only taking the time to shoot it when she was home alone on the ranch. Many memories had been spent in their shop where their dad had hung a hoop so his kids could play every day growing up, no matter what the weather outside was like, and she had felt herself called to it time and time again to clear her head. Being in the school gym, meanwhile, was a different story.

Being in the gym was always a little uncomfortable for Kennedy since her sister's passing just because of all the memories that floated around in it. There were her brothers' senior nights, hundreds of practices and open gyms, laughter and sweat and tears... then there was the funeral, the white coffin on a stage under the north hoop, the overflowing amount of people, more people than had ever been in the space before. There was her sister's senior night, where her family walked out without their senior player, a picture frame tightly clasped in her mother's hands that was now being honored instead of an actual person.

Quitting volleyball had never crossed Kennedy's mind. While she had memories of playing with her sister, it was nothing like the memories of basketball and of her sister coaching her through the movements over the years. Jessica was an all-state selection her sophomore and junior years and was posthumously honored her senior year as well. She could see the court like no one else could, and she almost danced around, avoiding defenders and becoming a threat no matter where she was.

She so badly wanted Kennedy to be as good as she was; the two would spend extra time in the gym, practicing dribbling and shooting. Even though Kennedy wasn't the player her older sister was, she tried and was finally getting to see time on the court with her sister in the weeks prior to her death as the sixth man, moving up in front of some of the older classmen on the bench. Sadie McCallister, a then-starting junior, had been injured the last game that the two played together, hours before her death, and Jessica had excitedly whispered that the two were finally going to start together when they got back onto the bus that night to head home post-game.

"Are you sure?" Kennedy had asked, her heart jumping slightly in her chest.

"It's not good, they're taking her to Billings tomorrow for x-rays," Jessica had answered. She quickly added, "I feel horrible of course but, oh, my gosh, can you imagine both of us being announced as starters next weekend?"

Yet in some twist of fate, Sadie only suffered a minor ankle sprain and finished starting the season, Kennedy didn't get her name announced because she couldn't bring herself to dress out, and Jessica had never stepped on the court again.

Principal Johnson began talking and pulled Kennedy back to the first day of her own senior year. She realized she had been digging her nails into her pants and quickly relaxed her hands. She glanced around. No one seemed to have noticed her reaction, and she felt herself relax fully. Her anxiety had gone down a lot lately, and the full-born attacks she had been having the past two years had faded greatly over the summer.

"Good morning, Pirates!" Principal Johnson called out from the center of the gym. When Kennedy had been in junior high, there used to be sixty students in the room for his first day of school speech. The number had dwindled down to just over twenty-five in six short years, and she realized how ridiculous it was to be having the meeting in the gym in the first place.

"Welcome to another exciting year at Hysham Schools. We have a few new additions to our staff this year…" he continued on, and Kennedy felt herself slipping away into her thoughts again. She wondered what they would be doing at practice that day—their volleyball coach had been running them hard the last few days, and her muscles were pretty sore. She was hoping they would get a break and maybe get to scrimmage for a bit with games coming up that weekend finally.

Kennedy scanned the teachers along the wall. Mrs. Kiefer, the varsity volleyball coach, was near the end of the line, whispering back and forth with Ms. O'Brien; Kennedy tried to make eye contact with her. but the two seemed too involved in their conversation to notice Kennedy's intense gaze. Slowly, she took in the other teachers in the line. Most of them had been in the district for years and were friends with her parents and had known her since she was in just a toddler whose entire world was the ranch. There were a couple of young, new faces: the business teacher and the special education teacher. Mr. Bailey was back for another year, as was Mrs. Lambert. Her husband, Mr. Lambert, was nodding enthusiastically alone with Mr. Johnson's comments.

Kennedy's eyes slid to the door and there Coach—no, Mr. Davidson… he wasn't her coach anymore—stood, looking right at her.

They made eye contact, and Kennedy pursed her lips. They held the gaze for a moment before she looked away. She already knew what was going to happen during seventh period today, when she got to his government class.

He was going to ask her to play basketball. And she was absolutely going to refuse.

2

Each class left the gym individually to go meet with their class advisors, starting with the seventh grade. As the junior class left the gym, Principal Johnson turned to the three seniors in attendance. Grace looked over at Paul, who had been sitting with the rest of the football team on the opposite end of the bleachers. He looked back at her but didn't rise to come sit by the two girls at the top of the rows.

"Well," Principal Johnson said, stopping to clear his throat. He glanced at his papers for a moment before folding them and tucking them into the back pocket of his slacks. "Are you all ready for your final year?"

Kennedy and Grace stole a glance, and Grace quickly covered her face with her hands to keep from laughing. Principal Johnson was known for the awkward speeches that he would give to the senior class from time to time during the year, with topics usually about the "life after your formal education" or, his most well-known in the spring, "just get your work done and please don't put a live goose in my car again."

The girls nodded their heads and Paul must have as well because Principal Johnson began to talk about how their class would be small but mighty and how he expected great things from the group in their final year of school. "I hope," he began, "that this will be another eventful year for your class. The volleyball team seems to be in excellent shape for another run to divisionals and perhaps back on to state, and Coach Melvin tells me the football team is looking solid." He looked at the three students, and his normally professional appearance relaxed a little. He had known these kids since they were in elementary school and had watched them grow up. While graduation was still a few months away, watching seniors leave was always hard. "I hope you all enjoy it while it lasts. Soon we will be back in here getting ready for your graduation."

The three students looked at him quietly. The group sat in silence for a moments before Johnson collected himself. "You're all free to go with Mr. Lambert to discuss your schedules now. Have a great day."

The group met in the library, and their official schedules were handed out, though they already knew the classes and their teachers. They had all basically known their entire schedule for four years since they were freshman and the novelty of getting locker assignments had worn off long ago. Kennedy listened to Mr. Lambert, the athletic director, school counselor, and the all-school PE teacher, talk about some of the events the group would be in charge of running in the coming months. There was the homecoming pep rally and bonfire that their class would lead, and then they would need to start planning for graduation near the end of the semester. "Though," he added, "your colors are already taken care of, so there is that."

Mr. Lambert knew the group in front of him had their schedule down pat—not much had changed in Hysham in the last few years— and spent the rest of the period talking to them about how their summers were. His daughter, Natalie, had been in Jessica's class as well, and he told the girls about the trip she and his wife had taken over the break before talking to Paul about the football season. Finally, the bell rang and the girls shuffled off to first period while Paul shrugged his letterman's jacket back on and continued to talk to Mr. Lambert in the library.

The next few periods passed by in a blur. Their teachers all knew them, and they spent time catching up and discussing their future plans, as well as the projects they would have in the upcoming year. Mrs. Jentz and the seniors had a discussion at length about the FFA and the future of the chapter for the year during second period; Grace and Kennedy sighed at the complex chemistry notes that Mrs. Kiefer had already penned on the board for the combined junior and senior science class.

The day flew by, with Paul joining Grace and Kennedy off-and-on with his slightly different schedule. At lunch, all of the high school girls sat together and talked about practice and the season-opening tournament they would be attending the next weekend. The boys nearly started a scrimmage across the room, throwing a container of milk around until Mr. Lambert told them to stop being knuckleheads.

Back in Ms. O'Brien's room, the small drama and creative writing class did an activity, and the already shortened period flew by. Before she knew it, the bell for seventh period was ringing, and Kennedy felt her heart seize up in her chest. Grace began to gather her things and head to the room directly across the hall; Kennedy slowly gathered her own materials and said she would see Ms. O'Brien in a bit. Slowly, she slid across the hall.

Allen looked up from the papers he was shuffling as Kennedy entered the room; she pursed her lips at him again as she went to sit next to Grace, who glanced at Allen before she started whispering to Kennedy.

Allen had always given Kennedy the space she needed after what had happened—he had never questioned her decision to not dress out again at the end of that season and hadn't pressured her to step on the court again last season. But he was getting a little desperate... and so were her parents.

Scott had called Allen the week before and explained that he and Kathy were worried about Kennedy. While she seemed to be doing okay, there was still a lot of tension in their house, her father had explained, and they weren't sure what to do about it. Kennedy had grown up in the gym, which Allen was well aware of, and now she could barely be in the school if there was a game going on. "I don't want to force her," her father had said, "...but...we don't want her to regret it in five, ten years." He had hesitated before noting the last part. "She's been shooting around last two years. She doesn't know we know—she hides the ball in her room."

Allen had listened to his friend, who normally stayed out of the realm of coaching since his kids had started school. He knew what Scott was asking him to do though. He was asking him to be the bridge that her parents couldn't be, the one who picks up the player after they fall from grace, the disciplinarian that a child would willingly listen to... he wanted him to be her coach.

Allen had told Scott he would talk to Kennedy. It was a decision that he was dreading but also one that was getting his hopes up again. Would she play? Would they have enough for subs during a game? Could it be the year that basketball became a star in the community's eyes again?

Allen casually flipped through his syllabus with the three students in the class before launching into the first chapter of the book. He knew none of the other teachers would be likely to assign homework that first day, but the government books were notoriously hard, and he wanted to get an early start on them. First, he would bring them back to the beginning of their junior year, when they learned about the foundations of their government from a historical perspective. Then, he would shift into teaching about the actual process of government and its modern-day practices.

Before he knew it, the bell was getting ready to ring. He looked at the stack of extra books he had brought down from the supply closet, partially in a desperate hope the class size would triple and partially because he knew he couldn't carry them all back alone, and slowly cleared his throat as the long buzz filled the room.

"Kennedy," he said casually, "care to help me carry these down to the office?"

She looked at him, her light brown bun flopping around as she turned. Her mouth was a thin line. "Sure, Mr. Davidson."

Grace sped out of the room as the bell rang, solidifying what Kennedy already knew: she was involved in the process of recruiting Kennedy for the team. She also suspected her parents were involved, based on the comments her father and older brother had made about pickup games the last few weeks. Her mother was a little more forward, point-blank asking her if she had thought about playing. Subtly was not her strong suit.

She went and gathered the small stack of books that Mr. Davidson handed her and headed out the door. Davidson cheerfully told Ms. O'Brien that she was going to be a few minutes late, they "just needed to get these down to the front or they would sit on the counter all year." Ms. O'Brien nodded and began talking to Mrs. Lambert again as the junior high and high school students rushed to where they needed to be.

Kennedy walked silently alongside Mr. Davidson. Slowly, the halls quieted, and, as the last junior high student rushed into the band and choir room, the bell rang. Mr. Davidson slowed his pace, and Kennedy felt herself slow too, though all she wanted to do was bolt.

"So, Kennedy," he said, adjusting the weight of the stack of textbooks in his arm. "How was your summer?"

"Alright," Kennedy answered in a monotone voice. Allen, as she called him in the summer months, when he was her dad's best friend who drank a beer in the heat of June in their garage, had just had dinner with his wife and the Helland family. He knew how she was.

Mr. Davidson nodded. "Yes, dinner was great the other weekend," he answered. "Your mom makes the best potato salad."

The hallway seemed to be getting longer and longer, and Kennedy wondered if they would ever make it to the front office or if she would spend eternity walking through the dim overhead lights while her flip flops slapped on the dingy tiles.

Mr. Davidson cleared his throat, "You know, Kennedy... grief is a weird thing."

Kennedy's heart leapt in her chest. She hated that word, the word everyone used around her—grieving. She was fine.

"Your parents, your friends, the town... we're all worried about you," he continued. "Hiding from your fears isn't the way to deal with this and Jessica would want—"

"I don't care what Jess would want!" Kennedy snapped, her temper flaring. Mr. Davidson didn't answer. And the two walked in silence for a moment. Kennedy felt herself calm a little, and she added, "I've never liked basketball. My not playing has nothing to do with Jessica or her death. I don't like it and I never have and I would rather do things I enjoy all winter."

Mr. Davidson once again didn't answer as the two rounded out the corner by the office and Evelyn, the school secretary, popped up from her desk. "Putting these back in storage?" she asked cheerfully. Mr. Davidson nodded. "Didn't get the influx of students I was hoping for again," he answered, and Evelyn giggled. "Never works out that way." She looked at Kennedy and smiled. "Oh, honey, thank you for helping him with these, but I can help him put them back in storage. Get back to class."

Kennedy looked at Mr. Davidson, and he nodded at her. "Have a good day," she said as she turned to go back to Ms. O'Brien's room.

Grace immediately knew that the conversation had not gone well and that Kennedy was not happy with her. She sat near Grace but didn't talk to her friend as they worked on brainstorming ideas for the yearbook theme. Instead, she pushed her headphones in and made her own list of themes. Grace respected her space and didn't say anything until the two headed to their lockers at the final bell.

"So, did Coach talk to you?" she asked timidly as Kennedy pulled her volleyball bag out of her locker.

"About how everyone is worried about me?" she snapped back and slammed her locked door. "Yeah, he did. And I'm fine."

"Kenna," Grace began, but her friend whipped around and stormed off to the gym, her locker slamming shut behind her. Grace followed along, starting a conversation with one of the sophomores as they made it to the locker room. Kennedy changed immediately and didn't stay to gossip with the other girls, and by the time Grace emerged, she had found a junior to warm up with. The girls didn't talk the rest of the practice as Kennedy would immediately begin talking to Coach Kiefer when they took a break. It wasn't until the final ball was picked up that Grace finally got a chance to talk to her friend.

Grace went and sat next to her friend as she slid her shoes and kneepads off. "Kennedy, please listen," she started. Kennedy went to turn away, and Grace quickly put her hand on her arm. She knew that Kennedy hated being touched, but it was the only way she knew she would stop and listen. "I'm not worried about you, but I think it's odd you are refusing to play a game that you loved for so long and... I miss having you on the trips with us. Will you please reconsider?"

Kennedy didn't move, and Grace continued to sit on the hardwood floor, her hand resting against her friend's arm.

Finally, Kennedy turned and looked at her. "I hated basketball," she answered. "I never liked it. and I only played because my parents made me. Now that they aren't, I'm not playing." She looked away from her friend. "Please don't ask me again," she said wearily.

Grace removed her hand and her friend went to stand. "Okay," Grace said meekly. "I won't ask again."

Kennedy strolled off to the locker room, and Grace slowly removed her own shoes and rose, plodding along after her.

3

Kennedy took Grace home but didn't speak to her in the car. Normally she would stay at her house for a while before heading home, but she was still furious with her friend. The Hysham Hills that framed the town and county were in the distance and growing as she continued on the road, her thoughts swirling around in her mind.

Normally, the silence she had on the car ride home was a welcome time for her to collect her thoughts and relax after a day of being around people, but at the moment, it was all a little too much. Grace's meddling, the conversation with Mr. Davidson, her parents' worrying, the relationship with her mother, her hanging the tassel from Jessica's rearview mirror... she felt herself reaching for her radio and clicking it on the first preset station.

Immediately, a radio station out of Billings, filled the car. The DJ's deep voice was talking about upcoming events in the largest city in the state. Kennedy relaxed some as the host and a couple of guests chatted about a concert that was coming up with a somewhat well-known country artist. It was going to be out at the zoo, a popular venue.

Listening to the DJ talk about the outdoor show brought back the memories of standing on the road during a street dance, listening to a local band. She missed those days and nights of laughing along with her sister and Jessica talking about how excited she was to go to non-country concerts in bigger venues when she made it to college the next year in Seattle. A few places around the state had offered her scholarships for basketball, but a family trip to the Pacific Northwest before her senior year had made her happy—a kind of happy none of them had ever seen on her before. She loved the feel of the culture, the rainy days, and the idea of living in a big city. Sometimes, Kennedy wondered how Jessica had lived in a small town in eastern Montana for so long with such a big personality—she just fit into the city life so much better.

Jess was the one who would pull you onto the street to dance at those concerts, who flirted with the new hired hands in town, flipping her long blonde hair around as she shot the young men sly smiles, who never judged but embraced everyone and their differences. She was a wild spirit who some people were overwhelmed by, but she didn't ever seem to care. Sometimes, Kennedy wondered how she was related to her older sister, with her quiet demeanor. Jessica was not one to shy away from a conversation, no matter how difficult the topic; Kennedy would rather have hidden away then addressed something head on.

Kennedy left the station on the rest of the drive home. The day had been a rare occurrence of her showing emotions in day-to-day life. The one similarity that she and Jessica had personality-wise was they both had worn their hearts on their sleeves, even if Jessica presented hers more readily than Kennedy did growing up. They both felt the world in not only black and white, but shades of grey. They both felt every emotion, though Jessica always seemed to feel the positive ones more while Kennedy felt the darker shade.

The days following Jessica's death were hard, as was to be expected. There was the moment Kennedy found out, the shock and disbelief that filled her soul when her mother's screams of agony had woken her up. Her own overwhelming urge to drop and scream; she had fallen to the kitchen floor beside her, but no sound came out, no matter how hard she tried to force it to. The alternating anger at night and the sadness during the day alongside the denial that cropped up when she least expected it had been hard those first few days. Then, the day of the funeral, the numbness that filled her. The stoic face she held as the priest spoke, as Jessica's friends and classmates shared stories, as her coaches remembered her and the traits of leadership and athletics she held on and off the court, and the members of the community recalled watching her grow up as they all sat in the high school gym. No emotions came through her.

To be honest, no emotions really had since then. Kennedy had been living mainly in a fog for the last year-and-a-half. Sure, there were times when anger or sadness would escape her, but for the most part she kept those pesky feelings neatly filed away in the back of her mind, tucked between the memories she didn't want to relive.

For nearly two years, Kennedy had kept her feelings in check, whether she was around her friends or family members. Her parents still made her attend therapy once a month, and she knew her therapist had voiced concerns to her parents. Her mother, in turn, would appear randomly and ask her daughter "how she was" and if she "wanted to talk." Kennedy would always say she was "fine" and excuse herself from the conversation her mother was cornering her into. Her mother was the one who normally was meddling, calling her teachers and talking to her friends. But she wasn't the one who had driven the conversation with Mr. Davidson today. Her father was the culprit here.

Her dad never wanted his children to live in fear. For as long as even his oldest, Kris, could remember, he had helped his kids overcome what scared them the most. If they were thrown off the four-wheeler, he would pick them up and dust them off and put them back on it the next day. The second oldest, Hunter, was known for throwing the ball away on the football field when he started playing because he was scared of getting tackled and hurt; her father took him out to the shop, where he had piled mats, and would knock him over again and again until her longer flinched when he was hit.

Scott had used a similar tactic with Jessica when she was afraid of driving into the paint. Jess had been knocked down hard her freshman year of basketball going up for a layup. She had the wind knocked out of her and couldn't catch her breath. Coach Davidson helped her off the court and set her on the end of the bench so she could calm down some, thinking that would be the end of that, but the fear clutched Jessica for the remainder of the season. She would change the plays that were being called and would refuse to drive the ball. Coach and her father had discussed her timidity after the season ended and her father got involved. That summer, he would be in the shop with Jessica, telling her to drive the ball. At first, he would just put an arm up in her face, making her lunge to the side. Slowly, they progressed until her father was swatting at her, jamming into her, and knocking the ball out of her hands. They worked on posting up, on getting physical both on offense and on defense. By the start of her sophomore season, Jessica had become a driving force on the basketball team both literally and figuratively. The next three years of her high school basketball career were marked by her fearlessness inside the paint and her ability to body up with players that were half-a-foot taller than her.

Her father's encouragement to get back to the court was his way of helping Kennedy "get over" what was bothering her, but Kennedy was still against what he was trying to do. He was the one who dealt with problems one-on-one, yet now he was bringing Allen into it, and it frustrated her; this was the same issue she had with her mom. Nothing ever felt like it was actually just between them.

Kennedy turned onto the gravel road—Helland Lane—that would take her back to the ranch. Her mother would probably be in the kitchen, finishing dinner. Her father would be in from checking on the cows and the fields; Kris would likely tag along with him for dinner with the family. He lived alone, and his mom always had more than enough food. She was still used to cooking for seven rather than four. Jackson would roll in soon and start eating out of the pan or bowls that her mother would be setting on the table in the kitchen. Kennedy would go in the kitchen door and her mother would ask her how her day was while her father slipped out of the room. Kennedy would slide past her mother, saying she had homework already—yes, already, even on the first day—and bolt herself into her room until Jackson would come and knock on the door and tell her to come eat.

Kennedy slowly turned on the side road that would take her to the main house: Fort Orchard Circle. The sun was just starting to set and the lights in the house were burning brightly. Kris's work truck was sitting in the lot beside the house, and Kennedy sighed, thankful someone else would be there to distract her mother. She pulled into her spot beside the house next to her oldest brother's vehicle. Her father's pickup was parked near the shop door, along with a few other vehicles. One looked like Allen Davidson's.

Kennedy cut the engine of the vehicle and pulled her stuff out of the car. She lugged her bags onto her shoulders and stomped up the side steps. The smell of tacos hit her before she even made it to the top step, and her stomach growled in anticipation. For all her mother's pitfalls, her cooking was never something Kennedy complained about.

She opened the door and braced herself for her mother's questions but, as the door swung open, was met with silence.

Kennedy peered around the kitchen curiously. A bottle of beer was sitting on the kitchen table and a chair had been pulled out, but the room was empty. She kicked her shoes off in confusion and shifted her bags. Otis, one of the family dogs, trotted in, and Kennedy dropped down to greet the old, black lab. "Hey, boy," she said, burying her face into his fur. "How are you doing today?" He panted in her ear, and she laughed.

"Oh!" The surprised voice said from the doorway. Kennedy looked up. "I didn't hear you come in, honey." Her mother was wearing jeans and a loose tank top, a glass of wine in her hand. Kennedy slowly rose from the dog.

"I just did," she answered, feeling herself begin to close herself off.

"We have company," her mother answered. A laugh floated into the kitchen like an exclamation point to her comment. "I was just grabbing more wine." She moved across the room to the sink where two bottles were sitting in a bowl of ice. "They're staying for dinner. Why don't you go say 'hi' to everyone in the living room before you go shower?"

Kennedy raised her eyebrows. Whoever was in there must be a big deal.

Her mother grabbed the bottles, and Kennedy followed her out of the kitchen. Now, she heard more murmurings from the dining room and living room area. Her mother slipped into inside the doorway, and Kennedy turned the corner.

The first thing she saw was Hunter, her second oldest brother; immediately, her face broke out into a grin. She dropped her bags and rushed across the room and threw her arms around him. He was laughing and put one arm around her into the traditional side hug of the Helland family. He was thinner than Kris and favored their father both in appearance and often behavior, as she did—tall, and lanky—though he, like Jessica, had more of their mother's confrontational personality. He was the one with her mother's natural, dark hair as well, and a smattering of freckles like his sisters that often made him look younger than he was. He smelled good, and as Kennedy buried her face into his shoulder, she realized he was wearing the cologne that Kennedy and Jess always used to buy him for Christmas.

"What are you doing here?" she asked, pulling away enough that she could look into his face. Hunter had been living in Denver for an internship over the summer months and hadn't been home since early May. She had thought, based on their conversations, that he wouldn't come home until his fall break from college once he returned to Spokane, so seeing him here was a bit of a shock.

Hunter dropped his arm away from her and gave her a crooked grin. "Well," he said, "I have some news for you all." He picked his Coors Light up from the table and took a swig.

"Not yet, not yet," her mother chided from across the room. "Your grandparents haven't arrived yet." She noticed her daughter still in the room. "Kennedy, run up and shower and then we can all sit down."

Kennedy resisted the urge to roll her eyes and threw her arms around Hunter again. He returned her embrace with another side hug before striking up a conversation with Coach Davidson, who had appeared as if from nowhere, and a couple of the other local ranchers. Kennedy felt her anger return a bit, and she quickly stepped away. It wasn't surprising that he was here with how close his family was to hers, but the conversation from earlier in the day was still fresh in her mind, and she wasn't ready to move past it quite yet. She looked around and saw Kris and her father deep in conversation nearby and her mother was visiting with Allen's wife Marty. Their cheeks were both flushed. and each loosely held a glass of wine as they conversed. Her mother and Marty had been friends for years—they were the backbones of the friendship between their husbands and children. While their husbands were content to sit in silence, however, the two women were known for their constant chattering, regardless if they had seen each other all day or two weeks previously. A few of Hunter's friends who hadn't gone to school or who had returned with degrees to work on their family farms and ranches were also milling around the room, chatting with his two high school coaches in attendance. She guessed that the football coaches were likely on their way out now, along with Jackson. Whatever was happening was going to be a big deal.

She dipped out of the room and headed for the stairwell. Suddenly, though, someone else was in the staircase, and Kennedy's cheeks flushed bright red.

Adam's smile, as he realized who was walking up toward him, warmed her from her head to her toes. and Kennedy quickly looked away, hoping it maybe looked like she was still winded from working out at practice.

"Hi," she said, looking anywhere but at him.

"Hey," he answered.

The two stood at the foot of the stairway for a moment before he held open his arms and she fell into them. He pressed his lips to her hair, and she smiled into his chest. For a moment, she forgot that she was covered in a thin layer of died sweat and her anger at her parents and her former coach as she felt his heartbeat under his t-shirt, his arms around her.

Just as quickly as they embraced, they pulled apart. "What are you doing here?" she asked finally making eye contact with his piercing, blue gaze.

"Couldn't miss the big news," he answered, his grin still resting on his face, "and I never say no to a trip to the ranch.

Her face turned scarlet again, and she looked away. She saw his hand come up, almost as if he was going to reach out and pull her in again, when suddenly he froze and drew his hand back.

"Hey, sport," he said lazily to Jackson, who had just started up the stairs behind them. Kennedy turned as her little brother walked up and shook Adam's hand. Her heart panged—when did he get that old? And she made eye contact with the man in front of her again. "Shower," she murmured and slid past the two and up the stairs to her bathroom.

She pulled her practice clothes off and slid into the scalding water, her skin reddening once again, but this time only from the temperature. As she washed her hair, she thought about how Adam's lips had felt pressed against it, and her thoughts drifted to him and their relationship.

She had first met him when she was a seventh grader. He was escorting Jess to her freshman prom and he had just shown up to take her to town. He was younger, his black hair longer, and his shoulders not as broad.

The two had been posing for photos on the front law with a group of other Hysham High schoolers. He was from Terry, over two hours up the road, only a year older than Jess, and a friend of Hunter's: a sophomore who played all three sports and who had done extraordinarily well at track his freshman year. Jess and her mother had spent nights giggling in excitement that he had agreed to go to prom with her (much to Hunter's annoyance). The two went dress shopping several different times until they found one that, according to Jess, "perfectly matched his eyes."

So began the trips back and forth to Terry between Jess and Adam, the late-night phone calls that Kennedy would sometimes hear through the wall, and the flowers that would occasionally be delivered to the school or basketball games. For over two years, until right before Adam left for college, the two were high school sweethearts who spent every minute together that they could, despite over a hundred miles in between them.

Kennedy had known something was up when she came down for breakfast the morning after they broke up. Jess had been sitting at the table, eyes red and swollen. Hunter was home still, and he was sitting with her in silence. Kennedy's heart had seized in her chest, and immediately she had asked what had happened. Jess's head had drooped in response. Hunter had looked at her sadly before turning to Kennedy and mouthing "broke up" and making a "breaking heart" emotion with his hands. Kathy flittered in asking if anyone wanted to get off of the ranch for the day and, when met with silence, filled the void by proclaiming it a "girls' day!" in Billings.

Jess's usually bubbly personality didn't appear on the trip. Instead, for the first time Kennedy could ever remember, the car ride to town was mainly in silence. Occasionally, Kathy would say something, but neither daughter would respond. When they got home that night, Jess went straight to her room and shut the door.

For several days, she rarely emerged from her room. Kennedy's worry grew for her—normally she was the one who spent all her time locked away in her room. It wasn't like Jess to act this way. At the same time, a hatred began to fester in Kennedy's heart for the person who hurt her sister in this way. Adam, who for two years Kennedy had viewed as a fun guy to be around and tag along with, suddenly became everything wrong with the male population: he was too clingy, too possessive; he only cared about appearance; he was sleazy; he broke girls' hearts. None of this was founded on much, of course, since Jess wasn't talking. But in Kennedy's head, Adam was the root of her pain.

The hatred continued to grow for him, even after Jess emerged from her room and life returned to normal. Hunter and Adam, who had become close over the years, remained good friends, and Adam's name would occasionally come up in conversation, which angered Kennedy; she couldn't believe not only Hunter, but her parents, other brothers, and even her sister, could still talk to him even after what happened between Jess and him.

Adam was going to school in Spokane, Washington, like Hunter, the two would take turns driving home for breaks, and Adam would sometimes stay with the family. Kennedy would join Hunter, Adam, and Jess, along with anyone else who made the trek out to the ranch, at the firepit in their yard. At first, Jess and Adam would keep away from each other, talking exclusively to their respective friend groups. But slowly, they would be brought back together like magnets.

Kennedy didn't understand what was happening in front of her. Adam had brought Jess so much pain just months before: how was she able to forgive him and laugh with him again?

The last night the two had spent together came at the beginning of January, just after the New Year. Adam and Hunter were to return to school in a few days and Adam would be leaving to spend time with his family before he returned to Spokane with Hunter. The girls had won their basketball game the night before, upsetting Ekalaka, the top-ranked team in the conference, and the entire girls' and boys' basketball teams had landed at the Helland house for the night to sit around the firepit and eat pizza. Kennedy was bundled under blankets, drowsy from the game. Slowly, everyone else had left, and she felt herself staring into the fire as her eyes drifted closed. When she woke up, she was alone. Barely awake, she began to gather her things and went to turn off the propane to the firepit, when she heard her sister's voice around the wall of the house. Butterflies entered Kennedy's stomach and a general discomfort filled her body. She felt bad eavesdropping, but she was anxious as to who her sister was talking to so late. Quietly, she crept to the side of the porch.

"Please, Adam," Jess was saying. She sniffled. "Don't make me do this again."

He quickly answered "Jess, just listen to me, ple—"

"No." She cut him off. Her voice was harsher than Kennedy ever remembered it being before. "You've been drinking, so I'm not going to blame you for the things you're saying, but you need to go to bed now. Go to Hunter's room or the guest room or even the living room couch for all I care."

"Jess," Adam's voice slurred out. Kennedy realized what was happening too late and before she could escape inside, she was looking down off the porch at her sister.

At first, Jess was surprised, doing a double take to look at Kennedy. The surprise rapidly turned to anger, however.

"Are you listening to my conversations?" Jess snapped. Kennedy tried to stammer out a reply but was cut off. "What the hell, Kennedy?"

Kennedy froze, not knowing what to say. Suddenly, Adam was there too. He looked surprised and confused to see her as well and awkwardly reached a hand out and put it on Jess's shoulder. The innocent touch set Kennedy over the edge.

"Don't touch her," she snapped glaring down at him. Adam yanked his hand back and took a few staggering steps backward, beer spilling out from the can he had in his other hand. His face, hidden mostly by the dark, registered a look of sadness.

"Kennedy," Jess hissed out. "What the actual fuck?"

"He doesn't get to break your heart again!" She looked at Adam. "Jackass," she muttered out.

Tears of anger had welled up in Kennedy's eyes, and as she looked at her sister, she saw them in hers as well, making her hesitate.

"Jess," she began, but her sister held up a hand, anger returning to her eyes.

"You don't know anything," Jess answered with tears now streaming freely down her face. Kennedy felt her own tears begin to fall.

Jess had turned to Adam. "And you, seriously. Go inside and sleep it off." She hesitated a moment. "We will talk tomorrow."

Jess rushed up the stairs and grabbed Kennedy's arm, dragging her inside and to the stairs before Kennedy could protest. "Go to bed," Jess shoved her up the first two steps and Kennedy had turned to look back down at her. "You *can't* get back together with him," she protested.

"You don't get to pick who I talk to or what I talk to them about," Jess angrily answered. The two stared at each other for a minute. "This is my issue, Kenna," Jess finally said. She added extra momentum behind her next words. "So, stay out of it."

Kennedy glared at her sister for another moment before turning and running up the stairs to her room, slamming the door behind her.

Adam had left by the time she went downstairs the next morning. She hadn't seen him again until the funeral.

When she saw his face in the sea of people seated in the high school gym, her heart had stopped a little. Kennedy had never actually spoken with Jess about that night again, which had surprised Kennedy. Jess was the confrontational type—normally if something upset her, she would make it very clear. The fact that that night had never come up again was nothing short of shocking. Even when their mother had brought up "a lot of noise outside last night," Jessica had made eye contact with Kennedy before brushing it off as "everyone leaving at the same time."

Adam had made eye contact with her before quickly looking away as Kennedy slowly walked to the first row of seats with her family.

She didn't remember much of the funeral. Someone had recorded it, so she guessed if she ever wanted to remember it, she could. It had been so hot in the gym, even in the middle of the winter, with so many people in the domed room. It made it difficult for her to concentrate, and Kennedy found herself lost in her thoughts most of the service. She came out of it when her mother nudged her. The priest had finished talking, and Coach Davidson had taken the stage.

Kennedy gripped her program had as one of the most influential people in Jess's life spoke about her. He talked about her leadership on and off the court and how she was always a team player. A few tears fell from his eyes as he said how he would miss her. Slowly, others rose to talk about Jess. Some of the girls she was close to from other towns and teams, her friends from Hysham, upperclassmen from throughout the years, community members... Kennedy felt herself becoming overwhelmed, and her hands felt numb. The program had been crumpled beyond recognition, and her breathing was getting heavy. Finally, it was the family's turn to speak. Kris went up, followed by Hunter with Jackson tagging along.

The priest returned to the stage, and Kennedy felt his eyes slide over her, a weight she couldn't shake. She had agreed to talk today when the funeral arrangements had been made, to appease her crying mother, but now the last thing she wanted to do was stand. She could barely breath.

"Kennedy," the priest had called out, his voice booming through the school's speakers. "Can I invite you to the stage?"

Kennedy had frozen again. Her mother nudged her again, and she felt herself, shakily, stand, though she wasn't sure how. Slowly, she shuffled to the stage where the casket was perched, surrounded by flowers. She heard the priest introduce her to the crowd, but his words sounded like gibberish to her. Somehow, she was on stage, and he was looking at her and gesturing her to the microphone and podium. Her heart felt heavy, and her throat was closing. "Was this what Jess felt like when she was dying?" she wondered.

She was at the stand now—oh god, what was she supposed to do with her hands? She put them up on the podium, but that felt wrong, so she quickly dropped them to her side. That still felt wrong. Kennedy cleared her throat and leaned into the microphone. Immediately, feedback screeched out over the crowd. Gentle laughter answered the horrible sound, and Kennedy looked over the group.

The gym had never been so full. The bleachers along both sides were packed, and the metal seats set up on the court didn't have a single empty chair. Some stood along the back wall, and younger kids ran around in the school lobby while their mothers told them to be quiet and careful.

Kennedy had cleared her throat. "Hello, everyone," she began, before carefully clearing her throat again. She looked down at the binder in front of her, where the speech she had written with help from her mother and Ms. O'Brien was neatly tucked. She swallowed hard and began reading.

"Thank you all for coming. My family and I greatly appreciate the support we have gotten over the last week-and-a-half." Kennedy knew she sounded like she was regurgitating information. Her mother had taken the helm during much of the writing and editing process—something Ms. O'Brien had noticed and gently pointed out to Kennedy when she proofread the speech for her. She had asked her if she was sure this something she was comfortable reading since it didn't sound like her style of writing. Kennedy had nodded along, but now she wasn't sure. She stared at the page in front of her for a moment and then looked up and scanned the crowd, where she found Adam's face.

What she saw had broken her. Tears rolled down his cheeks—she hadn't been able to openly and honestly show that emotion all week— only when she was alone. Yet, here was a college guy, crying in the middle of a high school gym over his ex-girlfriend.

She looked again at the speech in front of her and slowly shut the binder and suddenly, as if she had planned it all along, words bloomed from her heart and out of her mouth.

She still wasn't exactly sure what she said, but as the receiving line met her at the reception, everyone had told her how wonderful her comments were. She hugged Jess's friends and the community members one-by-one, thanking them again for coming. She was visiting with her kindergarten teacher when she turned to greet the next person in the thinning line and realized who it was—Adam.

She stared at him and he looked back, holding her gaze. Finally, she opened her arms and he did too, and they fell into each other, not saying anything.

Later, at the less-formal celebration of Jess's life, high schoolers, alumni, and friends from out of town gathered at the edge of the Yellowstone River. Even though the basketball teams were still in season, there seemed to be a general knowledge that no one would ever tell about the toasts that were going on throughout the night for Jess. Kennedy wasn't a big drinker, so she hung near the edge of the group and sipped a single beer throughout the night. As she mingled, she felt better than she had in weeks: she laughed as friends shared stories about her sister and her sassiness, forgetful moments, and learning to compete at the high school level. Eventually, the fire dwindled, and everyone began heading home, the sober friends having six or seven people cramming into their pickups and a few hopping into the back of the truck beds. Kennedy helped in making sure that everyone had a ride home. One of the girls who was in Hunter's class grabbed Kennedy and told her Kris needed a ride home and nodded to his pickup where he was vomiting profusely. Kennedy cringed and apologized to her repeatedly. She was making her way over to him when Hunter and Adam appeared. Hunter was telling Kris to get it together as Adam pulled him over his shoulder.

"Wait!" Kennedy had said as the trio marched off, running to catch up. "Are you okay to drive?"

"I haven't had a drop all night," Adam called back. "I'm taking these guys to Kris's house. Your parents don't need to see them like this. Go home, Kennedy." He hesitated before adding, "Let me know you made it, please."

Kennedy didn't answer, though she came to a stop in the dirt. "Okay," she had finally said. She wasn't sure if they heard her.

The drive home in her father's pickup was silent. She had clicked off the XM radio and instead listened to the sounds of the vehicle as it rolled down the gravel road. As she drove, though, the loneliness she had felt since her sister's death caught up to her again.

The lights were on when she got home. She came in through the kitchen door and found her mother reading at the table. A cup of untouched tea was steeping next to her. She looked up as Kennedy came in, but her face shifted to panic as she asked where Kris and Hunter were. They had kept Jack home for the night, knowing what shenanigans were going on.

"Kris's." Kennedy answered, shrugging off her coat. "Adam took them there."

Her mother sighed heavily, "Adam is a good egg."

Kennedy didn't answer as she slid off her boots. "Maybe he is," she finally responded.

Kennedy had gone up to her room, but she didn't go to sleep. Sleep hadn't been coming easily to her. Instead, she sat in bed and clicked on the TV. She scrolled through the channels until she found a true crime documentary to watch. She fell into a light sleep to the sound of the narrator detailing the exact way a woman had been kidnapped.

It was nearly 3:00 a.m. when a knock sounded at the door. She started, confused, and slowly slipped out of her covers to open the door. It was Adam.

"Hey?" she said, confused as to what he was doing there.

"You never told me you made it," he answered.

"Oh." She looked around. "I made it."

Adam just looked at her.

"I'm sorry," she finally coughed up. "I forgot I said I would."

"Well," he said, "you're here." He nodded at her.

The introduction track to the show she was watching suddenly blared from her TV and Kennedy rushed to her nightstand to turn it down.

Adam was looking at her quizzically when she turned to look back at him.

"Are you watching a true crime doc right now?" he asked.

Jen felt the blood rush to her face. "Yeah," she replied. "It was—"

"—what Jess always watched to follow asleep." He smiled. "I know. But it's been a long day for you and the burial is tomorrow—shouldn't you be sleeping? That's what I figured you were doing when you didn't get ahold of me."

Kennedy looked away, shaking her head and giving one dry laugh. "I haven't slept in days."

Adam nodded slowly. "I get it." He looked at the TV, where a family member was now giving an interview to the camera. "Mind if I join you, then?"

Kennedy looked around the room and was thankful not to see any bras lying on the floor. "Uh," she answered, "sure."

Adam pulled the door shut behind him and slowly crawled onto the opposite side of the full bed. He smelled good, like the cologne she and Jess would buy their brothers for gifts. She wondered if Jess had given him some on a holiday, once.

The two watched the show in silence, each on their own edge of the bed, shoulders barely touching. Soon, Kennedy felt her eyes begin to droop—she knew she wouldn't sleep for long, but Adam was right— it had been a long day. She slowly closed her eyes and crossed her arms over her chest. "Just a quick nap," she thought to herself.

She woke up with a start with her head nestled into Adam's chest, her right arm and leg flung over him. Kennedy blinked, confused as to how this had happened.

"Morning." Adam's voice startled her and she quickly scooted back to her side of the bed.

"I'm so sorry," she blabbed out. "I move around a lot when I sleep, and I usually cuddle a pillow."

Adam laughed. "It's fine. I'm just glad you were able to get some sleep."

Kennedy looked around for her phone and yanked it off the charger. "What time is it?"

The glaring brightness of 6:37 a.m. glared back at her. She sighed. Two hours more than she had been getting.

Adam also sat up and dangled his feet over the edge of the bed. "I'm going to Hunter's room to catch another hour or two before we head out." He stood up. "Will you be okay?"

She nodded, not looking at him.

Adam had moved across the room and was pulling the door open when she spoke.

"Adam?" he turned and looked at her. "Thank you…" she hesitated, "…and I'm sorry about before."

He gave her a half smile and nodded, pulling the door shut behind him.

That had been the start of their talking. The fact that they talked, that they were friendly, was pretty public knowledge, but her family thought it was a friendship as far as she knew. They did not, to her knowledge, know about the feelings that had developed behind closed doors over the last year-and-a-half.

Kennedy turned off the shower and quickly stepped out, flinging a towel onto her hair. She dried herself off and rushed around the room, throwing on a pair of jean shorts and a t-shirt. Before going downstairs, she ran some mousse through her wavy hair and finger-brushed it as fast as she could. She was about to head down when she gave pause and ran back into the bathroom she once shared with Jess. Most of the makeup had been her sister's and scared her as she didn't know what to do with it, but one tube looked familiar. She quickly ran some mascara over her eyelashes before rushing back downstairs.

Chuck and Gigi, the family's affectionate names for her mother's parents, had arrived, as had the football coaches. The both gave her hugs as she came down the stairs. She could see the football coaches in the next room over as well and knew it was quickly becoming a full house. She anxiously looked around for Adam and finally caught sight of him standing next to Hunter.

However, as she began to walk across the room to meet him, her mother appeared. "Honey, can you please help me get everyone a drink?" she asked, walking away before she could get an answer. Kennedy sighed and dutifully head back to the kitchen.

The older Helland child, Kris, was in the room when she walked in, snacking out of a bag of open chips her mother must have set out.

She rolled her eyes at him and mouthed, "Mother," and he snickered slightly in response. He opened up an arm, and she came and wrapped her arms around him. Out of all her siblings, she was currently closest to him. She thought it was because, unlike Hunter, who would push her buttons, or Jackson, who was completely disinterested with everything at the moment, Kris was content to sit in silence for a while but still managed to feel present all the time. He was a comforting force in her life, the one she would seek out when she needed someone not to listen, but to just be there for her.

"Any ideas as to what this is about?" he asked. She shook her head.

"No idea," she answered, "but Mom is in all sorts of a mood about it." She nodded at the porch. "Did you see a cooler when you came in, by chance?"

He nodded.

Kennedy rolled her eyes. "How much do you want to bet she's going to tell everyone she's sorry she wasn't prepared to have this many people over?"

It was Kris's turn to roll his eyes, and he playfully shoved his sister. She laughed and tossed her hair before stepping on the porch to gather an assortment of drinks from the cooler filled to the brim with ice.

As she came in and began passing out her selection of beer and pop to those in attendance, she overheard her mother telling the wife of one of the football coaches that she was sorry that the house was such a mess, she had no idea that all these people would be coming out. Kennedy scanned the room and stared at Kris until he looked over at her.

"You. Owe. Me." She mouthed and gestured at her mother with her head. He shook his head at her and turned back to his conversation with one of the neighboring ranchers.

Kennedy wandered from conversation to conversation, stopping back in the kitchen to gather more drinks from the porch every few rounds. She was giving one last look around the room to make sure that everyone had a drink when she spotted Adam again, this time alone. Assuming that everyone now had a drink, she beelined over to him, her own beverage in hand.

He was holding a beer in his left hand, his phone in his right. As she sidled up beside him, he slid him phone into the back pocket of his jeans.

"Hey, stranger," he said, and her heart fluttered slightly.

"Hey," she said simply.

He nodded at her brother, who her mother had cornered and was reverently talking to on the other side of the room. "You ready for this?"

She scoffed. "Is he?"

Adam chuckled beside her and bumped her hip with his. Immediately, she stepped to the side, and he blushed. "Sorry," he said.

She looked around the room in slight panic. Had someone seen that? Would they know? Her eyes scanned from group to group, trying to determine if anyone was looking at them. It didn't appear so, so she relaxed again.

It would be easier if everyone knew about her and Adam; she knew this. But she couldn't deal with everyone else knowing... at least not yet. She knew that Adam and Jess had broken up before she died, but there still seemed to be something... well, she didn't quite have the word for it. "Wrong" wasn't quite right, but at the same time, there did seem to be something wrong with the situation. She was dating her dead sister's ex-boyfriend. That wasn't something that was normal in most people's books.

She imagined, for a moment, what it would be like to be like to tell everyone she also had an announcement. To step forward and weave her fingers through Adam's and to triumphantly hold their interlocked fingers up in the air for all to see. She imagined the joy that would come, for a moment, as everyone stared at them.

Then she realized the shock that would spread across the room. How Hunter would immediately become pissed at both his best friend and his younger sister—he already had to go through this with one of them, and now another (never mind he repeatedly dated Jess's friends growing up). How her mother would burst into tears and ask her how she could do this to Jess. How everyone's faces across the room would not be of happiness, but of shock and disgust.

She quickly pushed the thought out of her mind.

Luckily, at that moment, her mother stepped into the middle of the room and cleared her throat. "Everyone," she said, and the chatter across the room died down. Kennedy glanced at Adam through her peripherals: he was looking at her mother intently.

"Everyone," her mother repeated again, "thank you all for coming out here on such short notice. We—Scott and I—are so happy that you could all make it out here to celebrate Hunter and his big news." She held up her glass. "I know he hasn't told you all what it is yet, but it's absolutely amazing, and we are so proud of him. So, if you all could raise your glass," everyone around the room raised their drinks into the air, including Kennedy and Adam, "here's to Hunter, and the new journey he will soon embark on."

"To Hunter," the group repeated, raising their glasses slightly more before sipping from them.

"And now," her mother looked behind her until she made eye contact with her second oldest son. She looked back over the crowd, beaming with pride, "Hunter, can you please share why we are all celebrating tonight?"

She moved out of the way, and Hunter slowly shuffled forward. Kennedy could tell he was uncomfortable with the attention that her mother had just thrown upon him, but he wouldn't complain about it until later.

He looked around the crowd for a moment and then nodded slightly, taking a drink of his beer.

"Uh," he began, and suddenly Kennedy felt like she was watching him talk in front of a pep rally again, a younger man appearing in front of her, "well, thank you all for coming." Slowly, as he continued to speak, his confidence came out and he seemed to age before her eyes.

"Like I'm sure all of you know, I spent most of this summer interning down in Denver with their baseball program." Heads around the room bobbed up and down. Kennedy rolled her eyes; like her mother would have let anyone forget.

"Well," he hesitated again, before continuing. "I just found out yesterday that they would like to offer me a full-time job pending my graduation in the spring."

Silence blanketed the room as the news sunk in, then suddenly excited chatter filled it. A few of the men in attendance raised their glasses again, and immediately the football coaches began clapping. Most people in attendance followed suit.

Hunter was beaming with his own pride now, standing in the center of the room. "I wouldn't be getting this opportunity if it wasn't for people both inside and outside this room. My professors, my high school teachers, my coaches... you all helped instill a love of sports and writing in me. Without your guidance, I never would have gotten there." He hesitated once again, looking at his drink. Suddenly he thrust it into the air. "So, here's to you all as well."

Laughter filled the room as everyone raised their drinks once again and drank. Within moments, Hunter had a small group congratulating him.

Adam turned to talk to Kennedy, only to find empty space beside him. She was no longer in the room. He looked around curiously, confused as to where she had gone. She had just been *right* there. When had she slipped away?

Kennedy had felt like the room was closing in on her when Hunter announced the news. It was hard enough having him in Spokane—but at least he came home during his breaks. And she had planned to have him closer to her next year, when she went to school in Missoula. The news that he would be moving to Denver suddenly made it seem like he was moving to a different planet.

She had slipped out the front door undetected while everyone was toasting each other in excitement. She had not raised her glass this time.

The sun was just setting as she walked across the parking lot to the shop. Her emotions were strained at the moment, and she needed to be alone to collect herself before she went back in to talk to the crowd and mingle. Her mother would expect a smiling face. She wanted to smile, this was big news for Hunter and something he had been working toward for years; she just couldn't quite get her face to make that expression quite yet. She needed to compose herself first.

The one thing she had noticed that had changed the most within herself since her sister's death was her emotions. They always seemed to be spiraling just beneath the surface, so it was often easier to just keep them buried. It was only when she was totally alone that she could finally open herself up to the chaos within her.

She felt herself drawn to the shop; specifically, her feet seemed to carry her to the basketball court in the building. She would come out here, sometimes, when her family was gone or she needed to clear her head at night. She knew it seemed backwards: to find peace on something she so vehemently refused to talk about or step on in public. But when she was alone, with no expectations... somehow it brought her comfort. For a very long time, basketball had been where she took out her emotions on something else. It was hard to cut something so big and transformative out of your life, she figured.

So, when she needed to be alone and think, she found herself out on the court. She kept a ball hidden underneath her bed, where her parents wouldn't find it and ask about it. Now, however, there was nothing to bounce or throw; there were just her emotions swirling around her, making her dizzy.

Kennedy crouched on the floor and tried to breathe as they overcame her. So rarely did this happen anymore: she had gotten good at pushing everything down, deep down, until she was alone and could deal with it. But sometimes her feelings would bubble up inside her and make appearance when she least expected them. She tipped over, the sobs ricocheting throughout her body and into the expansive space around her. Curled into the fetal position, she truly felt the feelings of grief and loss for a little while.

Once she had composed herself, she wiped under her eyes, praying the mascara she had foolishly put on had not run down her cheeks. She slipped into the shop bathroom and was glad to see it had stayed right where it should be. Minus red and puffy eyes, she looked relatively normal.

As she left the shop, dusk was falling and guests were leaving, piling into their cars. She went and hugged her grandparents goodbye, careful to stay in the dimly lit areas of the parking lot just in case her crying was noticeable. She then said goodbye to a couple of other guests, making her way back to the house. She was hoping she could slip upstairs un-noticed, when Hunter stumbled out of the doorway with several of his friends, followed by Kris and Adam.

"Sister," he spread his arms wide and bowed to her. She rolled her eyes; sometimes he was too much.

"Brother," she answered, though, playing his little game. He held out his arm and she took it, letting him lead her to Kris's pickup.

"We are off to party the night away," he said, and his friends began slapping him on the back. She raised her eyebrows at Kris.

"*Hunter* is off to party the night away," he clarified. "I am just along for the ride... which is ironic because I will be driving."

"I see," she answered. She threw her arm around Hunter and pulled him in for a side-hug. "Congrats," she whispered at him. She looked around at the group of guys. She had grown up around them and knew how rowdy they could get. "And be safe," she said. She made eye contact with Adam. "All of you."

He winked at her, and she was confident this time that no one else would notice through the hubbub around them.

Kris nodded at her as he got into the driver's seat, and the rest of the gang crawled in as well.

Hunter rolled down the window as Kris backed out of the spot and pointed to Kennedy. "You'll be coming to visit me every chance you get," he called out as the group drove away. She smiled sadly after him. "At least I get the chance to visit him," she thought to herself.

Kennedy managed to slip upstairs without running into anyone else that night. As she curled up in bed, her phone went off. She rolled over and picked it up and smiled.

Adam and she wouldn't usually talk if he was around Hunter; she was nervous he would look at the screen and see her name. It was a fear that had grown months after Jess's passing, when he had once mentioned it seemed like the two of them talked an awful lot. Kennedy had shut down and not spoken to Adam for several days and had been careful with her actions around brother ever since.

"Sorry couldn't stay, will stay at Kris's for night. Sleep tight" flashed on her screen and her heart fluttered just a bit again. She rolled back over, waiting for sleep to come.

4

The following day at school was uncomfortable for Kennedy. In a class of three, there wasn't much opportunity to avoid Grace. Kennedy chose to eat lunch in Ms. O'Brien's room instead of in the cafeteria, taking her tray through the line and then hightailing it to the room. When she appeared, Ms. O'Brien looked at her quizzically, but Kennedy just muttered something about wanting to get ahead on reading the plays for the spring semester and holed up in the computer room for the rest of the lunch break. Ms. O'Brien disappeared for a bit but reappeared just before the bell rang as Kennedy was going to clear her tray.

"I heard about Hunter," she said as Kennedy passed by the door. "That's an exciting opportunity for him!" Ms. O'Brien and her husband weren't the most social, but she knew that the English teacher had greatly influenced Hunter when he was in school. She was sure he had stopped by to let her know or had called today to tell her his news himself already.

Kennedy gave her a small smile in return and went into the nearly empty cafeteria. While her brother's news was exciting, it was also just another thing that she needed to process, on top of Coach Davidson trying to get her to come back for basketball and Grace going behind her back to help him do so.

Kennedy cleared her tray and hustled back to her locker. She had managed to sneak around Grace most of the morning by carrying the majority of her textbooks in her bag, but she needed to switch things out for the afternoon periods now. As she turned the corner to the hallway to the lockers, she saw Grace sitting on the floor in front of her locker, reading the book Ms. O'Brien had just assigned to them today. Grace looked up and made eye contact with Kennedy, and Kennedy hesitated, not knowing if she should proceed or turn around. She began to take a step back when Grace called out, "Hey."

Kennedy froze again and looked at her.

"Can we talk?" she had shut the book onto her hand. "I feel like you've been avoiding me all morning. You didn't answer my texts about cruising before school."

Kennedy slowly began making her way down the hallway. "Hunter was in town last night," she said. "And I was running later this morning."

Grace smiled. "Yeah, I figured when you came in pretty much as the bell was ringing for O'Brien's class."

Kennedy didn't answer and instead began shifting the books in her bag around and putting them back into her locker and grabbing what she would need for the afternoon.

"Kennedy." Kennedy looked at her childhood friend, now sitting on the floor cross legged. "Don't be mad at me, okay?"

Kennedy felt herself begin to sweat. Confrontation stressed her out for many reasons, but confrontation with her friends hurt her even more. "I'm not mad." She shoved the last of her books into her bag.

"It's just, you're not thinking about the rest of us. We barely have enough girls to make a team, and you know that I'm trying to get recruit—" Kennedy slammed her locker, and it crashed together before creaking back open. Grace looked up at her in shock. Kennedy stared back down at her.

"Would it kill you to *not* make this about you for once?" she snapped, dragging her bag up onto her shoulders and turning to leave.

"Make this about me?!" exclaimed Grace. She rose from the ground. "You're the one making a decision that impacts everyone else about you, and for such a silly reason."

Kennedy whipped around. Hot tears were burning in her eyes. "My sister died, Grace. I don't think that's a silly reason."

"She died two years ago, Kennedy! We've all moved on and healed," Grace paused, letting the words sink in, "but you don't want to. Even your parents agree with me!"

"Why are you talking to my parents about me? And when?" Kennedy sobbed out, the tears now running freely down her face.

Coach Davidson suddenly appeared. "Ladies," he said, trying to step between them. Kennedy shoved past him.

"Why are you talking to my parents about me?" she repeated through her haggard breathing. Coach Davidson put his hand on her shoulder and began pulling her back.

Grace looked at her sadly. One of the other teachers had appeared from her classroom and was ushering Grace back toward her room. She began to say something but couldn't seem to get what she wanted to say out and closed her mouth. Instead, she shook her head as the math teacher led her back into her classroom.

Kennedy began to cry harder as the bell rang. Most of the faculty and students had been outside, so they hadn't heard the argument between the two girls, but now the students were going to flood back through the doors. Coach Davidson grabbed her and put his arm around her and led her back through the hallways to his classroom. Kennedy made her way to the desk she had sat in for the last four years and dropped her bag off her shoulders before sitting down and putting her head in her hands.

"Uh," Coach Davidson stammered out. "Kennedy?" She looked up at the man who served many roles in her life, tears streaming down her face. "I'm going to go talk to Ms. O'Brien and let her know you'll probably be late. And I'm going to check in on Grace and Ms. Smith as well."

Kennedy nodded her head before placing her head back in her hands.

She wasn't sure how long he had been gone, but it was long enough that she was able to compose herself and wipe away the last few tears with the scratchy tissues the school provided. The feeling was familiar on her face—she had used gone through quite a few boxes of those in the weeks following her sister's death, alone in the nurse's office. He came in and nodded at her before sitting down behind at the desk beside her.

"Mr. Johnson wants to talk to you before the end of the period," he said. "Grace is in there talking to him now."

Kennedy nodded. She wasn't surprised. The outburst that had occurred in the hallway was uncharacteristic of her, so Mr. Johnson would likely want to visit about it.

"Kennedy," Coach Davidson began, "can we please talk about what is going on?"

Kennedy didn't answer and a drawn-out silence began. Finally, Coach Davidson broke it.

"Grace isn't the only one worried about you. A lot of us are." Kennedy began to protest, but he held up a hand, "Please, let me finish." Kennedy froze and slowly leaned back in her chair, suddenly exhausted.

"You are withdrawn a lot of the time. And I know you've always been quiet, but there is something different about you now. I can't imagine the pain you went through when Jess died... and we all heal differently. We're just concerned that you aren't healing in a healthy way." Kennedy felt tears falling off her face again, but the sobs weren't coming. "We—I—don't want you to come out for the team if it is going to cause you this must distress. But I think getting back on the court could help bring back memories of Jess you maybe haven't let yourself remember for a long time—good memories. There might be pain at first, but do you remember the times you spent playing one-on-one on Sundays? The way you two hugged each other at half court after we upset Wibaux on their come court, the night before she died? Or how fun it was to finally play alongside each other during a game?" Kennedy looked up to see Coach Davidson was also crying now and quickly looked away. Other people's tears made her as uncomfortable as her own did. "Jess was special, and

I know it is hard without her here. But she wouldn't want you to pull back into your shell and forget the things you loved to do—and yes, I know you loved basketball even if you told me you didn't."

The two sat in silence for a few moments before he spoke again.

"I'm not going to ask you to play again." Kennedy looked up again in surprise. The two made eye contact, and this time she felt compelled to hold it. "But I want you to remember the times that you two had on the court, and I want you to really think about if you want to never get the chance to play again, to make her proud from wherever she's watching you from. Is it worth it to you that you end this thing you two shared, that you were so passionate about together, on this note?" He went silent again and Kennedy looked away, but she could feel his eyes on her still.

"The season doesn't start for three months. Enjoy your last year of volleyball and all the other lasts you will soon have. But keep it this in the back of your mind: is this a last I am willing to miss out on?" Coach Davidson let his words sink in, and Kennedy felt them weigh down on her more than anything else had before. Coach Davidson clapped her shoulder twice and stood up. "Let's get you to Mr. Johnson." Kennedy stopped up and pulled her bag onto her shoulder and began to walk to the door.

"Oh, and Kennedy?" She turned and looked at her teacher. "Just a heads up—your parents are here."

Kennedy closed her eyes for a moment and breathed out. "Thank you," she said as she began to walk out the door. She hesitated before crossing the threshold into the hallway, "For everything." She slipped out the door quickly, and Allen Davidson sat down heavily in his chair and put his head in his hands.

Kennedy slowly made her way to the front office. The always perky Evelyn greeted her warmly with a "Hi, sweetie, how are you?" and a sympathetic look. "He's in his office and your parents are too, you go right in."

"Thanks," Kennedy said as she shuffled into the room.

Hysham's principal's office was housed in the center of the building. As such, there were no windows in the wood paneled room. Instead, Mr. Johnson had put up a multitude of "motivational posters" that included people skydiving and running long distances with fonts underneath that were too small to read. So, it was only assumed that they were motivational. Kennedy always thought it would be hysterical if one day she went up and read one and it was an unmotivational poster instead: the ultimate prank.

Sure enough, as she entered the room, her parents were seated right across from Mr. Johnson, and her mother was in the middle of a long-winded comment and was so focused she didn't even hear her child come into the office. Kennedy perched at the seat next to the door, sliding her bag off her shoulders and onto the floor.

"...and I really just don't know how else we can help her, I am at a total loss for what else we can try. Maybe drugs? But I don't know if she'll take them, and we can't force her to take them. I mean, Scott has taken them since his mom died right after we got married, but I am not really sure if they would help her or not and what if they make things worse? I just don't get how Jackson has healed so differently than she has and even the older boys and I'm just so worried about her..." her mother trailed off, so Kennedy finally chimed in.

"I don't like the idea about medication," she said. "I've talked to the therapist you make me see every month, and I've told her I don't want it. And I'm seventeen, almost eighteen, so no, there isn't really a way you can force me to take it. As for my brothers: We're different people. We all heal differently."

Her mother looked back at her in shock, having missed her entering the room. Her father gave her a small smile, and Mr. Johnson just looked at her in exhaustion.

"Hello, Kennedy," he said.

"Hello, Mr. Johnson," she replied. "Mom. Dad." She nodded at both her parents.

"Oh honey," her mother got up to hug her, but her father put a hand on her arm. She looked down at him, sighed, and sat back down.

"You guys didn't need to come in," Kennedy said, leaning back in her chair.

"Yes, we did," her mother snapped. "You were in a screaming match with Grace in the hallway, Kennedy."

"I just lost control of my emotions," Kennedy answered, trying to keep herself level-headed. "And it wasn't a screaming match."

"Regardless, that's concerning to us," her mother replied. "We—" her father cleared his throat, "fine, *I*, am very concerned about you and your actions today, honey. Is the therapist not working out? Is there something else we can do to try and help you? What do you need?"

Kennedy sat in silence for a moment, staring at the ground. Finally, she looked up. "I just need some space, okay? I need to not have people asking me about Jess all the time and for people not try and force me to fit in their preconceived box of how I should heal and how I should grieve... and for people not to try and force me to heal with it on their terms."

Her mother looked hurt, but Kennedy plowed on with her speech. "And I need to make my own choices about how I heal, too. That means not forcing me to play basketball or trying to get Allen to get me to play, or anything like that. Okay?"

Her father looked a little hurt now too, but Kennedy didn't care. This was something that everyone needed to hear, before it got even more out of hand.

"Well," Mr. Johnson looked quite uncomfortable from behind his desk. "This seems like a family matter more than anything. So, I'm not quite sure how much help I can be. Kennedy," he looked at the senior, "are you okay to go back to class?" She nodded. "Good, you can sit in the library until the bell rings then. And you know you are welcome to my office or Mr. Lambert's or the nurse's office if you ever need a moment." Kennedy nodded once more.

"Thank you, Mr. Johnson," she answered. "And thank you for understanding what I may need. Or not need. And for giving me space."

Her mother's face soured, and her father looked down. Mr. Johnson continued to look on uncomfortably. As Kennedy swung her back onto her shoulders once more and trotted down the administrative hallway back to the library to wait for the bell to ring.

Halfway down the hall, though she turned and went back, knocking lightly on the frame of the door. Her parents and Mr. Johnson were still sitting in uncomfortable silence. "Just one question: Did Mr. Johnson call you two today?" Her mom's face turned bright red. "That's what I thought," Kennedy said. "Keep my friends out of this, okay?"

She turned and sauntered off again.

5

Scott Helland pulled himself into the driver's seat of the work pickup as Kathy slammed the door more aggressively than normal. "'Keep my friends out of it,' what is that supposed to mean?" she angrily asked her husband as she shoved the seatbelt clip into place.

"Probably exactly what it sounds like," he answered, backing out from the parking spot at the front of the school.

"Well, she isn't talking to us, she I'm not sure how else I'm supposed to get information about how she's doing," Kathy snapped back. Her husband didn't answer, knowing more was likely coming. "And thank you for letting me be painted out to be the bad guy in this situation, by the way. So much for a united front."

Scott looked over at his wife. "I believe she called me out for talking to Allen as well." He pulled out onto Main Street. Normally the drive to town was twenty minutes, but the two had already been in town at the hardware store when his wife had gotten the text from Grace and insisted they stop by the school "just in case." He had felt uneasy about the situation to begin with, but after seeing Kennedy and hearing about how she wanted space felt even worse. Jessica and his wife had similar personalities: bubbly and open, willing to talk with any stranger about any topic. Kennedy favored him and his quietness, chiming in and opening up only when it was necessary. He could admit that it led to some difficult times, not knowing what she wanted but also not wanting to pry, but keeping a distance and letting her come to him when she needed something always seemed to work. His wife's desire to want to talk about every issue that came up though, definitely put a strain on the relationship between the two, so, he wasn't surprised that much of the blame had been placed on her. The boys she was willing to leave alone more often, though Kris and Jackson were generally open with her about their thoughts and feelings more than Hunter was; but you could usually gauge how Hunter actually felt even through his sarcastic and annoyed comments. Since Jessica had died, it seemed Kathy wanted to have that same relationship with Kennedy more and more; and the more she pushed it, the more it drove a wedge between the two.

The two drove on in silence, getting on the road to head back to the ranch. Scott knew his wife was upset because normally she chatted to fill the silence. As they drove past the white, wooden cross, surrounded by flowers and mementos that marked the spot where their daughter had died, her crying became apparent to him.

He reached out and took her hand. And she shakily whispered, "I just miss her so much." He didn't answer for a moment. "I do too," he finally replied.

His wife shifted in her seat and brought a tissue from her pocket up to her face to wipe away the tears. "Not just Jessica. I miss Kennedy, too. I know our relationship has always been tense, but it seems like it is more now than it ever has been before, and I don't know how to help it."

He let the silence take over again as he drove the rest of the way home. As he parked the truck in his parking spot, he turned off the engine and leaned back in his chair. "She's telling you how to," he answered. "She wants space. We need to give her it unless we have a reason not to do so."

"It's just... it's so hard to do that," she answered, wiping her eyes again. "I don't like to see her hurting. It hurts me."

"It hurts me too," he answered, "but she will come to us if she needs something."

"Will she though?" she asked, looking at her husband, her frustration evident in her voice. "Because she takes after you, and you have a tendency to let things fester or to try and solve it on your own. I just wish I knew that she was talking to someone or doing something to help her."

He thought back to the times he had silently watched her play basketball in the garage the last two years, especially the first time, where she had sobbed openly on the floor.

"Maybe she already is," he answered as he slid out of the truck and shut the door firmly behind him, sealing away the conversation.

6

Kennedy didn't say much to Grace during the last two periods of the day. Coach Davidson shifted his lessons plans around so everyone was doing individual work rather than the group work he had planned, sensing the awkwardness that could ensue, and Kennedy played the clarinet while Grace played the trumpet, so band was not an issue. She was just thankful it wasn't a "paper and annual" day with Ms. O'Brien the last period.

Kennedy hung back to talk to Mrs. Jean, the music teacher, about some things at the end of band, and Grace waited for her as long as she could in the locker room before she had to go out to the court. Kennedy rushed in and changed in a couple of minutes before practice started.

Mrs. Kiefer had the girls warming up in rotating pairs, so Kennedy went and found her assigned partner and began warming up once she finished changing into her practice clothes. She kept her water near the coaches' things so she could strike up a conversation at a moment's notice if needed throughout the practice.

The time for competition was coming closer, so the last drill of the day the group was split up into the rotation for the upcoming tournament on the road. While Mrs. Kiefer stressed the rotation wasn't final yet, it was likely not going to change much, if at all. Grace had been a defensive specialist the last two seasons and would be filling the role again this year. Kennedy had been a middle hitter for most of her career but due to a lack of upperclassmen who were able to run the court had been shifted over to setter. Mrs. Kiefer had hoped to run a 6-2 play by the end of the season with one of the sophomores, but for now the group needed someone more assertive controlling the ball and making plays for the time being. Kennedy wasn't sure if she could fill that role, as assertiveness was not something that came naturally to her, but she would try as much as she could.

Kennedy helped organize the freshman who were confused by the rotation on the court. One, an outside, would be starting and another, a middle, would be playing front row while Grace filled in the back row for her. Neither seemed to understand the concept of a 5-1 offense, but Kennedy was patient and explained as best as she could. She knew the transition could be hard and thought about how thankful she was to have Jess there to explain it to her before she made the jump to varsity her freshman year. Grace hung back and watched the encounters: Grace had always struggled to help coach younger players and tended to become frustrated if things didn't go right but then wasn't able to help problem solve the situation much. That was where Kennedy came in. While her quietness on the court meant that she was often overlooked, it also helped her relate to the younger classman and be an encouraging force. She also had a deeper understanding of how the game worked, similar to her basketball knowledge, having watched her sister play for several years before she herself put on a uniform.

Finally, the scrimmaging began.

The group worked well together: Grace's passes were solid, and Kennedy worked to move her sets to where the hitters had been requesting them. After each point, whether they earned it or not, Kennedy would gather the team together just like they did during a game for a quick chat. She would clap hands with the girls who scored points or give a reassuring pat on the back when they needed it, including Grace. They were a team, working together for one common goal. And when they stepped onto the court, they would play that way, regardless of how they felt outside the painted line on the court. This was another lesson Jess (and basketball) had ingrained in Kennedy through her time in traveling sports.

At the conclusion of practice, Kennedy once again returned to the coach's area after the group's huddle. This time, though, Grace was not going to be shaken. She joined in on the two's conversation about some of the plays Kennedy was hoping to incorporate into the game as the season progressed and some of the drills she had learned at camps over the summer. Kennedy felt herself shutting down as Grace took over the conversation, spinning it to the way practice and rotations had gone that day. Normally, she would let her steer the way. But after the day she had had and the way she had spoken up to her mother, something inside her had shifted.

"...I'm not sure Ellie can handle that kind of pressure playing front row," Grace explained, shaking her head. "She just doesn't have the... she's not very good at hitting *hard*, you know?"

Ellie was one of the sophomores on the team. She hadn't had much playing time the previous year, but she was a hard worker. Kennedy had actually recommended to the coach she be placed in the offside position because she was smart about where she placed the ball and didn't just hit it as hard as she could, like some of the girls. She understood it was about strategy, not just strength. And she had a feeling that in the long run, she would make a good setter as well.

"Actually," Kennedy snapped, "I think Ellie will grow into that role nicely. She's smart about where she places the ball and can handle being a backup setter if she needs to be. She has gentle hands."

Grace and their coach looked at her in shock.

"It's not about how hard you can hit the ball. It's about earning the point: that comes from thinking through each play and changing things up. Who cares if you can smoke the ball for two plays if you're hitting it out of bounds or into the net the rest of the time?"

"But hitting the ball hard is the *point*," Grace counterstruck. "You want to earn a point, the best way to do that is to hit the ball hard enough that your opponents can't get to it."

Kennedy frowned. "It's about adapting." She looked at the coach. "Give Ellie a chance. You won't regret it."

The coach looked at her and at Grace then back at Kennedy. "You girls need to work this out off the court; I heard about what happened in the hallway at lunch. I don't want drama all season."

"'A house divided against itself cannot stand,'" muttered Kennedy.

Grace looked at her and cocked her head. "What?"

Kennedy shook her head. "Never mind."

She picked up her shoes and kneepads off the floor and tucked them under her arm. Coach Kiefer moved away to talk to her assistant coach, leaving the girls to their own devices.

Kennedy looked at her childhood friend. "It's a quote from Lincoln, about how if our government is divided, we will fail."

Grace rolled her eyes slightly. "Right. Look, I'm sorry about what happened earlier. Coach Davidson asked me to back off, so I will."

"Great apology," Kennedy said, turning around to leave.

"Hey, I'm trying here," snapped Grace, who ran to catch up.

Kennedy looked down at her but continued walking.

"So, you're just going to ice me, huh? After all I've been there for you for?" she asked angrily.

Kennedy didn't answer, and the two walked in silence into the locker room. The last of the girls were heading out as they came in, and Kennedy sat down heavily on the wooden seats that filled the room.

"I'm not icing you," she said wearily. She was tired of dealing with people and conflict for the day; all she wanted to do was be alone for a while. "I just am hurt. And need some space, okay? Can you, for once, just give me some space?"

Grace sat down next to her. "Kennedy, what's wrong? Like what's really wrong?"

Suddenly, the tears were flowing again, and she didn't know why. She tried to wipe them away before Grace saw, but soon her friend's arms were around her as she sobbed. "I feel like life is moving on and she's stuck here. And it's not fair. It's not fair! She never got to have all of the 'lasts' Allen mentioned today. Why her? Why not me?" she sobbed out.

Her friend didn't answer, instead letting the girl she was closest to break down in emotions.

Eventually, no more tears would come to the surface and the two would walk out together, past the framed basketball jersey for #12 that hung on the wall, always looking out over the gym lobby. And Kennedy would feel her heart break again, and her friend would feel it break as well, shattering into back into the pieces that hadn't fully come together yet.

The drive home for Kennedy was filled with silence yet again. When she saw the curve in the rode coming up, her knuckles turned white from gripping the wheel.

She didn't normally stop at the place her sister died. If she did, she usually stayed in the car while her mother laid her wreath or whatever token she had collected to put out there. Kennedy had never gotten out of the car to walk to the memorial; in fact, she actively tried to ignore its existence. It didn't feel right. This wasn't where Jess was, to Kennedy, but others seemed to memorialize it more than her actual resting place located on the family land.

The plain white cross put out by the State of Montana Department of Transportation marked the spot where her sister had rolled her vehicle and died. These white crosses dotted the state: some had more markers, others did not. Jess's was one that was personalized. Behind it, a steel cross made by the FFA chapter was staked into the ground, with "Jessica Francine Helland" and her dates of life etched into the thick steel. Flowers and tokens littered the ground—the pile grew and shrunk depending on the time of year and who was home from college. Some people tucked letters into the twisted metal, telling Jess how much they missed her or the impact she had in their life. Teddy bears and cards had filled the spot in the days and weeks following her death, but now things that would last longer seem to have taken their place. Other works of metal and wood and flowers growing in the spot rather than ones from the store made the location colorful against the blandness of the dry Montana summer.

Kennedy felt herself pulling to the shoulder of the road. She stared out the window for a long time. How many times had the two girls driven past this spot together or with their family? How could they have known that one day, it would be the spot where one of them took their last breath, alone, on a cold winter night?

So many had stopped here over the years… they would tag Jess in the photos, tell her how much they missed her. Kennedy didn't post about Jess or even talk about her. Instead, she kept her thoughts tucked away inside, until she could get up to the hill.

The hill was one of the only places she would feel Jessica. The other was in the gym.

That was one of the reasons why it was so hard for her to be in there sometimes.

Eventually, she made her way back on the road and headed towards home to her parking spot and into the door. Jackson looked up at her as she came into the kitchen.

"You don't normally stop at the marker," he said his phone still in his hands. "You okay?"

Kennedy smiled sadly at him as she slid off her practice shoes and ruffled his damp hair as she walked by. She had seen him pass by her while she was pulled off to the side of the road. "I'm fine, just having one of those days." She looked around. "What's for dinner?"

He shrugged. "Mom and Dad went to Forsyth, Hunter and Adam are in the living room."

"Oh, they're still here?" She tried to keep the excitement out of her voice. Spending time with Adam in person was a rare treat, but she wished he had mentioned it to her sooner. She wouldn't have taken so much time after practice if she had known.

"Yeah, for a few days, I guess. They were talking about catching our games this weekend before heading back."

Kennedy's face flushed and she quickly took a sip of the glass of water she had just poured. "Kinda hot in here, isn't it?"

Jackson shrugged in response and continued to scroll through the app he was looking at on his phone.

Kennedy rushed upstairs and quickly showered. She panicked slightly, not knowing what to throw on for clothes. It wasn't like she was ever dressed up when Adam was around, but she still didn't want to put on her clothes that were destroyed from helping move cattle in the summer.

She finally settled on a pair of black leggings and a long-sleeve t-shirt from the previous volleyball district tournament. Running some product through hair to help it hold its waves, she spritzed some perfume on and then headed downstairs.

Adam and Hunter were camped out in front of the TV in the main living room when she walked in. It was an odd moment since normally Hunter hung out in the basement living area when he was home.

"Hey, guys," she said as she strolled in, trying to act casual. "Didn't know you were sticking around for a while."

"Yeah," Hunter said without looking away from the flat screen. "Figured we'd stay and watch your games and Jack's."

"Sweet..." Kennedy was avoiding looking at Adam for fear she'd blush.

She sat down on the opposite end of the sectional from Adam. "What are you guys watching?"

"New cop show," This time it was Adam who answered her. She looked at him and felt her face turning red so she looked down and called Otis over to her. He happily trotted over, and she began petting him.

"Well, since you're home, I guess we can get dinner started," Hunter said. "Will you go grab frozen pizzas out of the garage freezers?"

"Mom's not cooking?"

"Something about needing to get out of the house for a night, Dad took her to Forsyth for a movie and dinner date," Hunter said. He looked over at his sister. "How'd you piss her off today?"

"Called her out on spying on me through Grace," Kennedy answered. He sighed. "She means well."

"Yeah, but damn."

Hunter shrugged, still engrossed in his show.

"So, pizza?" he finally said, as a commercial came on.

"Why can't you get it?" she asked.

He spread his arms out. "I'm a guest."

Kennedy rolled her eyes. "Fine, I'll get the pizzas."

Immediately, Adam hopped up. "I can help you."

"Bro, she doesn't need help with that," Hunter said. Kennedy looked at Adam in panic.

"Yeah," he said simply. "But I want a beer."

"Oh." Hunter looked at him. "Grab me a couple?"

"Sure." He looked at Kennedy. "Shall we?"

She nodded quickly and followed him out to the kitchen, where they let Jackson know their plans and slid on shoes. Otis followed along faithfully; the only member of the family Kennedy was okay with letting know her little secret was always welcome to tag along.

The freezer was out in the shop, along with what her father called "the pub." He mother hadn't let him put a wet bar in when they were renovating the main house, so he had built one out in the garage instead. It was where the other local farmers and ranchers came to celebrate after the harvests were done and where they would either toast their victories or drown their sorrows after high school games. Kennedy and Adam didn't say anything to each other on the way out to the shop and were sure to keep their distance. It was another story as soon as they stepped through the door, though.

She turned around and slid her arms around his neck and buried her face into his chest. He slid his hands around her and pulled her in.

"This was the day from hell," she said, her voice muffled in his sweatshirt.

"I'm sorry," he said. "What happened?"

"Besides what my mother clearly already told you about?" she asked. "Well, Grace and I got into a yelling match in the hallway. And then I cried in Coach Davidson's classroom for a while. And then got back into it with Grace after practice."

He didn't answer and instead pulled her in closer and gently kissed her forehead. The two stayed like this for a few minutes before he broke the silence. "We should probably grab this stuff before they wonder where we are."

"Yeah," she pulled back from him and pulled her hair back behind her shoulders. "You know where the beer is?"

He laughed in response. Adam had been welcome to the beer fridge long before he was legal, even when Hunter wasn't.

"Is Kris coming for dinner too?" She called out as she rustled through the freezer.

"I think so," he answered. "Think he'd want a brewski?"

"Doubtful, but maybe," she replied, pulling out several of the frozen pizzas from the freezer. Adam threw his arm around her shoulder as they made their way back to the door of the shop and gave her a quick peck before he pulled the door open for her. The closeness she could have with him when they were alone almost made up for how ostracized she felt most days.

Kris had arrived while the two were gone and had started preheating the oven. He was talking with his younger brother at the table when the two walked in, though he quickly stood up and took the pizzas from Kennedy as she walked in.

"Oven is going, I can pop these in there for you," he said as he took them. Kennedy smiled at him. While Hunter was more of a couch potato, Kris had always been a helper for his family. He had started coming over more often during the time after Jess's death, and the two had become a lot closer because of that: the only good thing she could ever imagine coming out of such a tragedy. Well, one of the only good things: Adam was up there as well. Kris had come back to the ranch after getting an agriculture business degree and joined the large multitude of single guys that the town housed. She knew he would make some girl who wanted to live in the middle of nowhere happy someday, but he seemed pretty content living his own life for the time being.

She sat down at the table. Adam was hesitating between going back out to Hunter and staying beside her in the kitchen. She looked at him for a moment and was about to nod to go join her brother and his friend when Jack spoke up.

"Hey, do you guys know what we haven't done in a while?" Everyone looked at him. "Game night."

The kids of the family had grown up playing board and card games. It was really one of the few things that they could do when they were stuck out of town in the dead of winter and it was too cold to be pulled on a sled behind a four-wheeler. Each Christmas, their parents would buy several new games they could play as a family. As they aged, other games entered, more adult ones that the kids would refuse to play around their parents. Their game nights used to be legendary, with most of the high school and friends from out of town holing up in the basement or around the firepit after prom to play.

For the first time all day, a smile spread across Kennedy's face. "Adam, go get Hunter. It's game night."

Kennedy ran up to her room and pulled out several of the games she considered her own before rushing back down the stairs.

Jackson, seeing the stack in her arms, had quickly grabbed the one from the top and proclaimed they would be playing that risqué option when he saw it in her hands and Kris immediately argued for one of the tamer options instead—Kris tended to get awkward with most of the cards in the game Jackson was pushing for. Hunter quickly took Jackson's side of the argument, and Adam became the tie-breaker by lazily casting a vote for the crowd favorite of questionable cards and answers. Kennedy held the game triumphantly above her head and perched her other games on the kitchen counter. Kris threw his hands up in exasperation as a joke and grabbed a few cans of pop out of the fridge and passing them to his underaged siblings before cracking one open himself.

The next couple of hours were filled with laughter. One of the best parts of playing this game with Kris was he was mortified by the majority of the cards in the deck; his face would turn bright red seeing his sister read some of the dirtiest submissions, and he got up and left the table several times with a "Jesus..." but always came back.

Sitting around the table like this made Kennedy forget about the day and forget that someone was missing for a very long time. It wasn't until Jackson spoke up from beside here, while the group took a pause between rounds for a bathroom break and to run and grab phone chargers or more beer, that she realized there were some empty chairs around the table that should be filled.

"We should do this more," Jackson said, sadness creeping into his voice. Kennedy looked over at her younger brother, and he was looking at her with big eyes.

Kennedy set her phone down. "Do what more?"

"Hang out, the four of us... and Adam, I guess. She would want it, you know?"

Kennedy looked at her younger brother and gave him a small smile. She forgot how much he looked up to Jess sometimes. And it blew her mind how old and mature he had gotten in the years since her death. She put her arm around him and pulled him in for a Helland side-hug. "Yeah, we should."

The group was fizzling on playing by the time her parents came back in that night. They had reverted to pulling the cards out of the box and were simply reading them out loud.

Her mother came in pulling off her scarf. When she saw the scene in the kitchen, a smile rose to her face.

"Game night, huh?"

Her husband followed in after her. "Looks like you guys had a fun night."

Cards were strewn across the table and most of the pizzas had been devoured, though the boxes they had come in were still strewn across the counter.

Kris immediately stood up when his parents came in. "I can clean it up, Mom," he said, and he began gathering plates.

Her mom waved her hand at him. "Leave it. I can deal with it in the morning."

The rest of the kids began gathering cards as their parents went to their room to change. Kennedy glanced at her phone: 10:35. It was getting late and she would need to be in town early for lifting. Adam noticed her glancing at the time and gave her a quick nod.

"Hey, Jack," he said. The youngest Helland looked up from his pile of cards. "Don't you guys have early practice tomorrow? Let Hunter and me deal with these."

Jack flipped the cards out of his hands, and they spread across the table while Hunter glared first at Adam, then at him. "You guys are *sooo* spoiled," he said as he began gathering the cards once again.

Kennedy gave him a thankful look and headed upstairs. She quickly read the assigned readings from Ms. O'Brien; that was really the only work she had to do. She slipped into her pajamas and waited.

The text message jingle came through just a few minutes later.

"Sorry for not telling you. Was with Hunter all day. No escape," Adam said.

"With that crab ass? No apologies needed," she typed back.

A few minutes later her phone dinged again, and she hurriedly read the message.

"You do actually need to go to bed."

"I know," she typed back.

"Will see you tomorrow," he replied.

She didn't answer, and a few minutes later her phone dinged again. "Goodnight," lit up her screen.

She smiled and turned her phone over as she pulled the covers up.

7

The next few couple of days went by as a blur. Things with Grace were still awkward, even after their conversation, so Kennedy spent a lot of time by herself at school, though the two did talk some. She focused on getting her work done each class to make sure she would have plenty of free time after she got home from practice and left as soon as she could to get home to shower. The next few hours were spent with Hunter and Adam, as well as occasionally Jackson and Kris and her parents.

Adam hadn't spent much time at the ranch this summer since Hunter hadn't been there and Kennedy didn't want to arise suspicion. This was the most time they were getting to spend together in person since right after Jess's death, when it seemed he and Hunter were at the ranch more than they were at school.

He had slipped into her room for a few minutes on two occasions, but it wasn't looking good that anything would allow them to have more than a few minutes of privacy. That changed, however, the day before Jackson's first game.

One Thursday a month, Kathy would drag Scott into town to attend a booster club meeting. Her mother was the president of the group and liked to have the extra body in attendance for moral support. This time, it happened to line up that the meeting was the same day as the day before the first home football game, so the two would be gone even longer making sure that everything was in order for the home opener.

Kennedy recognized the opportunity to spend some time together, alone, and in-person when Hunter and Kris went out to the garage to play one-on-one ball. Kennedy was not even asked to play (her brothers knew she wouldn't), and Adam told them he just wanted to "chill." Hunter had shrugged his shoulders, and Jack had grabbed the ball and rushed out the door with no answer. The two spent time lounging on the couch, their lips coming together. However, Kennedy found herself on high alert, waiting for the two to throw the kitchen door open with a bang or her mother to come in with a perky "Hello!"

Adam noticed and leaned back on the couch. Kennedy sighed and tipped over next to him, letting her knee rest against his.

"It's hard," he said.

She nodded in response.

"We could tell them?" he tentatively ventured.

Kennedy began laughing. "And watch my mom bust a gasket? Yeah, okay."

Adam had no response to this and instead turned his attention to the TV. A few minutes later, he ventured a "Why would she do that?"

Kennedy looked at him in disbelief. Adam was smart, studying pre-law in school, but sometimes she swore he had no common sense. "Um, probably because you dated my sister? Who died? Do you not see something fundamentally wrong with this?"

Adam looked at her. "Jess and I dated over three years ago, and she passed after we broke up. Maybe they would find it comforting and understanding?"

"No way in hell my mother would think that," she said, rolling her eyes. "She thought you two would get married."

Adam looked at her in confusion and let out a small laugh. "Why would she think that?"

Kennedy shrugged. "Dad and her were high school sweethearts. I guess she just assumed the same for you two."

Adam looked at her again, in silence now. Finally, he shrugged slightly and chuckled. "That's crazy. We were just kids. Your parents are great together and that may have worked for them, but there's no way that would have worked for us."

Kennedy felt herself tense up slightly, though she wasn't sure why. She shifted a little on the couch. "You were kids?" she asked.

He was watching the show again and absently answered with "Yeah, I mean, we were young. I loved her, but we both had a lot of growing up to do."

Now her entire body froze up. She paused for a moment before moving slightly away on the couch. Adam looked over now in curiosity.

Thoughts were bouncing around her head now, but she was having trouble deciding which part of his statement to address first.

Finally, "You loved her?" fell out of her mouth.

His eyes were suddenly wide. "Well," he started to stammer out but she cut him off.

"When did you stop loving her?" she asked. Her sister had never used that word to describe what she had with Adam, and suddenly everything just seemed really weird, to be asking him when he loved her sister.

He opened and shut his mouth a few times, but nothing came out. Kennedy put her hands on the couch and pushed herself to the side, away from him now, staring at him. "Adam," she said softly, "when did you stop loving her?"

He pursed his lips now, staring back. "That first love when you're a kid cuts deep," he answered finally.

Kennedy looked back at him. Laughter suddenly bubbled out from somewhere deep inside her. "I don't know if it's worse that you keep calling her a kid when I'm the age she was or if it's worse that you won't tell me when you stopped having feelings for her."

He tried to backpedal now. "It was different for us, we weren't as mature as you are," he stammered out.

"Still not answering that question on being in love, are we?" she asked, standing now. She suddenly had the urge to run, to hide, to lock herself away. Jessica would be pushing this conversation, demanding answers. She couldn't even bring herself to look at him now. Everything about him, about this suddenly seemed... icky.

She felt her feet carrying her to the kitchen. The couch creaked as he stood as well and began to follow her.

At the threshold of the kitchen entrance, she turned and faced him. He was closer than she thought, and she took a step back, startled slightly. "What do you mean I'm more mature than her?" she asked when she got her bearings back.

"We talk about deeper stuff than the two of us ever did," he answered. "Life and death and the future. Jess and I never talked about that."

She began playing with her hands now absentmindedly, staring at the ground in front of her. When she looked up, the tears were hot in her eyes. "Am I your second chance with her?" she asked.

Adam's eyes got wide now. He took a step forward and she instinctively shrunk back. He froze. "No, not at all."

She just stared back at him, the tears blurring her vision. She looked at the floor again. "When did you stop loving her?" she asked again. He didn't answer. She let out the air she didn't realize she had been holding in her chest and looked up. He was standing there with his hands held out, shaking his head.

Her flight response was at an all-time high now. "Oh my god," she whispered. She held up her hands and turned to the side. She needed air, she needed to breathe.

"Kenz," he said.

Her hair now stood on end at the nickname the Jess called her; it felt surreal to have to coming out of Adam's mouth in this way.

"Don't call me that." She whipped back to look at him.

Adam looked at her in alarm. "Kennedy?" He stepped toward her, extending his arm to reach out to her but she pulled back. The walls were closing in around her now.

"Don't," she said, stepping back. She was starting to get tunnel vision. "I need some air," her voice breaking again.

"Kennedy..." he began.

She looked him in the eyes now. His face, that had been a comfort to her for so long, suddenly seemed unfamiliar. She shook her head and turned, fleeing out the door.

Again, her feet carried her out the door and across the parking lot. Jackson and Hunter were on their way inside from playing basketball. She blew past them, not saying anything.

"Kennedy?" Jack asked in surprise. "Where are you going?"

She hopped onto one of the family four-wheelers, turned the motor on, and revved the engine on in response, jerking the gear into drive and flying out of the spot.

"Hey!" Hunter yelled after her. He looked at Jack. "Mom is gonna skin her alive if she sees her riding that thing without a helmet."

Jack shrugged again. Suddenly, Adam was there, albeit slightly flustered.

"Where's she going?" he said, slightly panting and with a wild look in his eyes.

Hunter shrugged. "Who knows, who cares." He looked at Adam. "You good, man?"

Adam coughed slightly. "Yeah, just coming out here to see what you guys were up to."

Hunter looked at him again, still confused but deciding getting to the bottom of it wasn't worth the effort. "Well, I just schooled old Jackson here at a game of...." but Adam didn't hear him. He saw the four-wheeler disappear up a hill and knew exactly where Kennedy was going.

The burial was more private than the celebration of life had been. Instead, it was just family and some of Jessica's closest friends. The lack of access to her grave was likely why the spot alongside the road had turned into such a memorial today.

Nestled back in the rolling hills of Treasure County, there was a spot that looked out over the entire valley. Getting the casket out there was difficult, but the family was bound and determined to have Jessica buried at her favorite spot, the place she often ran to when she needed to get away and think. The lack of access to it in the winter months was likely what drove her to cruise the backroads to clear her mind the day of her death. Or at least that was the only reason anyone could come up with for why she had been on the road that morning.

The high point of the land looked out over the entire Yellowstone Valley. It was dark enough at night that you could lie on your back and watch all of the stars overhead and even the Northern Lights if they were dancing far enough south that night. Jessica had loved chasing them, pulling Kennedy, the deeper sleeper, out of her room and into the pickup to try and find them many a time when they were out. In the summer, she would take the snowmobile out and watch the early sunrises and late sunsets that turned the sky shades of pink, purple, and peach. When she was upset, she would escape there to be alone. It only seemed fair to let her rest there for eternity.

In the two years since her death, her close friends and family members had really turned the place into a nice place to visit, even if it wasn't as adorned as the marker on the road. The headstone had been put in and her two closest friends from the FFA had built a bench, so that others could sit and talk to her. Her mother and Coach Davidson's wife had planted flowers; her teammates had put in trees. Her father had fenced the area off to keep animals out. It had become a beautiful spot, and the beauty would continue to grow as the land matured.

The day of the burial, however, her mother was in a panic.

"Maybe we should wait," she was anxiously saying as Kennedy came downstairs in her jeans and a nice sweater early that morning.

Her father was drinking coffee at the table, his chew can out waiting to be opened and a plug of tobacco put in. "I plowed a road, we can all get out there in the right vehicle." He stared at his drink for a moment. "Even the hearse can manage."

Her mother was jetting from spot to spot around the kitchen. "But maybe the spring would be nicer for everyone." She poured herself a cup of coffee. Kennedy watched the conversation from the doorway; neither parent had seemed to notice she was there. Her mother was right: the fact that they could bury her now, in the middle of a frigid Montana winter, was somewhat of a miracle. But her relatives and neighbors had been determined to make it happen thanks to her father's wishes.

"Kathy," her father said gently. "It's happening today."

Her mother looked up, and Kennedy saw the tears streaming down her face.

"I'm not ready," she whispered.

Her father shook his head. "And I'm not either. But the funeral home is bringing her at 10 a.m. And the…" now his voice began choked and thick, "the grave's been dug."

Her mother looked at him and suddenly crumpled into him, sobs echoing throughout the room. Kennedy took a few startled steps back and felt herself run into something.

She had turned and began to open her mouth, but Adam shook his head and nodded at the living room. She had nodded back and followed him out.

"I thought you were going back to bed," she had said simply. He had shaken his head. "I was going to, but I heard your parents in the kitchen, and Hunter texted me to tell me he and Kris were up and needed a ride since I," he put up air quotes for this next part, "'stole the damn pickup and ran off into the night last night.' I didn't even know he knew I left to be honest."

Kennedy froze. "What are you going to tell him?"

"That Kris's couch is complete shit and there was no way in hell I was getting any sleep on that thing." He shrugged. "It wasn't a lie."

She nodded at him. "Um," she began, "thank you again."

He winked at her. "Of course." And Kennedy had felt her face turn scarlet.

She was saved from answering by the Davidsons' sudden arrival. Marty had arrived with Mac, her older daughter Courtney, and the coach in tow, a breakfast spread in all of their arms. Her mother's chatter had echoed out across the house, and Kennedy looked at Adam. "I should go help."

He smiled. "Yeah, and I should go help your hungover brothers make it here in a timely manner." He reached out to hug her but stopped short and dropped his arm. She had caught her breath when he reached out and let it out slowly as his arm fell down. She gave him a small smile and turned away.

The two didn't see each other for a while. While Adam was hustling Hunter and Kris through their getting ready, Kennedy got to play hostess alongside her mother, welcoming those as they came through the door, passing out fruit and muffins. There would be a luncheon after the burial, out in the shop, which her father and some of his friends had painstakingly cleaned earlier in the week. It should have been a family project a few months later, for Jess's graduation party, but Kennedy tried to push this out of her head and kept herself busy making sure everyone was comfortable.

The house filled quickly with people, tears, and laughter. Kennedy moved from friend to relative to neighbor and back again, thanking them for being there. They reiterated to her what a great commentary she had given on her sister's life the day before, and she nodded along, smiling painfully.

Suddenly, her father was at the door, and a silence fell across the room. Kennedy was talking to one of the girls a year or two older than Jess when it hit her. She turned and looked at her father, looking out the window. He turned and nodded at the crowd who had gathered in the dining room.

"It's time," he said.

The somber mood took hold of the room immediately as everyone gathered their jackets and coats and trinkets they had brought to place in the grave: anything from flowers to books. Outside the house, people were figuring out carpool opportunities. The hearse wasn't here yet, but it would be any moment. Her father was standing near the edge of the main house property. She ducked up beside him.

Tears flowed down his face as he turned and looked at his younger daughter. He opened up an arm, and she slid into his reach. "Any minute now," he muttered. She pressed her face into his coat.

Suddenly, she heard tires on the packed snow, and she pulled away, only to realize it was Adam and her brothers sheepishly pulling into the driveway. She looked at them with wide eyes, and Kris looked miserably back out. Her father tensed and dropped his arm away from her shoulder, his gaze following the truck.

"Where the hell have they been?" he asked no one in particular. Kennedy immediately said, "Dad, not now." He looked at her, and she could see the anger in his eyes, so she dropped back and turned to walk back to the group.

It appeared most people had found rides at this point, in vehicles that could handle the rough terrain. Some were still milling about, though, waiting for the hearse to arrive. Kennedy found Jackson standing by himself and pulled him in for a hug. He had been so quiet and withdrawn over the past week, so unlike his normally chatty self. Sometimes she felt like he was being forgotten.

Her brothers and Adam slowly made their way over to her mother, who was standing with Marty. She couldn't hear what was being said, but by her mom's body language and her brothers' drooping heads she could tell it wasn't good. She then reached out and pulled Adam in for a hug as well as each brother. They continued their slow march over to Kennedy and Jackson.

"And how are we feeling?" she asked coyly. Kris groaned in response, and Hunter glared at her, his eyes bloodshot.

"We're Irish, we were doing an Irish send off," he replied.

Kennedy rolled her eyes in return. "I think that happens after you bury someone."

Hunter had nothing to say to that.

In the distance, the hearse could be seen slowly coming up the drive, and Kennedy felt all the air leave her body in one fell swoop. She stared in pain at the slowly moving vehicle that was bringing her sister home for the final time. But she couldn't look away. She couldn't miss this.

The hearse slowly pulled up to the gate to the main property, and her father met the driver. They talked for a moment before her father stood and tucked his hands into his Carhart. The Davidsons and her mother met him, and the group talked for a moment before coming over. "We are going to lead the way," her father said. "Marty and Allen are going to drive for your mother and me." He looked over the kids. "Adam offered to take you all out. You'll follow the hearse and help them if there is any trouble, alright?"

His children had nodded back, and he had grimaced at them.

"Then let's go say goodbye."

The group wove through the winding road the neighbors and her father had plowed in the days before, out to the spot where they had dug the grave with a backhoe. Fifteen full vehicles followed behind the family, holding aunts, uncles, extended family members, and friends. The car full of kids didn't say much as they drove. Kris learned against the cold window, and Kennedy could feel him swallowing hard every few minutes. Hunter sat in the front with Adam and would occasionally make a comment about the plowing job, but little else seemed like an appropriate topic to broach.

The drive was only about ten minutes, even with the shoddy road; it would likely be walkable in the warmer months. Soon, they were parking the vehicle to make the final walk to Jess's resting place.

The hearse continued up the road, led by her father who was walking in front of it. The group followed behind him, now bundled in coats and blankets and their fingers covered with gloves. Kennedy wished she had thought to grab a blanket, when she noticed Adam digging around the back of the truck bed. He tossed several of Kris's throw blankets out to the siblings, and Kennedy looked at him in thanks. He came up to her with the last one and held it out: it was huge, likely a comforter that Kris had long since retired. She smiled at him and pulled it to her chest.

At that moment, Otis and the brigade of family dogs came trotting up the road, and Kennedy found herself laughing. Of course, they wouldn't miss out on this.

The group slowly continued up the hill to the hole in the ground. Kennedy hadn't been out to the spot since they had dug it, and she felt her heart seize again looking at the pile of dirt. The group from funeral home was setting up the area, making sure the equipment would work correctly to lower the casket into the ground. Her father talked to them easily: he had grown up with the family that owned the funeral home, and they were doing him a favor by allowing the burial to take place here and now. The priest from the previous day, a man from Forsyth with a southern drawl, moved toward the front of the group, and those in attendance gathered around him. Kennedy pulled out the blanket and realized she had more than enough fabric to cover her and someone else. She looked at Adam and held out a corner, and he pulled it around himself, stepping closer to her.

Slowly, her brothers, cousins, and some of Jess's closer male friends moved over to the hearse, where they pulled the casket out for the final time. They gave their own blankets to one of the attendants and slowly marched her the short distance. Adam stayed beside her.

As pallbearers moved her for a final time, the sun came through the clouds and lit up the land, and everyone around them gasped. It felt like the first time they had seen the blue skies and the sun in months. Even the priest stopped speaking and looked up as the group of boys and men had set her down on straps above the gaping hole in the earth. Kennedy felt her arm go rigid from the shock and suddenly her hand was in Adam's. She froze, but he didn't say anything and instead twirled his fingers through hers.

The priest looked out over the group once again and held out his arms. "God and Jessica are here to tell us she has made it into the gate of heaven. We may weep the loss of her on Earth but can rejoice knowing her soul lives forever beside Jesus." The pallbearers had all stepped away now, and only the attendants remained near the casket. They began to lower it, covered with a bouquet of pale pink roses and sunflowers, her favorites, as the priest continued to speak in front of the crowd.

"We all have loved and cared for Jessica on this earth, but now we say our goodbyes to her. Please bow your heads."

Kennedy could see her family members and friends doing so out of the corner of her eyes, but she couldn't bring herself to. She felt eyes on her, and she turned and made eye contact with Adam.

"Receive the Lord's blessing," the priest said, his arms spread wide and head bowed down. "The Lord bless you and watch over you. The Lord make his face shine upon you and be gracious to you. The Lord look kindly on you and give you peace; In the Name of the Father, and of the Son and of the Holy Spirit."

"Amen," said the group of mourners. Kennedy quickly broke eye contact with Adam and pulled her hand away. "Amen," she murmured.

Her parents moved to the front of the crowd next. Her mother had tears flowing down her face and tissues gripped in her hands. Her father was the one who spoke. "Thank you all," he began before becoming choked up. He took a moment of pause and looked up before looking back over the crowd. "Thank you all," he began again, his voice shaky but confident, "for being with us the these last few days. This is a pain we never knew we would go through…" tears began to fall from his eyes now and Kennedy felt her own welling up, "and there's a long road ahead of us before we get back to normal. Or what our new normal is. Not just for our family, but for everyone here and for those across the state." He took a long breath. "Jess was… well, Jess was something special." The crowd laughed gently. "And there is no way for us to repay you all for the kindness you have not only given us the last two weeks, but the kindness you gave our daughter growing up. It takes a village to raise a child, and we are very thankful to have you all here to say good-bye and so that we can thank you for all you have done." He turned around and nodded at the attendants from the funeral home. "Thank you," he said, nodding at them each. "We can let her go now."

As the sun dipped behind the clouds once more, Jessica Francine Helland was laid to rest. Each person in attendance went up to her and threw in the customary fistful of dirt, along with things they may have brought from home. Flowers, a basketball shoe, some books, photos… everything fell into the pile in the center of the grave, landing with a dull thud on top of the box that held her body. Kennedy watched from several feet back as her extended family, some teachers, neighbors, her sister's friends, and her teammates went through the line.

Finally, her parents and brothers went one by one to throw dirt onto the casket. The white was barely peeking through now. Kennedy followed Jackson with trembling hands as she picked up a cluster of dirt and threw it into the air.

The spot looked nothing like it did that day, with the snow melted away and new pieces throughout the area. Kennedy parked the four-wheeler and walked up to the headstone trembling from head to toe. The wind from the four-wheeler had made her eyes water, but now they were solely tears falling.

She stood at the gravestone, looking down at it, not knowing what to do. She knew that Jessica wasn't here: at least, she wasn't here spiritually. Her body was below her feet, sealed away in her casket in her favorite dress with her childhood stuffed animal and a basketball. There were times when she swore she could feel her, her touching her in the breeze, whispering in her ear, but today was not one of those days.

Maybe that is why it was a little easier for her to let go for a bit and let her emotions fall.

Screaming at a headstone was perhaps not the most effective way of handling emotions, but the anger that Kennedy had felt for two years and the added information from today had brought her to this point.

Alone, overlooking the valley, she had it out with her sister until she found herself on the ground, just sobbing. It was difficult to argue with someone when they couldn't answer. Curled on the ground, Kennedy softly whispered out, "Why did you leave me?" to the stone. No answer came.

Adam was looking out the kitchen window, worried.

Kennedy had left over an hour ago, and it would be getting dark soon. Hunter and Jackson seemed unconcerned, sitting at the table talking about the game the next night.

Adam looked over at them. "Aren't you all a little worried about Kennedy?"

"Nah," Hunter answered. "She's always needed to be alone when something upsets her. Grace probably just pissed her off again or something. Normally, I would blame our mom but couldn't have been her this time." He juggled the basketball back and forth between his hands.

"Mom's going to be pissed that she took off without a helmet though," Jackson threw out into the room.

Adam looked out the window again. He had never really thought about the question Kennedy had asked him—about when he stopped loving her. Now, as he sat there, he wasn't sure if he ever actually had stopped.

His ponderings were interrupted by Scott and Kathy coming home.

Kathy was abuzz with excitement for the first home game of the year the next day when she came in. She had thrown food into the slow cooker before leaving and began dishing out the homemade chili as she chattered about the signs they had gotten made for the team and some of the events they would be hosting later on in the season. She pulled out the cinnamon rolls she had baked that morning as well, sliding them out onto plates. Adam wasn't listening, still waiting for the sound of the four-wheeler to reappear.

Finally, Kathy seemed to notice that one of her children that still lived at home was missing. "Where's Kennedy?" she asked, looking around the room.

She went over by the doorway to the kitchen and called up the stairs "Kennedy?" When there was no reply she looked at her sons. "Where is your sister?"

Jackson and Hunter began shoveling food into their mouths to stall for time. Adam internally sighed and answered for them.

"She left on one of the four-wheelers a while ago."

Kathy looked at him. "To go where?"

He hesitated a moment, then finally told her the truth. "We don't know. She was upset when she left."

Scott sighed from the other end of the table. "She'll come back when she's ready."

"That's why I said!" Hunter grumbled. "Adam is over here acting like a mother hen, worrying that she isn't back yet."

Scott looked up at Adam, and Adam felt the color drain from his face. "That so," Scott slowly drawled out. Adam gulped.

"Yes, I didn't know she usually acted like that when she was upset," he finally stuttered out, well aware that everyone was looking at him now.

Kathy sighed. "Jessica would chase her problems down; Kennedy runs away from them."

"Not sure why that surprises anyone," Hunter said as he got up to get more food. "They're different people."

"Yes, they are," Adam thought to himself.

Kennedy roared back into the family's parking lot shortly after sundown, the dim lights of the vehicle barely lighting the way. She sat in silence for a moment as the vehicle quieted down; the roar of the drive still echoed in her ears.

She slowly slid off and walked toward the steps the lead into the kitchen. As she neared them, the door opened up and Otis and Sawyer came trotting out to meet her. She bent down and let them lick her face; then she noticed the figure silhouetted in the doorway.

"Hey, Dad," she said wearily, standing up and brushing herself off.

He came down the steps and stopped right in front of her.

"Hey, pumpkin." His hands were tucked into his jean pockets and he had his boots on. "You okay?"

She nodded slightly, feeling tears come back to her eyes. She was glad the night could cover them some.

He stood in front of her in silence for a few minutes, then opened his arms to her. She felt herself moving forward and rushing into them, her tears falling freely now.

"I miss her so much," she sobbed. Her father slowly stroked her hair, not saying anything.

8

The next few weeks passed somewhat uneventfully in the lives of the high school students. Jackson's football team had won the first game of the season, and Kennedy's team had finished second at their opening tournament. There was room for improvement, but it had been a solid start overall.

Hunter and Adam had left town the day after her first volleyball games. Adam had snuck up to her room early in the morning to say goodbye, but things were still uncomfortable between them, and he had only stood at her doorway, simply letting her know that he would let her know when they made it back to Spokane. She had nodded along with the things he said, as he told her he would come back for Thanksgiving and Christmas and tried to make plans with her. Finally, he had shoved his hands into his basketball shorts and nodded and told her he'd talk to her soon. She had shut the door wordlessly and laid back down to stare at her ceiling.

Things with Grace had improved some, especially after playing together on the court. Kennedy even offered to cruise with her for a while before she took her home after the games. It was nice to have someone to talk to again after what had happened with Adam: the two hadn't spoken much since he had left town either. Actually, they hadn't spoken at all minus him telling her when he and Hunter had made it to Spokane, just as he promised. Kennedy wasn't sure how to start the conversation, and he hadn't reached out.

Her monthly appointment with her therapist came and went. She asked her about the mood Kennedy had been in near the beginning of school, but she had shrugged it off claiming it was due to stress. She didn't like opening up to people she knew, let alone people she barely knew. The therapist had suggested possibly talking about family therapy to help mend things between her and those of her family who could be there, but Kennedy had adamantly asked her to not set that up for the next time they met.

As the cooler air began to come in, the school's seniors had begun applying to schools. Kennedy was accepted into one of the larger state schools in October, and Grace got her acceptance letter to the other shortly after. Paul told everyone he had changed his mind about schooling and began applying to diesel technology programs around the area; Kennedy was surprised since he had never expressed interest in continuing his education, but she was glad he was doing something to get him out of town for a while, even if it wasn't that far away in Billings. She suspected his recent success in fall FFA events had encouraged him to continue on.

Lunchtime meetings were also in full swing. Kennedy was honored to serve as the FFA president of her chapter her senior year, and she ran through meetings once every few weeks. Her paper and annual class also kept her busy as she worked on editing and getting things put together to start on the yearbook. Her days seemed to be getting fuller and fuller even as the sun set earlier and earlier.

As the fall sports seasons continued on, the volleyball team was doing well, as was the football team. Soon the post season was on the horizon, and Kennedy, Grace, and Paul worked on getting their things put together for senior nights. While Hunter wouldn't be able to attend her night, Kennedy wanted both her other brothers to walk her out, and she requested that Jess's volleyball warmup also be carried onto the court.

Her mother had slid her hand through hers and she looped her arm through her father's as Mr. Lambert read off her future plans and "thank you"s to various members of the community. After, her team swarmed her and Grace, pulling them in for hugs. Kennedy found herself laughing and remembering the time they had done the same thing to Jess. A happy memory in the gym.

As the conclusion of the season neared, the Lady Pirates were ranked third in the district and, with only one weekend left in conference play, had the opportunity to slide up into second place for seeding before heading on the bus to Glendive. Practices were going longer, pushing the "three hour" limit by far; Mrs. Kiefer seemed to have lost her mind and had given up on teaching for the time being. Kennedy hadn't been assigned homework in her class in weeks, and they spent an extended time period each week watching science videos online.

It seemed as if everything was going to plan, but Kennedy had something lingering on her mind. Each day, when she went into Coach Davidson's room, the conversation he had with her about lasts had come to mind.

She was rapidly coming up on the lasts that Jessica had gotten to experience during her life, and his comments about regret rang around her mind every time she stepped foot onto the court for volleyball practice. In a few short weeks, the net would come down regardless of how she felt. That chapter of her life was closing. For a very long time, she had thought that the basketball chapter had closed too. Now, she wasn't so sure.

She knew what Jessica would want her to do. Play, of course. Jess was nothing if not a team player; one plea from Grace and she would have been all over her sister, telling her that it was something she needed to do, even if she didn't want to. But Kennedy wasn't Jessica, and she wasn't as keen to give up everything to help others.

Stepping foot in the gym when a basketball game was going on was enough to send her into a panic attack sometimes. She wasn't even sure if she could play a game without losing it. But still, Allen Davidson's words bounced around her head every day, with increasing velocity as the basketball season neared.

Insomnia had been a part of Kennedy's life since she was young, but it especially held her in the years since Jessica's passing. She usually watched TV, but sometimes, when her family was sleeping late at night, she would go walk around outside, looking up at the stars that covered the night sky. She would think about how her siblings would try to find constellations on the way home from late night games, pointing them out to each other in excitement. Kennedy would walk into the yard and sit in the silence, looking into the great beyond above her. It was there that she really thought about basketball seriously, for the first time in two years.

She remembered the first time she touched a ball after Jess's funeral. Her mother had sent her out to pull meat from the garage freezer for dinner that summer after the accident. Kennedy had wandered out, thankful to be out from under her mom's watchful eye for a few minutes. She was taking her sweet time, wandering around the building and looking at the workbench where her father kept his projects he would work on in his spare time. He had told her he was building her mother new bedside tables for their anniversary, so she stopped and admired his handiwork. Jessica's car was on the other side of the building, covered in a thin tarp. Kennedy felt her breath catch as she walked by it, moving toward the freezers to retrieve the meat. She gathered what her mother asked for into her hands and was just shutting the door when she noticed the ball sitting on the floor next to the couch her father kept in the building.

A women's basketball.

Kennedy was confused. She hadn't seen one of those around the house in months. Where had it come from? Jackson had switched over to a men's ball during the previous basketball season when he was brought up as an eighth grader to help the guys have a JV squad. And it certainly wasn't hers. She stared at it for a moment, not sure what to think. She finally shrugged her shoulders and assumed her dad had it out for some reason.

She pushed the door shut with a dull thud and began to walk out when she stopped and looked back. Really, the ball could be in a spot where someone could trip over it, she thought to herself. She sighed and tipped the burger meat onto one of the stacks of boxes he had with new parts for one of the ranch's vehicles.

She moved slowly back to the ball. It wasn't right next to the couch, but a few feet out. Almost like it had rolled into the furniture and then back out.

Kennedy's hands trembled as she reached out and picked up the ball. Its shape felt strangely unfamiliar in her hands... larger than she remembered. More awkward to hold. It had been nearly six months since she touched a basketball.

It was quiet in the shop. Her father, brothers, and Adam were out working in the fields, moving water for irrigating. The late evening sunshine was streaming through the bank of windows near the ceiling, catching the dust particles that were floating in the air constantly. It was peaceful.

She hesitated, slowly turning it in her hands. Then, as if she had never stopped, she put it to the floor.

The thud echoed back to her, the sound of her youth and summers. The hours spent in the gym and shop, shooting free throws and practicing moves with her father and brothers. Jess driving past all of them, her small frame letting her have rapid bursts of speed that Kennedy couldn't fathom, much less do. She caught the ball and everything came crashing into her as the sound bounced around the acoustics of the place.

The sadness of losing her sister would sometimes catch her off guard. A certain smell of perfume or hairspray that Jess used would hit her out of nowhere in the grocery store; a song would come on that the two used to sing along to in the car when they were driving home; a stranger would walk into her peripherals and suddenly her sister was strolling alongside her, her blonde hair softly swinging back and forth. And then suddenly these moments were gone, and she was alone again.

The dull thud of the basketball against the ground brought back her sister for that moment, and all the memories they shared playing the game. And just as suddenly they were ripped away.

Kennedy stumbled back slowly sat down on the floor as the sobs shook her body. This was one of the moments she wasn't expecting to have a reaction to, but there were just too many ties to cut away from the game. She gripped the ball in her arms and let go of the emotions she had been holding onto for days, weeks, months, fall out in her tears.

She wasn't sure how long she sat there alone. But finally, her sobs became less and less until they were a whimper. She wiped the drying tears from her eyes and stood up shakily, tucking the ball under her arm the way she had thousands of times before. She looked around. She had fallen at the top of the paint, just below free throw line her father had painstakingly painted on the floor years ago. She looked down at the black lines and at the ball in her hands. Slowly, she had stepped backward.

The rhythm of her free throw tradition came back to her naturally. Three solid bounces, readjust foot line up, eye up the hoop, bend down, then shoot with an extended follow through. She had been doing the same routine since fifth grade. When she eyed the basket this time, however, she had hesitated. It felt weird to be shooting out here alone, without her sister there to ball shag for her when it bounced off the rim. She honestly couldn't believe that she was able to do this, about to do this, to stand here and prepare to shoot. But there was something different about doing these actions, these almost sacred actions alone, alone rather than in front of a crowd where everyone was expecting something.

She took a few steps back, still eyeing up the basket. Then she moved forward again and the rhythm came back out.

Three dribbles.

Shuffle feet.

Eyes up to look at target.

Bend down.

Shoot.

Follow through.

And the ball bounce around the rim, slowing with each bounce.

It balanced perfectly on the rim for a moment, and then fell through the net.

"Like butter," her dad thought, watching her shoot. He had arrived just as she had turned back to collect the ball and had watched her through the shop window as she fell back and sank down while her sobs echoed off the walls. It had taken all his strength not to go out to the court and pick her up, like he had done when she sprained her ankles in traveling ball.

Instead, he had watched, silently. He watched her rise again and realize where she was. How she had lined up just like they had practiced for years. How naturally it still came to her. How she had hesitated, but ultimately stepped back to the line.

She didn't need him to come in and rescue her right now. So instead, he watched, heart swelling with pride, as she chased the ball down and returned to the line. Shooting again and again and again. All shots sliding through the rim with ease.

Kennedy had found herself drawn out to the makeshift gym more and more on her sleepless nights the last few months. She would wait for whichever parent went to bed last, usually her mother, to go around and turn out all the lights. Then she would wait for the inevitable snoring from her father, usually around 11:30 p.m. She would give it a few more minutes, then creep down the stairs, the basketball she had snuck out of the shop and into her room in hand, and sneak across the parking area in the cold autumn night.

Out on the painted lines of the court, those first few times, she would stare at the hoop, not sure where to begin. There was a big difference in playing alone after spending years playing around others.

Usually, she ended up shooting for a while, just wherever felt comfortable to her. Her height meant that she was a post player, so she would start at the bottom of the paint and work her way up and around. She wouldn't let herself move to the next spot until she had made a shot from where she was at on the court. Next, she would go around the three-point line. While she didn't have great aim from out this far, there was what her sister had called her "sweet spot": the area to the left of the center of the basket at the top of the arch. If she was going to make a three, for whatever reason, it was going to come from this one spot on the court.

She was more forgiving of herself in the case of three-point shots since they weren't what she normally would play. If she missed two or three, she would move on to the next spot, though she tried to get the rebound and go for a layup if that was the case.

She could practice the steps of a post player, but it was difficult without someone guarding her. So, she would do a few moves until she got bored. Then it was back to free-throws.

Coach Davidson had always put a lot of emphasis on free throws at practice. "They're how you win a game," he would say over and over again. In the Hysham main gym, there were six hoops to shoot at. At the beginning and end of each practice, each girl would be required to shoot sixty free throws and keep track of how many they made and missed. He echoed her father's favorite saying: "free throws win games." Kennedy would think of this each time she made it to the line, her dad's voice rattling around her brain. The team ultimately had one of the highest percentages for free throws in the conference, all due to the effort they put into them during practices.

Eventually, Kennedy would find herself bored or finally becoming tired of what she was doing. It was hard to keep one's focus when there was no one to play against. Times like these were when she really missed Jess, but she also missed her brothers. The girls had grown up playing against them and with them, and this was an aspect of her relationship she had also lost with them after their sister's death.

She would finally take the ball she had stolen and head back inside, ready to finally slip under the covers for a couple of hours of sleep. She didn't think anyone knew about her late-night escapades or how she sometimes did this ritual during the day if her family was gone. She wouldn't go out anymore if they did know: it would just be another way to pressure her into playing and that was the last thing she wanted. She enjoyed the silence when she was in the shop by herself and the comfort it brought her. It was like she didn't have to think for a little while in there. Having anyone else there would change the dynamic.

For the last few weeks of volleyball, her trips out to the shop increased. Her parents started going to bed earlier, waiting to hear the sounds of their daughter's footsteps on the stairs going out and her eventual return to the house. Kathy found herself smiling. This was a kind of sneaking out she could live with.

Finally, district volleyball was upon the team as well as all the hoopla that came with it, and Kennedy found new ways to distract herself. There were pep rallies to plan and the need to decorate the hallway lined with lockers, as was tradition. The football team was also having play-offs at home for at least the first round, so the boys were needing things done as well.

Finally, she was seated on the bus across from Grace and the rest of the team was on the bus that was being escorted out of town by the sheriff's department, ambulance crew, fire department, and parents.

It was a custom in Hysham to do this when leaving for tournaments or after qualifying for the next round. Kennedy had grown up waiting up for the teams to make it back so her family could parade them around; getting to be on the other side was just as thrilling as partaking in the ritual was for a seven-year-old, in her mind. This was why she loved her hometown: the sense of community that came out when you needed it the most.

The team had landed in second place in the conference and easily won the first game. The second brought them up against another team they handily defeated, just as they had throughout the season. Jordan, the team in third, had been upset by the sixth-place team from Circle and had dropped them into the losing side of the bracket.

On Friday night, the Pirates fought hard against the Bulldogs, but came up short in five matches. Kennedy was frustrated. She just wanted to beat them *once* this year. But she picked her head up and tried to rally the troops. They were guaranteed another week of playing: they could focus on having fun now.

And have fun they did. Bright and early Saturday morning, they finally got the chance to play Jordan at the tournament. The game was tough, and the Mustangs took them to four, but Kennedy and her team managed to come out on top. On to the championship they went for a rematch against Ekalaka.

This was fun, but in a challenging way. Each point mattered immensely, and Kennedy was proud to see the way the girls shifted and moved and how everyone contributed to the game. Ellie in particular made some great contributions, and Kennedy felt pride at sticking up for something she believed in. The girls came out on top, meaning a consolation game would need to be played. The team worked hard, going to five, but ultimately fell in the second match.

After the trophies were awarded, Mrs. Kiefer told the girls to go out and thank the fans before going into the locker room, and Kennedy rushed over to where her parents were, where her dad was beaming and her mom pulled her in for a full hug, which Kennedy was not expecting. She slid into her dad's side hug and did the same for Jack—normally she would rustle his hair, but seemingly overnight he had shot up and was now taller than her and just as stringy as her father and Hunter. Kris appeared moments later, slightly red in the face, and also threw an arm around her.

"Proud of you, Sis," he said.

The group began chatting about how the games had gone and how thrilling it had been to watch.

"I was on the edge of my seat the entire time, really!" her mother proclaimed loudly. Kennedy blushed at the outburst but felt happiness seeing how happy her mother was at her daughter's achievements. She often felt overshadowed by her siblings, especially doing so much of what Jess had done while alive, but now she could see her mother's excitement for her.

Suddenly, someone was covering her eyes and she froze. "Yeah, kept us on the edge too," a familiar voice said.

Kennedy reached up and removed the hands from her face and turned and threw her arms around Hunter.

"I can't believe you're here!" she exclaimed. "When? Where? How?" she blurted out.

Hunter laughed. "Took classes off on Friday and Monday and convinced Adam to come so he could see his parents since we were driving through and all. Scared the hell out of them last night."

Kennedy's heart leapt into her throat. "Adam's here?"

"Sure am." He had walked up beside them while she was embracing Hunter. "Can't ever say no to a trip to the ranch." He looked at Hunter. "Though I'm not sure we're going to actually make it out to the ranch?"

Kennedy felt breathless looking at him. The two hadn't spoken much the last two months, and she wasn't sure how she would feel the next time she saw him. Now, however, she remembered the comfort he brought and before even thinking about it she rushed into his arms.

He squeezed her for a moment, but quickly let go and she remembered where they were. She hurriedly stepped back and looked at Hunter again. "I just..." she threw her arms around him, hoping she could continue to feign shock, "I just really can't believe you guys came," she finally got out.

Hunter was looking at her strangely and then looked at Adam, who looked amused. He seemed like he wanted to say something but finally shook his head.

Kennedy felt happiness spread across her. She was going to play volleyball another week, Adam was in town, and everything seemed to be going okay.

Someone tapped her on the shoulder and she turned and saw Coach Davidson and her mood dropped several levels.

He nodded at her as Marty pulled her in for a hug. "Great ball, today," he said simply. Marty added an "I've missed watching you all play. I'm glad we made it up."

Kennedy gave her a small smile. "Thank you for coming."

Coach Davidson nodded at her. "Another week to play. That's a big deal." He looked out over the crowd. "Half of the girls your age don't get that chance."

Kennedy's annoyance shot up. He had promised not to do this to her again. He seemed to sense the change in her demeanor and quickly backed off, shaking her father's hand. "Scott," he said. Scott answered with an "Allen."

"S'pose I'll see you out at the pub tonight?" her father asked.

Allen chuckled. "I'll be there. Courtney is on her way to town, too. Might bring her along; she's been asking how you all are."

"Oh, that would be great," her mother answered. "I'll pick up some things on the way back through Miles City."

Marty immediately sprang into action as well, helping her mother plan and delegate who would get what. Kennedy snuck off during their excited chatter and slid back into the locker room, where the rest of her team had gathered. Grace came up and threw her arms around her and soon the girls were all hugging in the middle of the room. Even though they had been here before, there was always something exciting about getting to play another game with the people you loved.

Kennedy fell asleep on the bus ride home, and Grace woke her up just as they were passing the county line. Two miles out of town, at the Sarpy Creek exit, the welcome home sirens began, and the cars followed them through town and to the school, where Grace and Kennedy hoisted their second-place trophy with pride.

9

Kennedy drove home wearily. She was tired: more tired than she had been in a long time. She turned the music on to have something to listen to in order to stay awake as she drove the two-lane out to her house.

As she pulled into the drive, she saw the pile of cars in the parking lot, and she smiled softly. Adam had texted her and let her know that he and Hunter had made it out and were staying the night before heading out the next day to begin the trek back to Spokane. They had friends in Missoula they were going to stop and see on the way back, to help break up the trip. She was happy she got to see him and was hoping they could talk some about what had happened the last time he had been in town.

She pulled her duffle bag out of the car and tossed it onto the porch. She shuffled across the lot to the shop, realizing how sore her muscles were.

"I should have invited Grace out for the night," she thought. The two hadn't been spending a lot of time outside of school and activities together, what with the weirdness from the beginning of their year and how busy senior year was keeping them. She was looking forward to the break before basketball started where they could spend a day in Billings together.

The door to the shop was open, and Otis came trotting up to great her. She bent down and breathed in his musty scent, and he panted in excitement. Having visitors always got him riled up. He ran off as one of Allen Davidson's cow dogs came flying by, barking enthusiastically.

In the shop's make-shift bar, things were in full swing. The neighbors had stopped by for a bit, including some of the beet farmers who were just finishing up their harvest seasons. As they saw her coming in, a few held up their drinks to her and gave a celebratory cheer.

She blushed and slid into her father's side hug and went to get a plate of the pizza her mother had gotten in Miles City and piled on some chips as well. She found a seat and neighbors came up to say hello to her and ask her how she was.

She smiled politely and made small talk as she ate her food.

Her mother fluttered by with a round of appetizers and squeezed Kennedy hard. Kennedy leaned into it, feeling how tired she was yet again.

She went and hugged her father again and told him good night just as Jackson and some of his friends came in and the celebration started again. They had won their football game the previous night, and this celebration was just as much for them as it was for the girls' team.

She was thankful for the distraction as it let her slip out unnoticed. She was starting across the lot when the door to her house opened and Hunter stumbled out, Courtney Davidson gripping his arm.

Kennedy rolled her eyes. The two had dated in high school and everyone could see it was a horrible fit but them it seemed. She should have known that alcohol and both of them being home from college would start this up again.

"Sister!" Hunter held his bottle of beer in the air triumphantly. "Making another run for state." He saluted her. "I'm so proud."

Kennedy rolled her eyes as Courtney giggled harder and pulled herself into him. "You're such a good brother," she cooed. Kennedy faked a gag and Hunter glared at her.

"Come on, Court," he said. "Adam and your friend are waiting for us."

"Her name is Sa-man-tha," Courtney stammered out. She had grown up around the family, and Kennedy normally enjoyed being around her, but she and Hunter were some of the most annoying people in tandem she could be around: either they were all over each other or they were screaming at each other. There was no in between. Now was apparently a loving moment; five minutes from now could be the total opposite.

Kennedy rolled her eyes and continued walking when she realized they had said Adam was with Courtney's friend. "Who's Samantha?" she casually asked, pulling her long brown hair over her shoulder.

"Oh, Kenna, you will LOVE her!" Courtney cried out, finally letting go of Hunter to rush over and grab her. "She's the *sweetest* girl. I'm trying to set her up with Adam."

Kennedy could smell the alcohol on her breath she was so close; it took a lot to not step back as she processed the information she had just been given. "Oh…" she answered finally.

Hunter was looking at her hard.

She nodded. "Well, I won't keep you two then," she finally said, stepping out of Courtney's reach.

"Have fun," Kennedy added, feeling the lump in her throat grow; she quickly swallowed it down and rushed up the steps, grabbing her bag and dragging it inside. She dropped it inside the door—she was sure her mother would comment on it later—and rushed upstairs where she fell into the comfort of her bed, different tears from the ones she had cried earlier coming now.

She woke up to a light knocking at her door. She looked at her phone she had fallen asleep clutching. 3:13 a.m. Slowly she sat up and swung her feet over the bed and shuffled to the door.

Adam stood on the other side in sweats and a hoodie.

She stood with her hand on the door and finally turned and walked back to her bed, leaving the door open for him to follow.

He shut it quietly behind him as he came into the room.

She sat down on her bed and looked up at him expectantly.

"So," she said, trying to remain casual. "How's Samantha?"

Adam sighed. "Courtney told us they ran into you when you were coming out of the house." He sat down on the bed next to her. "They started fighting soon after, so not much happened. I spent most of the last few hours trying to get him to cool down."

She nodded. "Right."

"Kennedy," his voice was different right now. He seemed almost in pain.

She looked at him and felt her heart begin to break again. She shook her head.

"Don't," she whispered.

He sighed. "I care about you so much. And I want you to be happy: that's all I've ever wanted. But...I don't think either of us is happy right now."

Kennedy felt the tears fall down her face.

"I want to give you happiness, Kennedy." She looked up at him and saw he was crying too. "You throw a lot of positivity my way, and I hope that I have been giving it back to you as well. But this isn't the way to do it. I think we are both holding onto something we shouldn't be."

Kennedy was sobbing now. Adam went to put an arm around her but stopped himself short. They say in silence for a few minutes, the quiet only broken by the sounds of her sniffles.

"For almost two years now," he said slowly, "this has been something that we have kept hidden. I wanted it to be out in the open... I wanted to show the world what a beautiful thing came out of such tragedy. But every time I almost told Hunter or grabbed your hand in public... I couldn't. And the last time I was here, what you said about when I..." he was starting to get choked up now, "about when I stopped loving her... it made me realize something was holding you back and I'm not sure you'll ever move past it." Kennedy had stopped crying now and was simply staring down at her feet. They were dry and rough-looking from the volleyball season. "I should paint my toes tomorrow," she thought.

"Kennedy," he sighed, "you've helped me heal a lot these last two years. When I lost your sister," he was crying now, "I lost my best friend. I lost the person that I could confide in, that I could call at any time, the person who was always there for me... but then, there you were.

Someone who felt the same pain I did, who understood what it felt like. We were two lost souls that could come together to heal... but I think for now we need to grow apart. We're holding onto something that just isn't in the cards for us anymore."

Kennedy didn't answer, and the two sat in the silence. Finally, Adam rose.

"I'm sorry," he said simply. "You know that you can call me any time you need me or text me or whatever you need. I don't want us to change things—"

"Don't want this to change things?" Kennedy's voice was like a knife cutting through the room. "What exactly won't change, Adam? Are you going to come back here and kiss me and sleep with me in my bed? That's not what friends do."

Adam snapped back at her "Maybe those things will change, but the way that I care about you won't."

She laughed, a dry laugh. "Right." Kennedy hadn't been in a relationship before, but she had two older brothers and Grace was always talking up a new guy. As soon as things ended, there was no returning to what it was before.

Suddenly, Adam was mad. "You know, this isn't just something I want. You've barely talked to me the last two months."

Kennedy stood up. He was taller than her, but only just. She was nearly at eye level with him when she said ,"You should go now."

Adam stood too. "You know it's the truth, Kennedy. You have barely talked to me since I was here last time. Which is weird, because all we've done the last two years is talk. We never moved out of talking." He spread his arms out. "So really, nothing will change."

Kennedy stared at him with red eyes. "Get out."

He stared back, then turned and walked out, pulling the door shut behind him.

Kennedy stared at the door, her arms crossed over her chest, and sat back down on her bed, her body shaking.

The last time she felt this alone was the night her sister died.

10

Jess had driven Kennedy and Jack home after they got home from the ball game that night. She was driving one of her father's work trucks while he replaced a part in her car. It was heavier, so her mother was more comfortable having her drive it on those roads anyhow.

A heavy snowfall, followed by a warming period and then a quick freeze, had left them slick.

After letting the vehicle warm up for a while, the Helland kids dropped Grace off at her house and then the trio headed home. Jackson quickly fell asleep in the back seat with their bags, leaving Kennedy and Jess alone to talk about how the game had gone.

"I really think this is going to be the year we finally make it out of districts," Jess was saying as she spun the radio dial. "It's finally going to happen, twenty years later."

Kennedy had rolled her eyes a little. Every year, the girls' team would say these exact words... and every year, something would happen and they would choke, like clockwork.

"I know you don't believe me," Jess had said, finally settling on a station out of Forsyth, "but I just have a feeling. These last few weeks are going to be special. We're always going to remember them."

The two had continued their drive with Jess focusing on the road. It was icy out, and even with the bigger vehicle, she seemed to be paying a bit more attention to the roads than she normally would. Kennedy reached back and gently shook Jackson awake as they turned onto the last stretch of road before their house. She could see all of the lights were on the ground floor. Her mother was up waiting.

The kids pulled their bags out and headed inside. They shuffled through the kitchen and out to the living room where their mom was bundled up on the couch, book in hand.

"You guys make it out here okay?" she asked. Jackson grunted a response and turned to head up to his room. Jess nodded her head. "Roads were pretty rough for us," her mother said.

Jess had laughed. "They were a little rough, but nothing I couldn't handle." She had tossed her newly short blond hair around slightly. She had just cut it the weekend before and the shoulder-length look was still something she and her friends and family were getting used to.

Her mom had sighed. "Well, I'm glad none of us have anywhere to go tomorrow. Hopefully they improve some by Monday." She had stood up and began folding her blanket.

"Are you two off to bed?" The girls nodded. She held her arms out. "I'm exhausted. It's been a long couple of days, driving to Custer and then to Ekalaka. Let's all sleep in tomorrow. Now, give me hugs, then bed."

Kennedy rolled her eyes but went and slid into her mother's embrace. Jess also hugged her mother, then both girls had headed upstairs.

Jess used the bathroom first, and Kennedy came in as she was brushing her teeth. She spit into her sink and washed her face as her younger sister brushed out her hair. Jess had then stopped for a second, leaning on the counter. Kennedy had looked at her in concern. "Are you okay?"

Her sister had looked at her and smiled. "Yeah, just tired," she answered. "Get some sleep. I'll see you in the morning."

Kennedy crawled into her sheets a few minutes later, an exhaustion had overtaken her. Her mother was right. It had been a long few days, and she was exhausted. She was looking forward to sleeping in in the morning; she pulled her phone out one last time and made sure her alarms were off. She was going to sleep in tomorrow.

The sounds that woke her were unlike anything she had ever heard before. It was animal, primal.

Kennedy rolled over and grabbed her phone. It was 4:53 a.m. Something was seriously wrong.

She pulled herself out of bed and flung her door open. Jackson was in the hallway already, looking around confused.

"What is that?" he asked. Kennedy shook her head; she had no idea, but it was scaring her a little. She had tried to smile at Jackson because she didn't want to freak him out too.

She knocked on Jessica's door, but there was no answer. She pushed it open slightly. "Jess?" Still no answer. She shrugged and looked at Jackson.

"Wait here," she told her brother.

The sound continued, but she realized now that crying had mixed into it. She could see the kitchen light was on as she crept down the stairs and she could make out voices now.

She got to the bottom of the stairs and turned the corner to a sight that she would never been able to fully erase from her mind.

Her mother was on the ground, screaming and sobbing simultaneously. Her father was sitting at the table, half reaching for his wife and half covering his own face with his hands. "Honey," he was murmuring, but he seemed unable to move. The county sheriff, Anthony, was kneeling by her mother in a pair of jeans and a hoodie.

"Mom?" Kennedy found herself saying. She seemed to be disconnected from her body. She felt herself speaking and walking, but she had no control over her actions. She walked into the kitchen, looking at the scene in front of her in pain and confusion.

Her mother looked up at her and began sobbing. "Kennedy," she reached out for her daughter. "Oh, Kennedy," she choked out.

Anthony had stood quickly, "Kennedy, come have a seat, please." He had looked at her father, who looked back with blank eyes, tears flowing freely.

Her mother was suddenly threading her fingers through her daughter's and Kennedy took a step back, ripping her hand away. She didn't want to be touched right now. "What's wrong?" she asked.

Her mother began sobbing again, and Anthony had bent down to her, encouraging her to get up and into a chair.

No one was answering her, and Kennedy was suddenly angry. "What's wrong?" she repeated. No one answered her again. Anthony had gotten her mother up to the table and was asking her if she needed a drink. She was shaking her head and putting her head in her hands as her daughter demanded, once again, "Tell me what is happening."

Kennedy was scared, and she knew it came across in her voice and in her mannerisms.

"Kennedy, please sit down," Anthony said, holding a hand out to her. She stepped back again and felt the wall behind her. She was shaking her head, looking back and forth between her parents. Her heart was pounding in her chest so hard she thought it would break through her ribs.

"Kennedy, sit down." She had never heard a tone like that come out of her father's body and she froze, but still she was shaking her head as tears fell from her eyes, though she didn't know why. She had never defied him like this before, but now she couldn't bring herself to sit. Her entire body was vibrating with adrenaline.

Her mother let out another sob and her father turned his attention to her, sliding an arm around her shoulders. She leaned into him.

Anthony looked at her. "Kennedy," he said. She could see how much this was taking out of him. "There's been an accident.

She would not remember the next few minutes in great detail. It was something that she would be thankful for later. That she didn't remember him telling her that her sister had rolled the pickup sometime earlier this morning, between them getting home from the game and now. That one of their neighbors had seen it upside down while driving to town and had called for help. That by the time the ambulance got there she was already gone. She wouldn't remember sliding to the floor in silence, collapsing from the shock and grief that hit her like a freight train. Her parents' hands on her as they joined her on the floor, now trying to pull her up to a seat. Jackson joining them, his own cries joining that of his mother's as Kennedy pulled him into her, trying to comfort him. The undersheriff, a friend of Kris's, arriving with him in tow, her own tears streaking her face as he came after her and fell into his mother's arms.

Kennedy didn't remember these moments precisely. But she remembered the pain she felt; the pain she felt as everything she had ever know was ripped away from her, shattered into thousands of pieces. That kind of pain was unforgettable. It shaped you, how you felt things in the future, what you felt within your soul.

And then the numbness would sink it; something that may be even worse than the pain. The lack of emotion where you felt completely cut off from the life that was going on in front of you. How when your older brother called after talking to your mother, you didn't even cry because there was no pain and no fear; there was nothing. How when the basketball team showed up at her house later that morning, she felt absolutely nothing: not their embraces or their comforting words. Nothingness.

The feeling clung to her for days, with breaks of sudden outburst that she didn't know how to control. It was like she was living in a fog. She could see things, but they weren't clear. Everything was smudged out, from her physical touches to her emotions. Nothing was sharp anymore.

She knew she was blocking it out, limiting her emotions, even today, two years later. But the pain she felt when she learned that her sister had died: it was a pain she had never felt before. And anytime she let the thin, foggy veil fall ever so slightly, it all came rushing back to her, stabbing her in the heart again and again. It was why she didn't open that door in front of other people: if she did, it would break her. And it had cost her a lot over the years, straining all of her relationships in new ways.

But the truth was she kept it up for one main reason: if she let it down and got close with someone again, she didn't think she could live through the pain.

11

She wasn't going to go down for breakfast the next day, for fear of running into Adam the next morning, but Hunter came up to her room. He was in a jacket and jeans, ready for the day when he knocked on her door.

She had cautiously pulled it open, not sure if it would be Adam or not on the other side. When she saw it was Hunter, she felt herself relax and pulled it open all the way.

"Hey," she said. She looked him up and down. "Are you leaving?"

He nodded, putting his hands into his pockets. "Adam had something come up and wanted to head out early. Something about a class and a group project, I guess."

Kennedy froze a little and nodded back at him. "I see." Hunter didn't say anything and looked down at his feet. Finally, Kennedy sighed "Get off the pot," she said impatiently.

Hunter looked at her. She shrugged at him.

"What's on your mind?" she said meekly.

He stared at his feet for a moment more before looking up at her. "Kenna..." he never called her that, so immediately her hair stood up on end, "... is there something going on between you and Adam?"

Kennedy felt all the blood leave her face. "Uh..." she stammered out, not sure what had happened that made him think there was. They had always been careful when they were around him and even when each one was around him alone. She couldn't think of anything they had done or said recently that would make him think this. And Adam had blatantly said last night when he talked to her that he could never bring himself to tell him.

She giggled, a nervous tic that sometimes made appearances again. For once, she was thankful for it. It made it seem like she found his questions funny. "Why would you think that?" she finally got out.

He looked at her, his eyes slightly squinted. Finally, he leaned back, shaking his head. "No reason," he answered simply.

Hunter held his arm out, and Kennedy gave him a quick hug before shutting the door. The entire family knew about her nervous laughter, so he knew that she wasn't telling him the whole truth. In fact, she hadn't told him anything, he realized as he headed down the stairs. She had answered his question with her own question. "Always the politician," he thought to himself. He also took after his father and was not one to share much, but Kennedy was truly the master of hiding things away.

Adam was in the kitchen saying goodbye to his parents when he came down. "Kennedy sends her best," he said, looking at Adam. Adam stared back with no emotion.

There had been a lot of things the last few months that made him question how well the two of them really knew each other. First, there were the messages that Adam thought he was hiding so well: he seemed to forget that Hunter would borrow his laptop occasionally and would see that he was getting texts from someone saved as "Kenna." While Hunter never opened the messages—he didn't want to know what the two of them were talking about for fear it would deeply disturb him—it was pretty frequent communication from what he had gathered. Then there was the two of them always going off alone together or volunteering to help the other one out; Adam's reaction to Kennedy being upset a few weeks back didn't help the situation either. Finally, the most recent piece of evidence had come the previous night.

He had tried to set Adam up on several different occasions, but he had always wiggled his way out of it. Then Courtney brought her friend along last night who was clearly into Adam, and Hunter had paid close attention to the two of them: enough that it had set Courtney off about how he never paid attention to her.

"No, baby," he had said, waving his hand at her while staring down Adam and Samantha across the firepit. "I hear what you're saying."

Courtney had started blubbering and Samantha quickly came over when she realized her friend was upset. Hunter slid up to Adam, asking him how it was going.

"Alright," Adam had replied. He seemed distracted.

"You good, dude?" Hunter had slurred out. His drinking made him more paranoid into what he believed was going on between his friend and his sister... for the second time.

Adam had shrugged in response. "Just a lot on my mind," he answered.

Hunter had nodded along, taking a swig from his beer. He could see the two girls talking in the shadows.

"Anything you want to talk about?"

Adam remained quiet for a few minutes. Finally, he said, "Hunter, why are you with Courtney right now?"

Hunter looked at him in surprise. This was not the conversation he expected to be having. "Well," he said slowly, looking out to where she was standing. Then he found himself falling silent. Why was he with Courtney again?

"Uh..." he began, pausing again. "I guess because she makes me happy?"

Adam looked at him. "Really?"

Hunter shrugged. "I don't know man, we're not really together, you know? We're just together right now because we're both here and...." He struggled to find the words he wanted.

"It's comfortable?" suggested Adam.

"Yeah," Hunter said. "It's comfortable."

Adam didn't answer for a while. One of the girls, Hunter thought it might be Courtney, was laughing now. He squinted, trying to make out which was which in the dark.

"Hunter," Adam began again. Hunter turned and looked at his friend. The patio was suddenly swaying left to right, making him sea-sick. The flickering light from the fire was not helping the situation.

"Why did you two break up for real?" Adam asked. Hunter swallowed hard. It was difficult for him to answer, but finally the words came out.

"Because comfortable doesn't mean that it's right or that everyone is happy," he said, his voice thick. "Sometimes comfortable is when you are familiar with something, so it doesn't scare you anymore. But if it doesn't scare you, it isn't making you grow." He knew he shouldn't, but he tipped his bottle up and finished off his beer. "Comfortable can be great when it makes everyone happy and brings you peace." He gestured out to the girls with his bottle. "Court doesn't bring me peace," he had continued. "In fact, she's a real pain in my ass." He paused thoughtfully. "But she is always here when I need her to be. So, we circle back around to trying to learn to love each other and failing miserably."

He smiled. "I know you all think we are idiots. I am; she's pretty smart. She just gets caught up in the idea of me. But I'm comfortable for her too. I'm not challenging her or making her grow like I should be. So when we're together we're miserable." He leaned back in his chair and closed his eyes.

Adam spoke again. "But you used to be happy?"

Hunter waved his hand. "Oh, sure. In the beginning. When we were young and naïve and didn't care about growing at all. Then, we were happy. But now we are both trying to move on, and we just keep holding each other back." He paused again. "It sucks really. I wish we both could just give each other what we need, but we can't."

Adam wasn't saying anything now. Hunter finally stood up, unsteady on his feet. He squinted out into the yard again and realized the girls were gone. "Damn," he muttered. He had looked down at Adam. "I'm going to bed."

Adam had nodded and told him he would as well in a few minutes.

Hunter had gone to bed but woke up a little while later. He had picked up his phone to check the time and realized it was dead and his charger was upstairs in his bag. "Goddammit," he had muttered, sliding out of bed and onto the floor. Still tipsy, he had stumbled up the stairs and was fumbling with his bag when he heard angry voices coming from upstairs. He stared at the staircase, unsure of who it could be at this hour, when Adam had come down the stairs and gone to the guest room, walking past Hunter unknowingly. Hunter had stared after him as everything clicked into place.

Now, though, his friend wasn't giving anything up and neither was his sister. Hunter sensed that something had ended between them last night, but he wasn't quite sure what it was yet. As the two finished saying goodbye to his family members, they hauled their things out to the car. Hunter wanted to ask him point blank if something was going on—Adam was an honest guy; he would tell the truth if asked a direct question. But something was holding him back. Clearly, the two of them were keeping whatever had happened or was happening quiet for a reason. Maybe it was best he didn't know.

12

Kennedy spent most of the day locked away in her room. Her mother came up to try and get her to come down several times, but she just kept saying she was too tired from the long weekend every time she knocked.

She finally left her room Sunday evening to go look for food. When she came into the kitchen, Grace was sitting there.

Kennedy looked at her in confusion. "What are you doing here?"

She grimaced slightly. "Your mom asked if I would come out. Something about being worried about you."

Kennedy replied simply, "Oh."

Grace didn't answer for a few minutes as Kennedy pulled up a chair. "They left to go to your grandparents for a while. Jackson was with them."

Kennedy didn't answer again.

Grace shifted around uncomfortably. She knew that Kennedy would be upset that her mother had meddled yet again, but when she had asked her to come, there was no way she would say no.

"Kennedy," her friend looked up at her. "Are you okay?"

Kennedy felt the tears come to her eyes as she shook her head. "No."

Grace sat in stunned silence as her friend recounted what had happened the night before and over the last two years. She had never suspected that Adam and Kennedy had a relationship that stretched beyond friendship, but now as she listened to her friend recount the tale, she found some things making sense.

Like how Kennedy had become so protective of her phone and how she wouldn't invite Grace to come out if Adam was around. The late-night phone calls she had gotten when they were staying in the hotel over tournaments. How she didn't seem to have an interest in the other guys who would try and talk to her.

When Kennedy finished explaining everything, Grace leaned back in her chair.

"Damn," she said. "I'm sorry, Kenna. I... well, I honestly had no idea... that any of this was going on. So, I'm a little shocked."

Kennedy wiped her eyes. "We... well, mainly I, I guess... didn't want anyone to know about it. Because I knew everyone would think it was weird."

Grace hesitated. She knew she was going to have to tread lightly here.

"Well," she began, "it's a little... surprising, I think. But," she added as Kennedy covered her face, "I don't necessarily think it is... was... a bad thing."

"Well, it doesn't matter what it was now, because it's over," Kennedy answered, going to the fridge and throwing her hands up in despair.

Grace shook her head. "I don't think it's fully over, Kenna."

Kennedy shut the fridge door and looked at her friend. Grace made eye contact with her and shrugged. "He wants to be your friend still."

Kennedy laughed coldly. "I know I don't have much experience dating," she said, now rummaging through the cabinets, "but I know that *never* works out. Just look at you and Jordan or Nick, and we all know Hunter and Courtney aren't friends when they aren't dating. and even Kris and Sadie have drifted apart and the only reason *they* broke up was because of college. Honestly, if she hadn't found another guy, they probably would have gotten married." Kennedy shook her head. "No, this is done. I know it."

Grace shook her own head in return. "Kennedy, the two of you helped the other heal for a long time; that's something that *none* of these relationships have in common with yours. Even your sister and Adam. There's a reason that none of those other relationships are working out or ever will work out, but I don't think you should cut Adam out of your life just like that. Clearly, he is someone you can turn to when you need him." She knew that last part had come out a little bitter, but Kennedy had clearly been seeking comfort out from someone else for a while; Grace felt a slight tinge of jealously in her stomach.

Kennedy sighed, sitting down. Nothing in the cupboards must have sounded appetizing so she was emptyhanded. 'I'm sorry, Grace. I should have told you about this a long time ago; you have no idea how hard it has been to keep it from everyone, but especially from you."

Grace shook her head again. "You did what you had to do, I get it." And she did. Truth be told, she was a little impressed that Kennedy had managed to keep this a secret for so long. Kennedy wasn't an open book, but if something was truly bothering her, she would tell somebody about it. This must have been eating away at her for a long time.

The girls sat in silence for a long time, long enough that Kennedy stopped crying and instead was staring off into space.

"So, like..." her friend hesitated before steamrolling on and finally breaking the silence, "absolutely no one knows?"

"Well," Kennedy sighed, "I think Hunter was suspicious something was up this morning, but as far as I know, no. No one else knows."

"Oh..." Grace leaned forward. "So... did you get anywhere?" Kennedy turned bright red. and Grace giggled. "Oh, come one. I haven't been able to talk to you about this at all during the relationship. and you have heard all about my boyfriends." She scooted her chair closer to the table. "Spill it."

The girls talked for a couple of hours, giggling the entire time. Kennedy told her all about the moves that Adam had put on her, and Grace listened intently, asking questions here and there. At around nine, she realized what time it was and she announced she had to leave before her stepmom freaked out and started calling everyone looking for her. She came up to her friend and slid her arms around her from behind.

"I know it hurts," Grace said. Kennedy felt the tears come again momentarily and she quickly pushed them back down, "and it's going to hurt for a while. My best advice is to get some good ice cream and watch a lot of bad reality TV. I don't know why: it just seems to help. And know you can call me if you need absolutely anything, okay?"

She pulled away and slipped into her shoes. As she went to open the door, she turned back to her friend. "And for the love of God, Kennedy... please tell me the next time something this exciting happens in your life."

Kennedy shook her head and laughed. It did hurt still, even through her veil that kept out most emotions, but sharing her thoughts and feelings with Grace had helped a tiny bit, at least.

Her phone dinged and she glanced at the screen. It was a text from Hunter. "Made it back," he said simply. She waited, wondering if another message would come through from Adam but then slid her phone across the table. "Waiting never did me any good before," she thought as she stood up and went up to her room to watch TV.

She heard her parents and Jackson come in a little while later. The first set of footsteps that came up the creaky stairs were clearly her brother's. The next set were her mother's. She hesitated a moment before knocking quietly.

"Come in," Kennedy answered, and the door opened.

Her mother seemed unsure of how to proceed and ended up hovering near the door of the room instead of coming fully in. Finally, she held out the phone that Kennedy had left on the table in the kitchen. Kennedy sat up and paused the TV, and her mother brought it in to her.

"Did Grace make it out okay?" she asked.

"Yes," she answered.

Her mother anxiously shifted her weight nodding. "And Hunter texted you?"

Kennedy nodded.

Her mother nodded back and an awkward pause filled the room. Finally, she spoke again.

"I'm sure you're upset I invited her out—"

"No." Kennedy said.

Her mother looked at her in shock. "You're not upset?"

Kennedy shrugged. "I mean, I am a little. But it was nice to talk to someone for a little bit."

"Oh," her mother seemed confused. "Okay, well. Good, then."

Kennedy raised her eyebrows and nodded again.

"Well," her mother looked around her room and picked up a loose sweater off the floor and set it over her dresser by the door, "I guess that I'll leave you to—" she froze, noticing the TV screen finally. "Which murder documentary is this?"

Night-time was harder for Kennedy, but she expected it to be. That was when Jess's death had always been harder for her too. There was just so much more to distract yourself with during the day, but when the night rolled around, a lot of those things disappeared. But her thoughts were swirling around her mind, and she needed to escape them somehow.

When she finally checked her phone a while later, she wasn't surprised to see no new texts from Adam, but it still stung a little nevertheless. She had cried again; they would normally talk on the phone at night, minus the last two months, when their conversations were a little more sporadic, but now that wasn't really an option.

Desperately trying to distract herself, Kennedy pulled out her favorite book, *Blind Your Ponies*, from her shelf and flipped through the well-worn pages for a bit, but soon she became restless. She got up and paced around her room for a few minutes before diving down under her bed and grabbing the basketball she kept hidden there. She peeked out the door of her room and saw the lights were all off. Everyone had gone to bed, so she slipped down the stairs.

She got into the rhythm of things out in the garage fairly quickly, the steady thumping of the ball on the cement soothing her. She pushed herself as hard as she could. She was sore from the weekend, but more than that she realized that it was hard to challenge herself when there was no one else around. However, for once, she didn't care that there wasn't another body on the court to push her and make her work. She found herself putting the ball down finally and sitting on the floor, a thin layer of sweat glistening on her shoulders under the tungsten lighting. She wasn't sure what time it was, having left her phone inside, but she felt like she had worked out enough frustrations to finally get some sleep.

She crept back into the house and crawled into her bed. She was tired and she was dreading waking up for school in the morning, but it had to be done. They had divisionals to prepare for, and she really didn't want to miss another day of school.

Her thoughts were still swirling around in her mind, but not as much as they were before. She rolled over and tried to push them down as much as they could, but they bubbled over as she fell asleep. Kennedy hadn't remembered her dreams in a long time—but that night, with so much on her mind and flowing through her brain, there was no way to keep them from coming.

She awoke with a start to her phone alarm blaring at her, and she groaned as she reached over to turn it off. She found herself looking at the screen, but when she didn't see Adam's name, she threw it across her bed and rolled back over, waiting for the next alarm to go off. When it finally did, she threw her legs off the bed with a sigh.

She winced slightly. She hadn't realized how hard she had pushed herself out in the gym trying to outrun her thoughts and feelings the night before, and her body was not happy with her on top of the weekends' games. She hadn't done moves like that and shot like that in two years; coupled with the soreness form playing volleyball all weekend, she was having a rough start to her morning.

She slid into the shower, trying to loosen herself up some but finding little relief. As she got dressed, she found herself crying in frustration over her favorite sports bra not being in the hamper. She knew there were other contributing factors to her attitude, but clearly it was going to be a long day.

She skipped going into the kitchen entirely and left without saying a word to her family. Instead, she shot Grace a text asking her to cruise for a while as she left the house. She would go to the town's small convenience store first to grab something for breakfast before picking her up so she had plenty of time to respond.

As she drove past where Jess had died, she felt hot tears come to her eyes again, and she tried to brush them away as she drove, her sniffles the only sound in the car at the moment. She cried the rest of the way to town and decided it was probably not the best idea to go into the store with her eyes red and tears rolling down her cheeks. Instead, she pulled into the school parking lot and checked her phone.

Grace had answered her during her drive to town. "Can't," the message said. "Dentist in Billings today."

Kennedy's stomach dropped slightly. While she knew her friend would be there if she needed her, she couldn't help but feel an intense loneliness swarm up inside of her without anyone by her side going into the day.

She stayed in her car as long as she could to avoid having to run into most people in the hallway. Finally, she got out and rushed to Ms. O'Brien's classroom; a few stragglers remained in the hallway, and she came into the room as the bell was ringing.

Ms. O'Brien looked up from her desk. "Cutting it close today, are we?"

"Sorry," Kennedy sat down in her desk as the bell finished ringing. Paul was across the room, working on the daily journal topic that was printed on the board.

"No Grace today?"

Kennedy shook her head. "No, she had an appointment in Billings."

Ms. O'Brien nodded. "Alright, get to work writing then."

Kennedy sighed and pulled out her journal from her bag. She stared at the prompt for a moment then turned to her journal. Most days she would dutifully write about whatever was on the board, but today it just wasn't resonating with her. Writing about what historical figure she would like to have dinner with just wasn't something that has been on her mind. Instead, she began writing about the feelings she was having in that moment. She knew she wasn't anywhere near writing for the prompt, but there was something cathartic about writing about her problems like this.

She left a small note for her teacher as she asked them to finish up writing: "Sorry," she scrawled. "Had to go off topic today."

The rest of the day dragged on. Kennedy moved from period to period, keeping mainly to herself. Her teachers congratulated her if they hadn't been at the games over the weekend and she would politely thank them, but then would become withdrawn again. She took her lunch into Ms. O'Brien's room. Her teacher was sitting at her desk, grading assignments that had come in from the volleyball girls. She smiled at Kennedy, then looked at her tray quizzically.

"Not eating in the cafeteria today?"

Kennedy shrugged. "Just kinda feel like having some time alone right now."

Her teacher nodded slowly, putting down her grading. "Kennedy, are you doing okay?"

Kennedy knew she would cry if she spoke right away so she took a few seconds to breathe. "Yeah, I'm fine," she answered. "Just one of those days, I guess."

Ms. O'Brien sighed and stood up. "I was cleaning out the closet the other day," she said, walking to her back counter, "and I found this tucked away in there. I thought you might like to have it."

She held out a pink binder, and Kennedy gasped when she saw the written neatly in the corner. "Jessica Francine Helland."

Ms. O'Brien's students were required to keep binders during their time taking her classes. The binders stayed in her room year-round until you graduated or moved; only then were you allowed to move them from her shelves. She had forgotten that Jess would have had one in her room.

"I'm sorry I'm just now getting it to you," she said as Kennedy sat her lunch tray down on a desk and slowly took it from her. "I must have tucked it away over the summer for you all, and the girls actually found it when they were in my room yesterday." She smiled sadly. "I should have given it back to your family a long time ago."

Kennedy shook her head and swallowed hard "No," she said, looking at the binder in her hands. "I... I forgot she would have even had this." She looked at her teacher. "Thank you. Thank you so much."

Ms. O'Brien smiled at her again. "You're welcome. Enjoy it."

Kennedy nodded, still transfixed by the binder. She went and sat at the desk that her tray was at, completely forgetting about her salad and soup that she had just gotten. Ms. O'Brien slipped out, giving her some privacy.

Kennedy slowly opened the cover. The thing was nearly exploding it was so full. Kennedy's was near this point, so she got it. Five years of assignments and projects would do that. She rifled through her sister's projects and her memories during her time in high school. She would pour over them all in greater detail later, but for now she wanted to a glimpse into her life.

Kennedy flipped through the art that filled one side of the binder and then flipped through a few of her papers, pulling a couple out. There was a letter she wrote to Scout telling her that she thought she was very brave and a paper detailing her thoughts on the relationship of Romeo and Juliet. A few of her editorial pieces from *The Cutlass,* the school newspaper, were tucked inside as well, including a piece she had written arguing against the dress code her junior year of school. She had been especially proud of that, even though it had gotten her into some hot water with her mother back at the ranch. Her journal from senior year was tucked in the back, behind some more papers. Kennedy hadn't known that she kept it inside her binder: she had always separated the two, but still she flipped through the little blurbs of her sister's life and her thoughts about the random topics that had been on the board that day. Kennedy began skimming through them.

"First day of senior year!" the first page began. "I can't believe it's finally here."

A few entries later she wrote "If I could have dinner with any group of people I wanted, one of them would have to be Jimmy Fallon."

"Basketball starts today," one later began. "This is going to be our year. I can feel it."

Kennedy stared at this line of writing for a long time. She remembered how excited Jess was for her first day of her senior year season. How she had basically sprinted for the gym that afternoon, hair still long and tied up into a topknot. How she had gotten up to speak next to Coach Davidson about expectations and where she wanted to see the season end. She had clapped her hands together at the end, before they broke out of their huddle to begin warming up. "This is going to be our year, girls. We've got this," she had said before calling out "family on three. One, two, three."

"Family!" they had screamed back.

The lunch bell rang, and Kennedy flipped the pages to the front. She knew she wouldn't be able to get through the entire thing during the lunch period, but the little taste she had had shifted her mood greatly—it was the connection she was missing with her sister, the missing link that Adam had been in her life for so long. She was about to shut the cover when she felt something under the pages: a bump. She looked at the pages in confusion. They should be lying flat. She picked all of them up and looked at the pocket of the binder, where she could now see something had been stuck into it that was not papers. She slid her hand into the tight pocket and pulled the thin, flat piece of plastic out. It was a flash drive.

The underclassmen were starting to come into the room now, and Kennedy didn't want to explain what she had. She quickly threw the flash drive into the pocket of her hoodie and set the tray on top of the binder to carry it out of the room.

Grace reappeared at the end of band class that day, just in time to make it to practice. She came in and sat down at the piano and began to play and sing. Grace had taken lessons for years and had a beautiful voice that floated around the room. Kennedy listened to her, and Mrs. Jean walked by and reminded her "There is a choir here." Grace shook her head. "No way in hell is that happening," she said under her breath to Kennedy.

The two walked out of the room together when the bell rang. "How are you doing?" she asked as they stopped by their lockers to pull out their things for practice. Kennedy shrugged. "I'm okay," she answered. Despite Grace reaching out and making the effort to talk to her, Kennedy still felt somewhat withdrawn from her friend with the feelings of loneliness swimming inside of her. The feelings had lessened as the day had gone on, but they still lingered inside of her.

"We should get you off the ranch, what if we went to a movie tonight in Forsyth?" she asked. "We could see if anyone else on the team wanted to go and make it a bonding experience."

"I don't have any other clothes with me," Kennedy answered, thankful to have an excuse. She really just wanted to go home, be alone, and look at the drive that was still in her pocket.

"Oh. Maybe tomorrow?" Grace asked as they walked into the gym.

Kennedy nodded. "Yeah," she said, distracted by wondering what could be on the drive in her pocket, "that could be fun, just let me know."

She rushed out of the gym when practice ended, only to realize she had promised Grace a ride home. She paused in the lobby impatiently, scrolling through the apps on her phone. As the other girls came out, she looked up and said goodbye. The third time, she realized she was standing across from the retired jersey of her sister.

They had retired the number twelve from the girls' basketball program in a ceremony during the all-class reunion over the summer immediately following her death. The jersey now hung in a shadow box right outside the gym, looking out over the lobby. A photo of her celebrating during the victory over Wibaux in Wibaux the week before her death was hanging as part of a plaque with her name, the year she should have graduated, and A.E. Housman's "To an Athlete Dying Young" printed beside it. Her sister had loved that poem; it was now a bit eerie to see it depicting her own life cut short as an athlete.

Kennedy didn't often stop to look at the memorial, but there was usually a crowd around it during the beginning of games as people looked at it. Basically, everyone in the conference knew what had happened, but it wasn't unusual for younger visiting players to not know who Jess Helland was. It made Kennedy's heart hurt that those conversations and questioning glances would continue to grow over the years.

Grace finally came rushing out of the gym with an "I'm sorry, I was talking to a few of the girls about maybe seeing the movie tomorrow, but they suggested Wednesday so now we might go then but normally that would be a team dinner night so we are still trying to figure it out..." she trailed off as she noticed where Kennedy was standing.

Kennedy turned and looked at her.

"You okay?" asked Grace.

"Yeah," Kennedy said. Her hands were twirling the drive in her pocket. "Let's go."

13

She was cornered by her mother as soon as she stepped into the kitchen. "How was your day, honey?" she asked. Jackson was already at the kitchen table with a plate of food, and she could hear Kris and her father talking in the dining room next door. There was no way she was escaping to her room like yesterday.

She dropped her bag on the floor with a resigned "Fine," as she made her way to the table in the room.

Her mother set a plate in front of her filled with casserole and salad. "Just fine?"

Kennedy shrugged. "Yeah, Grace wasn't there so it was pretty quiet overall."

Her mother finished dishing up two more plates for her oldest son and husband before sitting down with her own plate at the table. "I see," she answered, taking a bite of her food. She chewed for a moment before pressing on.

"Ms. O'Brien texted me," she said casually. Kennedy sat her fork down and leaned back in her chair.

"And?" she asked, crossing her arms.

"She just said that you had eaten in her room today and wanted to know if everything was going okay, she wasn't sure you seemed like yourself," her mother answered, taking another bite.

Luckily, before Kennedy could answer, Kris and her father came into the room, continuing their conversation from wherever they had been having it before.

"You know I'll work around your schedule, Kris," her father was saying as he came in. "This is a great opportunity for you, and I know it's something you've been wanting to do for a while. I'm just glad it finally worked out."

Kennedy looked at her father and brother as they sat down. "What's something he's been wanting to do?"

Kris smiled at her, suddenly bashful. "Coach," he answered.

Her mother immediately chimed in with an "Oh, I'm so glad you got it!" and even Jackson looked up from his phone long enough to give his brother a fist bump.

Kennedy blinked. "You're coaching?"

"Well, assistant coaching," he answered, stabbing his salad with a fork. "But yes, coaching."

Kennedy looked at him. "What exactly are you coaching?" she asked.

Kris hesitated and stared at his plate for a moment, chasing a loose tomato around with a fork. Finally, he looked up and made eye contact with her. "Girls' basketball."

Kennedy stared at him, not knowing how to react. First, she wanted to get up from the table and storm off to her room. Then, she wanted to cry. Finally, she settled on nodding slightly and looking down at her own plate.

"Oh," she answered. "Well... congratulations."

She could feel that there was some tension in the room, and no one really seemed to know how to handle it as sounds of clicking filled the room as they all turned to their food. Finally, her mother began talking about how excited she and the booster club were to get to help decorate the hallway again the next night.

Kennedy listened absentmindedly, stabbing some salad onto her fork. She wasn't really hungry, but she forced herself to eat enough that her mother wouldn't question it and waited for an opportunity to leave the table without upsetting her.

After what seemed like forever, her father tossed his napkin on to his plate and leaned back in his chair and told his wife that it had been "Delish."

Kennedy quickly jumped up and scraped the remainder of her food into the trash and thanked her mother before grabbing her bag and rushing upstairs.

She had an older laptop in room that was a hand-me-down from Kris's time in college. It took a while to boot up as she sat anxiously waiting. Finally, the screen kicked on and she logged in as fast as she could.

She pulled the drive out from her hoodie pocket, where it had remained all afternoon and plugged it into the computer and opened it up to see the files.

Jess had been a very organized person, so it was not surprisingly she had only a few folders to sort through. One was labeled "Photos." Kennedy quickly moved past that to "FFA;" "College;" and "English." The final one was labeled "Life Story."

Hesitating for a moment, Kennedy finally clicked on the final folder, and the screen took her to a window separated by chapters.

The life story was an assignment done in Ms. O'Brien's class during the last semester of your senior year. Jess would have just started working on hers, so Kennedy wasn't expecting much, but she was surprised that there were already a few documents in the folder. She clicked on the first one and Word slowly opened it up.

Ms. O'Brien had a set order and topics that one needed to write in for the assignment. While Kennedy hadn't gotten the handout on it yet, it was clear the first chapter was an introduction to who you were. "My name is Jessica Francine Helland," began Jess's writing, "and I am who I am."

I live on a ranch on the edge of eastern Montana. That's important, because it shaped who I am in many ways. I grew up with a strong work ethic and as someone who was always willing to get into the bullpen, even when my brothers were scared. But it didn't just shape who I was as a worker. It shaped me in what I love and what I want to do with my life

We live so far out of town that it was hard to have friends when I was younger. We didn't spend our days at the pool in the summers or riding our bikes around town. Well, at least we didn't most days. Instead, we grew up chasing each other around the open spaces that our family owns on dirt bikes or horseback. My siblings were, and still remain, my best friends. They were the ones who were there for every moment of my life until, one-by-one, we got our licenses and learned to make friends on our own. But my family has remained an important part of my life. They are the ones who are here for me when no one else seems to be, not even myself.

Basketball is my favorite sport. I grew up playing it one the ranch alongside my siblings. But the game has become more than a game to me. I don't want to be the person who defines her life as a game, but it is how I understand the world. You see, in life I have many coaches. I have many teammates. I have also had many games that challenged me to my core— both on and off the court. I have fouled and I have watched others be fouled. It just makes sense to me.

I know that makes my decision to not play basketball in college a little hard to understand. I have talked to coaches and even received offers. But this game has become a part of me. And I'm worried if I don't move on that I will never see what else life has to offer. So, I am beginning to say goodbye as I write this. I am saying goodbye to a lot of things in the coming months. But it doesn't make me sad. At least it doesn't right now. Instead, it makes me excited for the future and for what is to come.

I am not sure where I will be when I finish writing this or when I sit down to read it next. And I am not really sure how to define myself, to be completely honest. I hope the next few chapters help both you, and me, figure it out.

There were several lines of spaces now, almost as if the next part was added in as an afterthought.

"I sometimes feel a little lost on who I actually am," Jess wrote, "because everyone who knows me has their own preconceived notion of who I am or who I should be. I want to know who I am and who I am becoming, but really, I am just getting to know her."

"So," she continued. "To the woman who rereads this at the end of college or when maybe she gets fired from a job or maybe when life is going good: don't forget about the days that you questioned who you were and what you believed. You have grown so much from this moment, and I am so proud of you. We are so proud of you. You've got this."

Kennedy stared at the page. Clearly, this was a draft, as Jess was all over the place on what she was talking about. But, there was something else. It almost seemed like she wasn't sure where she wanted to go with it. The line "I sometimes feel a little lost" especially stuck out to her when thinking this.

This surprised Kennedy. Jess had always acted like she was calm and collected and knew what she was doing, whether it was on the court or in life. She hadn't known her sister had doubts like that.

Someone cleared their throat and Kennedy looked up in shock. Kris had opened her door at some point and was standing in the entryway looking at her.

"What are you reading?" he asked. "Must be pretty good if you didn't hear me knocking or opening your door."

"Sorry," she stuttered, quickly shutting the laptop. "Just... scholarship stuff," she finally settled on after quickly running a list of plausible responses through her mind.

He nodded, looking around her room. "Can I come in?" he asked.

"Well, you are already in here," she answered. "I feel like saying no at this point would be rude."

Kris walked over to her desk chair and sat down heavily. He rested his hands on his knees. "I just wanted to check in with you and see how you were doing," he explained. He glanced up at her before she could answer. "And don't give me the same bullshit response you give Mom about being fine."

Kennedy froze, shutting her mouth. While Kris was the one who would sit in silence with her, he was also the one who would call her out when she was lying.

"It's been hard lately," she finally admitted.

He nodded. "You've been acting different lately. Even different than you did after she died."

"Yeah," Kennedy answered. "I know."

"What changed?" her brother asked.

Kennedy hesitated again. "It's just... I've been doing everything that she has done, but I also have started doing stuff she didn't get to do," she explained. "I feel... I don't know, Kris. It's hard to explain."

"You feel guilty." She looked at him in shock and nodded slowly. It was weird to have someone else put it out there, how she felt. Not even her therapist did that.

Kris sighed. "I had wondered if that was it after Dad told me he caught you hanging one of her tassels from her rearview. How long have you felt this way?"

Kennedy knew the answer was from the minute Adam had spent the night in her room after the funeral, but she didn't want to get into that now. "I think," she answered slowly, "there has always been a little bit of guilt. Like, why wasn't I with her in the car, wherever she was going? But the last few months, it's just been overpowering. Every time I do something, I'm reminded of when she did it or how she did it, and this reminder is constantly hanging over my head that is reminding me that soon, there is not going to be any reminders because I will have passed her in life." She had rushed out the last part because she was scared if she didn't say it now that she never would.

Kris whistled under his breath. "Damn," he said. "I didn't know; I'm sorry Kennedy."

She shook her head. "I know it's silly," she said. "I know I shouldn't feel this way. It's just so hard to comprehend that in a few short months,

I will have lived more life than my sister; the one who was always carving the path for me. And I feel bad that I get to continue on, while she is frozen in time."

"There's nothing wrong with your feelings, Kenna," he answered. "Your feelings and your thoughts are valid. Every emotion you have felt since her death is valid, and there is no reason to explain it or try and change how you feel. It's how you heal." He sighed heavily before continuing on. "I think sometimes we are told there is a certain way we should heal, and when we don't heal in that way, we think we are in the wrong. But there is no timeline on our healing from something like this. And I honestly don't know if we every truly heal from it. It becomes a part of us and how we grow and live..." he paused, "and even how we love."

Kennedy felt herself flush, and she pulled her hoodie up over her face. Kris continued on. "But I also want you to know that she would never want you to feel guilt over living. That's not who Jess was or who she would ever be. She would be your biggest cheerleader if she was here today, and she would be excited about the things you will be doing soon. That doesn't change how you have the right to feel and heal," he added, "but I wanted you to hear those words from someone else."

He stood to go. "I love you," he said to her.

"I love you too" she answered.

He began to walk to the door when she spoke again. "Kris?"

He turned and looked at her. "Yeah?"

"Why didn't you tell me about the coaching job?"

He now looked a little guilty. "I didn't think you would care to be honest. You've been pretty distant from the game the last few years. I'm sorry, I should have asked."

"No, I'm not upset," Kennedy clarified. "It was just a little surprising is all."

He gave her a sad grin. "You heal by staying out of the gym, I heal by getting back into it," he answered as he opened the door back up. He gave her one last look. "Good night," he said.

"'Night," she answered. She knew it was going to be another restless night. Between the writing she now had of Jess's and the conversation with Kris, she had a lot on her mind.

Eventually, though, sleep found her, and she woke up a bit more rested than she had felt for several days. While it hurt to not reach for her phone to text Adam first thing, she pushed her feelings aside and committed to having a better mindset for the day.

Jackson was in the kitchen when she came downstairs and she tussled his hair as she went to grab a granola bar from the cupboard. He immediately tried to fix it in the camera on his phone, and she laughed and stuck her tongue out as he glared at her.

"You're in a better mood today," he said, trying hard to comb down the dirty blond locks.

"Yeah," she answered. "Sorry if it's been a little rough the last few days."

He shrugged. "I just figured it was your time of the month."

"Jackson!" she exclaimed.

"What?" he asked turning to look at her. "Jess always said we should normalize talk about our bodies and how they work"

Kennedy stuffed her fingers in her ears. "That doesn't mean I want to discuss this with you."

He turned back to his phone, and she unplugged her ears and dropped her bagels into the toaster. "Oh," he said as she adjusted the time, "I need you to give me a ride today."

Kennedy looked at him. "Why?"

"Flat tire," he answered. "Dad's dealing with it today."

Kennedy sighed. "Fine. We're leaving in ten then."

He shrugged. "Fine by me."

Soon the two were getting into her car. While Kennedy normally liked driving alone, she had to admit it was nice having Jackson along for the ride today. She tried to start a conversation with him as they turned onto the pavement.

"Are you ready for the game this weekend?" she asked.

He was playing with his phone, but he looked at her as he answered. "Yeah, I think so. No home field advantage this time, which sucks, but it should be a pretty even matchup against Westby."

"I wish I could be there." Playoffs and tournaments for volleyball always overlapped, so she had only gotten to see a few of her brothers' postgame runs over the years.

He shrugged. "Yeah, it sucks that you'll be in Sidney for it, but I'm sure Kris or Hunter will film it or whatever."

She looked at him in surprise. "Hunter is coming?"

He shrugged, his attention now back on his phone. "So he says."

"He didn't mention it to me," she said. Normally he would tell her when he was coming home because it was planned out so far in advance. The last two times when he had surprised her were exceptions to the rule. She hoped he wasn't going to make a habit of it. "Was he planning on coming home at all?"

"Doubt it," her younger brother said. "He'll probably just stay up on the Hi-Line."

Kennedy felt some relief. While she wasn't sure if Adam would come with Hunter or not, she likely wouldn't see Hunter either way which was some added security even if he did come.

"Can I play some music?" Jackson asked. She wordlessly passed him the auxiliary cord, and he immediately got to work shuffling through songs.

14

The rest of the week flew by. Between school and volleyball practice, Kennedy felt like she had no free time to look more in depth at the binder or at her sister's first writings for her life story. She did feel a sense of guilt over not giving her parents the binder, though, so she took it downstairs with her while packing to leave on Wednesday night.

Her mother was sitting in the recliner in the living room, reading when she came in.

"Mom?" Kennedy asked. Her mother looked up from her reading. Kennedy hugged the binder a little tighter.

"I have something I want to show you," she said. She walked across the room and handed it to her mother, who took it, squinting at the writing in the corner.

"It's Jess's binder for Ms. O'Brien's class," Kennedy explained. Her mother looked up at her in surprise. "Ms. O'Brien found it in her closet earlier this week, and I've had it the last few days, but I thought you might want to see it."

"Oh my gosh," her mother said, as she began rifling through the projects and papers. "I didn't even know she had this," her mother said. She pulled out her older daughter's grammar scrapbook, which had been done with comic strips from her favorite comics. She laughed as she opened it. "Goodness, I remember how much stress this brought her," she said with a sigh.

She was beginning to tear up, so Kennedy went and grabbed a box of tissues from across the room. Her mother took several as she came back.

"Honey," she opened her arms, and Kennedy bent down to hug her, "thank you." She squeezed her hard, and Kennedy felt a little warmth spread across her. She stood up, and her mother wiped away some more tears.

"I swear, things like this appear right when you need them to," she said. Kennedy looked at her curiously, and her mother sighed. She closed the binder. "I know it's been a hard couple of months for you; it has been for me too," she explained.

Kennedy crouched down and sat on the floor, looking at her mother. "Yeah, it has been rough," she admitted as she pulled her arms around her knees.

Her mother smiled sadly at her. "I would never wish this pain on anyone," she said. "To lose your child is like... it's like losing a part of yourself. And to lose your sister is similar, I'm sure: it's a pain you can't explain unless you've gone through it."

Kennedy looked away. She could feel tears coming.

"Sometimes I question everything," her mother said. Kennedy had tears running down her face now, and she wished she had grabbed some of the Kleenex she had passed to her mother. She wiped them away with the arm of her sleeve and sniffled. "I question what it was that made her leave the night. I wonder if I heard her leave but was just too tired to register it. I demand to know why no one else drove down that road until it was too late."

She sighed; her breath was shaky. "It can take you to a dark place, a sad place." She lightly drummed her fingers on the binder cover. "But then, something happens, and it makes it feel like she is here still," she said. Kennedy glanced over and her mother gave her a small smile. Kennedy returned one of her own. "My grandma called it a shoulder tap," her mother explained. "It's this little moment, when the people who have left us reappear for a second, and we just know it was a sign from them. A sign that everything is okay or that we are going down the right path or just them letting us know we are checking in on them."

She nodded, breaking eye contact with her daughter to hug the binder again. "It's like she was here herself."

Kennedy stood and went to her mother. She pulled out a few of the pieces she remembered Jess talking about or that had stood out to her from her skimming. The two spent a long time reading, talking, laughing, and crying over the things they found of Jess's life in high school.

Eventually, Kennedy went up to bed. She checked her bag over to make sure that everything was packed that she needed and crawled into bed. She turned her TV off and stared at the ceiling for a long time.

She and her mom hadn't been able to sit down like that and talk openly and honestly in what felt like ages. Her mother had talked about a shoulder tap before, and Kennedy had internally scoffed, but perhaps there was something to it. Jess had always hated when her mother and sister argued and it seemed like that was all they had been doing lately; perhaps this was her way of helping them bridge the space between them, by giving them something to read over together and reminisce with.

Kennedy's heart panged a little. She would give the world to have Jess in the room next door so she could talk to her, even for a moment. Instead, she closed her eyes and began to speak.

"Hey, Jess," she laughed nervously. "I know I haven't done this in a while. I'm sorry... you know how busy it gets sometimes." She paused, even though she knew there would be no answer. "Um... I just... I wanted to say that, if you were trying to send a message to Mom and me, well, it was received." She was crying again, and she wiped her eyes. "I'm sorry," she said, laughing again. "This is stupid."

She sat in silence for a few moments.

"I just miss you so much," she said, curling onto her side and sobbing, "and I'm so sorry." She repeated this over and over again into the silence of her room.

Soon there were no tears left in her, and she stared blankly at the wall across from her bed, the wall she shared with her sister. "I just wish you would give me a sign," she whispered. While her mother seemed to believe this was one, Kennedy wasn't so sure it was for her. Slowly, she closed her eyes and drifted off to sleep.

It was not often that she remembered what she dreamed, but for whatever reason, that night she did. She was standing in the middle of the court during a game. Everyone was running around her, and the crowd was screaming. She looked around her, slowly turning in circles. She felt so out of place. Suddenly, Coach Davidson's voice came over the crowd.

"Kennedy!" he was yelling. "Get down the court! Why are you just standing there?"

Her feet jerked her forward, and suddenly she was running. She got to the top of the paint and turned around. She didn't know where to go.

The ball hit her in her chest, and she said "Oof," taking a step back. Her mind said, "That's a travel," but there was no whistle so she just stood there as the girl defending her batted at the ball. Kennedy pivoted, and suddenly Grace was in front of her, wide open. She passed to her friend, and she shot.

"Three points from Larkin," screamed the announcer.

Kennedy stood on the court, not sure of where to go next. Coach Davidson's voice rang out again, and she looked at him, "Kennedy, Kennedy go guard her," he was gesturing wildly at the girl taking the ball out of bounds. She staggered forward again and put her arms up, waving them. The girl bounced it in, but Kennedy reached out and grabbed it. She looked at her coach again.

"SHOOT!" he bellowed, and she turned looked up. She was right under the basket, so she shot. The ball hit the rim and bounced out. One of the girls on her team caught it and pulled it back up to the middle of the court.

The girl guarding her shoved her from behind, and Kennedy stumbled. "Hey," she said turning. "Don't do that."

The girl didn't answer and instead pushed her yet again. "Stop it," Kennedy said. Coach Davidson yelled again: "Kennedy, get physical!"

She looked at the girl behind her and posted up. She was still shoving her, and now Kennedy felt a surge of anger; she stepped back hard and put her hands up, asking for the ball. Ellie passed it to her, and she dribble and stepped back before dropping her shoulder and going up to shoot. This one went in.

The crowd roared. Suddenly Kennedy felt much more natural. She ran back down on defense and settled into the groove of the game. Coach Davidson would occasionally yell out directions for her, but mainly she felt like she knew what she was doing and like she was doing it right.

She hadn't been paying attention to the score but now she looked up. They were down by two with only a few seconds left.

Somehow, the ball was in her hands again, and she was in her spot, the three-point spot she knew she could make it from. She shot and as the ball flew through the air, the buzzer went off. It bounced off the backboard and hit the rim, bouncing around, until finally it fell through the net.

The screams echoed around the gym as her teammates surrounded her -- they hoisted her into the air and she was laughing. She looked for her coach, ready to raise her arm into the air like he would when something good happened, but as her eyes slid over the bench it wasn't him standing there.

It was Jess.

15

Kennedy slid into her seat at the back of the bus feeling empty. It was a Saturday morning in November, and her team had just lost out of their post-season volleyball run. They had fought hard but had ultimately fallen to Jordan in five sets in the round to determine third place. Only the top two teams would advance to the state championships.

Kennedy and Grace had spent a lot of time crying in the locker room of Sidney High School. It was the first "last" that had really hit them hard. Kennedy had finally stumbled out and had fallen into the arms of her father, who wrapped her up and whispered that it was okay for her to cry. She had fallen back into shaking sobs. As she pulled away, she saw a tear glistening in his eye. Next, she wrapped her arms around her mother, who was full-on bawling.

"It's okay, Mom," she had said, squeezing her.

She went around and hugged her grandparents as well as the community members who remained by the locker room, waiting for each individual team member to come out.

Her parents had to leave to make it to as much of Jackson's game as they could later that afternoon, so Kennedy gave them one last hug as she finished making the rounds and told them to keep her updated on the game.

As she walked into the locker room, Ellie was the only one in the room. She was sitting on a bench looking at her feet in defeat. Kennedy felt her heart break a little. Missing a serve to lose a game was hard. Missing a serve in a loser-out game, she couldn't even imagine how the sophomore felt right now. She slowly made her way over and sat next to the younger girl on the bench. Ellie didn't even acknowledge her.

Kennedy wasn't one for physical touch, but she leaned over and began rubbing the younger girl's back. Ellie looked up at her with tears streaming down and her face.

"Kennedy," her voice cracked out, "I'm so, so sorry. I can't believe I missed that. I just ruined it for all of us."

Kennedy shook her head pursing her lips. "You didn't ruin anything, Ellie," she said. "We've all missed a serve."

The younger player looked away and let out a sob. Kennedy slid her arms around her and rubbed her shoulders. "It's okay," she re-assured her.

They sat in silence for a moment, Ellie still crying hard, and Kennedy finally sighed.

"Ellie, do you remember when you were a seventh grader and managing basketball?"

Ellie had looked at her, swallowed hard, and nodded.

"Do you remember the game against Custer that year, in Hysham? The senior night game?"

The girl nodded again.

Kennedy smiled at her. "It was Natalie Lambert's senior night, and she had just fouled out, so I got thrown into the game. There was only about a minute left in the fourth quarter, and we were down by five points. Ashley McConnor from Custer knocked the ball out of bounds, and we got to take the ball out. Coach Davidson had me throw it in bounds, and, instead of running our normal press breaker, he called timeout and wrote a play where Jess would break down the court off a screen, and I was supposed to throw it to her." She was laughing now, through the tears, and even Ellie seemed to be repressing a giggle. "I still have no idea why he had me take it out. But, he did, and I lined up under the basket, and the ref told me I could run the baseline if I needed to. Well, Ashley lined up in front of me, and she must have missed that comment, so I started moving as he blew his whistle, and she started waving her arms but didn't move as I did. Jess made the break, and I wound up to throw it and as it left my hand, I realized where I was at."

Ellie was full out giggling now as she remembered the play. "I threw that thing as hard as I possible could... right into the back of the backboard."

"And you and the ref had to dive out of the way to miss the ball ricocheting back at you guys," the underclassman chimed in.

Kennedy laughed out loud again. "I did," she said through the laughter.

Ellie wiped some of her tears away. "I remember, but why are you telling me about this?" she asked.

Kennedy sniffed and wiped her own eyes on her uniform. "Because after the game, Natalie came up to me and screamed in my face for about two minutes. It was probably her last chance she would get to play Custer, and she really did not like those girls. The rivalry was a lot stronger then," she added thoughtfully before continuing on. "Anyhow, I learned several important things from that game. One, absolutely no one will remember your mistakes. Natalie actually laughed about the whole experience this summer when I ran into her in town and apologized about the way she acted and told me she had forgotten about it herself. Two, never throw the basketball directly under the backboard."

Ellie giggled again. "That's sound advice, I'll remember that during basketball season." She fell quiet quickly, realizing who she was talking to.

Kennedy patted her on her back and gave Ellie a small smile as she glanced up, before the senior stood and went to remove her jersey for the final time. She hesitated a second before pulling it off, letting go of the sport she had thrown herself into the last two years.

She turned to look at Ellie again. "Enjoy the next few years, because you never know what game will be your last." She grinned. "I'm looking forward to following along."

Back on the bus, Kennedy waited for her parents to text her with a game update. The volleyball team had stayed to watch the championship game, and her parents had just made it to Westby for the start of the game. She had a few regrets that she hadn't gone with them to watch her brother play, but she wanted to spend a few more hours with her teammates. Plus, even though she knew it was selfish, she wasn't sure if Adam was there or not.

The bus ride home was fairly quiet, though the group did stop to eat in Miles City and had some fun laughing over dinner. When they finally rolled into town earlier that evening, the news was just spreading: the Pirate football team had won the game with an upset! They were going to the semifinals.

The bus cheered loudly, and Grace invited Kennedy to come over to her house to wait for the team to make it back to town so they could parade them in. The girls made a few loops through the town in Kennedy's car before heading to her house. They chatted with Grace's parents for a few minutes before heading upstairs to her room.

Her cat, Lily, was perched on Grace's bed when the girls came into her room. She gave them a haunting stare before scurrying out.

Grace shook her head. "I don't know why she hates you so much," she said, sitting down on her mattress. Kennedy shrugged, landing in her desk chair.

"Got me," she answered.

They sat in silence for a few minutes. Kennedy was just thinking that she could drift off to sleep when Grace spoke again. "I can't believe it's really over."

She had wrapped her arms around her knees when Kennedy looked at her. "Volleyball?"

Grace nodded. "Like, you grow up knowing that one game will be your last, but you're never really sure when it will be. And then it just suddenly hits you out of nowhere, and it's gone."

Kennedy let this sink in for a moment. Her friend was right: you didn't know when something would be your last. She finally spoke after a moment of gathering her thoughts: "Yeah, there are a lot of uncertainties in life, unfortunately."

Grace sighed. "Is it too early to start wishing we could rewind to the beginning of the year?"

"Aren't you the one who couldn't wait to get out of town?" Kennedy asked with a laugh.

Her friend shrugged. "Yes, but... the thought of actually leaving is scary, isn't it?" She looked around her room. "Everything I have done so far has been with you or my dad by my side. Next year, even the rest of this year... I'm on my own and... I don't know how I'm supposed to feel about it yet."

Kennedy nodded, looking around the room as well. Photos of the two of them were up everywhere, from elementary to the trip they had taken to Washington, D.C., together a few years before. All of their memories and their childhoods were intertwined. Grace was right: from here on out they would be growing separately.

"It is scary," Kennedy agreed slowly. "But, at the same time, isn't it exciting? We get to go out, to carve our own trails... without our parents telling us right from wrong anymore." She stood up and walked across the room, wrapping her arms around her friend in yet another uncharacteristic display of affection. "And you know I'm only a phone call away if you need me."

Grace squeezed her own arms around her friends for a moment before letting go. Kennedy released her and sat beside her, pulling a pillow into her chest.

"I know. And I'm the same for you," she answered.

Kennedy nodded, not answering. She didn't really know what else to say to her friend.

Grace turned and looked at her. "Are you sure you don't want to go to school in Bozeman?" her friend asked, a twinkle in her eye.

Kennedy flung the pillow at her, and the two dissolved into giggles.

Grace worked on some scholarship applications as her friend slept soundly beside her for a while. Kennedy stirred as her phone chime rang out in the room and she rolled over and pulled her phone off the bedside table. She froze a moment after looking at it and quickly set it back down.

Grace looked at her in confusion. "Are you okay?" she asked.

Kennedy looked like she might cry. "Kennedy?" Grace said.

"Adam texted me," was all she said. It was all she needed to say.

Grace froze too. Kennedy had never dated anyone before, so the news about Adam had come as a shock to her. The two of them hadn't really said much about it since the day Kennedy had revealed their secret relationship to Grace; she had thought that it was best to let Kennedy come to her if she needed to again, and she hadn't. She was guessing that this was the first time either of them had reached out based on her friend's reaction.

She wasn't sure how Kennedy would handle this situation, so she tried to play through a few different scenarios in her head of what could happen.

She decided to start with an easy question and work up to her friend's feelings. "What did he say?" she asked.

Kennedy closed her eyes. "I don't know," she answered, "I'm too scared to look. I just saw his name."

Grace paused again and then asked "Do you want me to read it?"

Kennedy didn't respond for a moment, and then she gave a slight nod. Grace remembered all the times that her friend had read messages out loud to her that she wasn't sure if she could read or not. Kennedy passed her phone.

Grace clicked on the message, and it opened up. It was the only one in the conversation, and all it said was "Sorry to hear you lost. You had a good career, and it was fun to follow along."

Grace said this out loud, and Kennedy didn't respond. Grace locked her phone and put it on the bed between them before lying down herself.

"Why would he say that?" Kennedy asked suddenly, startling Grace.

Grace turned her head so that she was looking at her friend. Kennedy was staring at the ceiling still, and a silent tear was streaming down her face.

"He probably knew that you lost out from Hunter and knew how much you loved volleyball," Grace answered. "I'm sure he was just wanting to check in."

"But why now?" Kennedy asked. "I had just gotten him out of my head for a few minutes, and he reappears again."

Grace didn't answer and turned to she was looking at her ceiling as well. She wanted to say it was because all boys were trash and knew exactly when they needed to reappear in your life like some sort of twisted sixth sense, but she knew that wasn't what Kennedy wanted or needed to hear at the moment. Instead, she racked her brain trying to come up with a response. Finally, she spoke.

"I don't know why," she replied honestly. While she had more experience in the relationship department than her friend, she was still mostly clueless when it came to guys. "Are you going to answer him?" she asked.

Kennedy didn't answer right away either. After a moment, she answered truthfully as well. "I don't know."

The bus got into town around ten that night. The girls joined in on the parade into town and cheered loudly as the boys exited the bus in front of the school. This was a huge win for them: the team was small, but they had outlasted the Thunder, who had over double the Pirates' numbers.

Even as she stood in the enthusiastic crowd, Kennedy found her mind wandering. She hadn't answered Adam still, and it was weighing on her heavily. She used to answer his messages as soon as they came in, as long as Hunter wasn't around; now she needed time to process and think about what to say.

She could tell Grace was concerned, but she hadn't pushed the issue anymore. Kennedy was thankful for that: something had shifted in their friendship after the fight in the hallway and Grace seemed more willing to let her approach her with her problems instead of asking her to talk about them. The same went for her mother, and she was noticing that relationship improving too.

She made Jackson take a picture with her so she could post it on her social media accounts before the two of them loaded up in their cars to follow their parents back out to the ranch. "Proud big sister moment," she had told him when he protested. Jess had always said the same thing to him, so he quickly relented and gave her both a serious photo and one where he was rolling his eyes.

Kennedy was tired, and she looked forward to getting home and to bed. She helped her parents haul in the groceries they had bought but slipped upstairs before the neighbors started appearing. She didn't have the energy to talk to them at the moment, and she needed some time to be alone after spending the last few days surrounded by people.

As she sat in her room with the TV playing quietly in the background, she posted the pictures of her and Jack to her social media accounts. She had just set her phone aside to watch her show when it lit up. Curiously, she picked it up and saw it was a notification from the app.

She unlocked her phone and saw Adam had liked her photo. Her stomach clenched slightly, and she put her phone down quickly, making sure the screen was down and hitting the button on the side to silence it in the process.

She could hear the group outside, and she knew she should go visit, but she really just didn't have it in her at the moment. Instead, she leaned back in her bed and thought about the ways that things had started with Adam.

There had been a luncheon in the garage after the burial. Once again, she was feeling overwhelmed by people, and she had tried to make herself scarce, sitting on the steps leading to the second story storage area, out of the way of the group. A few people had approached her, but most seemed content sitting in the groups they had come with. Grace had been the one to sit with her for most of the time, but she had slipped over to talk to the team and her parents, leaving Kennedy alone.

She was playing with the food on her plate, not very hungry. An olive had rolled out of the pasta salad, and she was chasing it around the plate with her fork when someone started up the stairs. She looked up and realized it was Adam.

"Hey," he had said.

"Hi," she had almost whispered back.

He nodded at the step next to her. "Mind if I..." he asked, trailing off.

She moved over a bit and he sat down.

"How are you doing?" he asked her. She shrugged in response.

He nodded again. "I feel the same," he answered.

She didn't respond and the two sat in silence for a few minutes, watching the crowd below them.

"Where did Hunter and Kris go?" she asked after giving the room a quick scan and not seeing them.

He hesitated. "Kris is... feeling a little under the weather right now," he answered finally.

"And my mom let them leave?" she asked in surprise.

"They just went into the house, it's better than him puking in here or right outside," he answered. "I'm sure they will be back soon."

Kennedy picked up her cup of coffee and sipped it. Adam eyed her and finally she turned to him and said, "What?"

"Sure you should be drinking that if you can't sleep already?" he asked.

Kennedy felt her cheeks flush, and she snapped back, "That's not really your business."

He opened his mouth to respond but after a moment shook his head and looked away.

Kennedy stared at him.

Adam seemed to feel her eyes on him, and he turned to look at her. She had held his gaze until he looked away again.

Kennedy looked back out over the small crowd that had come to bury her sister. She could see Grace talking to Mac and Coach Davidson. The next week was the last home stand of the season, and Kennedy wasn't sure how she felt about getting back onto the court. It seemed wrong, without Jess by her side. She hadn't dressed out this weekend either on the road trips to Terry and Jordan, though she had ridden the bus to support the team. The girls and parents from the two towns had given her flowers and hugs and offered a moment of silence before the games. Kennedy had to excuse herself after each, and the idea of being in her home gym right after the funeral seemed excruciatingly painful. She hadn't even been able to walk inside the domed building yet. And it was supposed to be her sister's senior night.

The door leading outside suddenly opened, and Kris and Hunter staggered in. Kris looked worse for the wear, and he immediately went to get a drink out of the coolers in the room. Kennedy stood up: she was done eating anyhow. Adam stood beside her, and she turned and nodded to him before making her way down to her brother.

Kris's eyes were bloodshot and tear-filled when she got to him. Luckily, her mother hadn't seemed to notice yet. Hunter was standing by him, looking slightly better than his older brother. Kennedy glared at him as he reached out and tucked Courtney under his arm; she gestured to the oldest Helland. Hunter had shrugged and looked away to Coach Davidson, who had also joined the group. Kennedy linked her arm through Kris's and dragged him out through the back door of the shop.

He sat down heavily on the pile of wood her dad kept at the back of the shop to heat it. She stood outside, looking at him expectantly. He turned, looked at her like he was going to say something, and instead turned and vomited again.

"Okay, okay," Kennedy said, sitting down beside him, after carefully selecting a dry log. "I've never seen you this hungover."

He had wiped his mouth and dry heaved a little again before sitting up and leaning back against the wood. His pants and shirt were going to be soaked, but that was the least of her concerns at the moment.

He shook his head. "I don't know if I ever have been this hungover before." He hesitated. "I didn't know it was possible to be this hungover."

Kennedy looked at him, feeling some hesitation herself. Actually, now that she had thought about it, she wasn't exactly sure when the last time she had saw him without a drink in his hand head been. "Kris..." she began tentatively.

He shook his head, looking at the ground. "It's easier if you can't feel the pain, you know?" he said. "It's easier if you wake up and you pour yourself another drink and then you just keep drinking. It makes you forget," he continued, "at least, it does as long as you're still drinking."

He looked at her. "I almost missed my sister's burial because I was so hungover from the night before, from drinking to forget what I was doing today." He shook his head as his eyes began to water. "That's not right, Kenna."

She didn't answer for a moment. "Well, none of this is right, to be fair."

Kris was angry now. "No, it isn't. I didn't think I would be burying one of my siblings when she was eighteen." The two sat in silence for another moment, and he sighed. "But that doesn't mean I should drink away my problems to keep from facing them."

"Every day the last two weeks," he was saying, as Kennedy looked on, "I have woken up and immediately reached for a bottle. And even before that, I was drinking almost every night. It's easy to do that, when you live alone, you know. Easy to hide the number of cans and bottles you're going through. But the last week, shit, two weeks, since the moment we heard the news, I have been drinking and drinking hard.

"But the thing is, when you've been drinking hard for a while, it's easy to hide it. I know it seems like that wouldn't be the case, but it's true. You learn to carry a thermos with you wherever you go, to always keep a six pack in the front seat of your truck. Everything is a reason to drink: when you're sad or when you're happy. And even now, people are offering me a beer or to get me a drink when they're in town next." He sighed heavily. "But I don't want that."

Kennedy was crying now too, and she quickly wiped at her eyes.

"Hunter offered me a drink when we were inside, to calm my nerves some," he said. "And I took it and I opened the bottle and I took a swig, and I... I knew if I didn't get rid of it right then and there, I would never not have one in my hand. Because if I didn't deal with the pain of this, with the heartache of this, I would never be able to face it head on." He took a long shaky breath. "I would be like Peter Johnson."

Kennedy shook her head. "Peter Johnson? That old, senile guy who drives around drunk?" She paused for a moment. Peter had also been the one who had called in the wreck, but she wasn't sure if Kris knew that.

Kris nodded in return. He was looking out over the vehicles now. "Did you ever think about why he was drunk?" he asked her.

Kennedy shook her head. "No," she answered.

"Peter used to date a girl in town," he said. He was tossing the bottle of water he had gently from one hand to the other now. "They were high school sweethearts, supposed to get married, the whole shebang. But, right after she graduated college, she took a trip to see her aunt back in North Dakota. She never came back." He shook his head sadly.

"Why not?" asked Kennedy. She had never heard this story before.

"Found another guy out there, I guess," he answered. "And now he can't deal with the pain of losing her, even fifty, sixty years later. Honestly," he said, "I think if he ever got sober at this point, he would die of a broken heart."

He shook his head again and suddenly slammed his water bottle between his hands. The top popped off, and some the water sloshed out. "I didn't want to be sixty-five and still unable to process my feelings about losing my sister," he said. "So, I went into the bathroom and poured the drink down the drain and told Hunter we needed to come back out here. But coming back out here made it real, and now I don't know what to do."

Kennedy was staring at her older brother, and she could feel her heart break. He had always been a rock, cool and level-headed. A pillar of strength in the family. The one who would pick her up off the floor when Hunter plowed her over during a game of pickup basketball. She slowly leaned into him, and he leaned back into her, finally letting go.

She had helped him back into the house once he had collected himself. She knew her mother would be furious to see that the two of them had disappeared after he did with Hunter, but he needed to change into something not covered in snow. She was praying he had left a pair of dress pants in his old room, at least. He could throw his coat on over his dress shirt if he needed to cover the melted snow on his back. His wider shoulders and hips wouldn't fit into his father's or Jack's clothes, and she was just hoping there was a pair of pants somewhere in the house that would fit him.

She was in the kitchen, her head swimming from the information he had just given her. She wanted to run out and ask Hunter or her parents if they knew, or even Jack, but she sensed the answer was no. This was a secret that Kris had entrusted to her, and she would never let it go.

The kitchen door opened and she looked over, expecting it to be her mother. Instead, to her surprise, she found Adam standing in the doorway.

He looked at her and she looked back as tears came to her eyes. "Kennedy," he began, but she hadn't let him say anything else before she crumpled into him, sobbing.

There hadn't been many days since then that they hadn't talked to each other over the phone. And when summer came, it only made sense to talk in person when he was basically living at the ranch, the summer between her sophomore and junior years. It was somewhere in these nights that they had grown closer than Kennedy thought they should be. But, as Adam always said: "Grief brings people together."

She missed being with him, she realized as she sat alone in her room. She missed turning to him in her times of need and even when something good happened. But she still didn't feel right about how things had played out between them. It was a thought that had been festering in her almost since that first day.

She slowly reached over and picked up her phone and scrolled through her apps to her messages. His message was opened, and she felt bad for leaving him on "read." She opened up the conversation and typed simply, "Thank you," and set her phone back down before picking it up again and staring at the screen. The little bubbles came up, signifying he was typing, and she waited, but eventually they stopped.

Feeling slightly disappointed, she set her phone back down and went to get ready for bed. She showered, letting the water run over her. The shower was one of her favorite places to cry, but the urge just didn't come to her tonight. She was just so exhausted, it seemed like a waste of energy to break down now.

She got out of the shower and changed into her pajamas and made her way back to her room. She glanced at her phone once again and saw more likes from her post, but no new messages. She wearily crawled back into bed and laid down, staring at her ceiling.

She wasn't sure how long she sat there, before her screen lit up again. She rolled over and picked up her phone. "You're welcome," he had answered.

She didn't respond and rolled over once again.

16

The next Monday was weird for Kennedy as there was nothing going on for her. No volleyball practice, no team meetings, nothing. She ate in the cafeteria with the team, and she felt sadness wash over her. While she still felt connected to them, she knew that soon she wouldn't, as they began practicing and talking about basketball and began taking more trips across the eastern half of the state.

She would be in the cafeteria after they left for games, alone. Spending her Friday afternoons in class, alone. Going home for the weekend, alone. She wasn't sure how she felt so lonely even before the season had started.

She tried to stay in the moment, but she could already feel the girls she had spent so much time with slipping away.

Her heart was heavy when she got home right after school. Grace had asked her to cruise originally before remembering that she had asked the girls to go to open gym to shoot; she had hesitated before telling Kennedy, but Kennedy had waved her off as best as she could. "No, no, I totally understand," she had answered.

Jack was still practicing football with the team's win over the weekend, so she set out for home alone. Sometimes they would carpool into town during the winter, depending on roads, and she would stay late while he practiced when he was playing a sport and she wasn't, but he was having a team dinner that night. It sounded like her parents were going as well.

When she got to the house, it was silent, and all the lights were off. It appeared that they had decided to go to the dinner; she wasn't surprised. Kennedy went inside and set her backpack down. Otis trotted out to meet her. It was nearing dusk and was one of the last warm afternoons of the year. She rummaged through the kitchen, finally deciding on a bag of popcorn for dinner. She stood in front of the microwave as it popped.

She pulled the bag out and went to sit outside on the patio off the living room. The sun was going down, and it was unseasonably warm for November, so she curled up in one of the chairs and watched the sun dip down behind the hills. Otis and two of their other dogs, Rogue and Huck, laid at her feet, panting away happily.

As the sun fell down and the golden hour spread across her family's land, Kennedy looked toward the hills that Jess was buried on. She could only imagine the view up there at this moment, as golden hour lit up the valley. Her loneliness grew, and she felt a few tears slip out.

The porch door slid open, and she turned and looked. Kris was standing there. She quickly wiped her eyes.

They looked at each other for a moment, and Kris nodded inside. "Come eat dinner."

Kennedy followed him in, dragging her uneaten popcorn behind her. The dogs came in as well as she slid the door shut.

Kris had only turned the lights on in the kitchen, and she staggered into the brightly lit space. He had a pot of water boiling on the stove, and he was peeking into the oven. He shut the door as she pulled out a chair at the kitchen table and went to sit at the other end.

She scrolled through her phone for a moment, feeling his eyes on her. Finally, she set her phone down and looked at him and tilted her head. "Why are you here?" she asked.

He looked back at her, leaning back in the chair. "Mom texted me and said she was going to a team dinner and so was Dad," he said, looking away.

She nodded, picking up her phone back up. "Figured."

"I didn't want you to have to eat alone, so I thought I'd make us some dinner and we could talk," he continued.

She glanced up from her phone. "We don't talk," she said, before she began scrolling again.

He nodded, looking above her. "You're right, we don't."

The two sat in silence for a while. Kris eventually got up and started stirring things and checking the oven. Kennedy continued to play on her phone. Eventually, he came and set a plate in front of her.

"Drink?" he asked, pulling the fridge open. She hesitated.

"Wine?" she asked. He looked at her and nodded slightly. He pulled an unfinished bottle of their mother's out of the fridge and pulled two glasses out of a cupboard, pouring each of them a glass.

She raised her eyebrows when she saw he had poured two glasses and he passed her one, shrugging slightly. "By the way," he said, "if anyone asks I didn't see you doing this. Coaching means I can't be your buyer anymore."

She rolled her eyes. "Like you ever buy for me anyhow."

He shrugged again. "You never asked."

Another eyeroll came from the younger sibling, and she twirled a noodle around her fork. She wasn't really hungry, but Kris had gone to the trouble of cooking for her, so she would eat as much as she could.

They ate in silence for a few minutes, and when she looked over at him, he was taking a sip out of his glass. She quickly looked back down at her plate.

She could feel him looking at her again and her heart sped up as she looked up. She nodded at his glass. "Didn't know you drank wine."

He set his glass down and looked at her. "I have a glass here and there, you know that," he said simply. "Just don't get drunk anymore."

She nodded and looked down at her plate. Somehow, she had made her way through most of it without even noticing. "Still kinda weird to see it though, with how you were that one day," she admitted.

He nodded. "That's fair," he admitted. He had finished his meal and stood to get more food. He looked at her and after a slight pause she passed him her plate. He scooped more spaghetti and bread onto their plates and brought them back to the table. "That was a low point for me," he paused. "A *really* low point," he reiterated, with a head shake. She took a sip of her drink.

"I hit rock bottom when she died, you know?" he said. "Alcohol had been a big part of my life since I started college. I didn't like how much I was drinking before and then… then Jess died and it was the only way to get through the days, those first few days.

"But," he continued, "I realized how bad it was after her funeral. Maybe I should have quit fully then," he said. "But I didn't. Her death made me realize how bad I had gotten, but the desire to drink like that… it was gone, after I realized I didn't like who I was becoming." He nodded at the glass of wine. "I can go to the bar and order a drink and leave without finishing it. Or drink some wine with my underage sister at a family dinner," he looked at her then and grinned, and she gave a tentative smile back, "and not have to finish the bottle with the meal." He shrugged. "It's all about focusing on the experiences, good and bad. Not forgetting them," he concluded.

She nodded. They had never talked about what had happened that day, but she hadn't seen him drink again. She had thought he might but wasn't sure if he did or not. That would answer it.

Neither one of them finished their glass of wine that night, and Kris dumped the leftovers down the drain as Kennedy helped him clean up from their meal.

She was finishing up rinsing the dishes and he was loading the dishwasher when her parents and brother came in. Her mother waved them away and told them that she would finish up in the morning, and her parents disappeared into the living room to watch TV while Jackson scampered upstairs.

Kris went to get his shoes on, and she watched him. He looked up at her as he finished lacing his sneakers.

"Thank you for coming and for dinner," she said. He nodded back at her.

Their dad came into the room and began talking to Kris as he stood in the doorway. Kennedy snuck upstairs and into to her room.

She laid in bed for a long time, staring at the ceiling, but sleep just wouldn't come to her. Finally, at 1 a.m., she sat up and slid out of the covers.

She crept down the stairs. The house was silent as she slipped out of the kitchen door and walked over to the shop, her ball tucked under her arm.

She turned on half the lights in the building and began her warmup. She had her wireless headphones in, and she found herself bouncing the ball to the beat. She began shooting, spinning, running. Working out what she didn't even know was inside of her.

She worked until she was drenched in sweat and breathing heavily. Rap was blaring in her ears, and she suddenly realized how loud it was. She pulled the earplugs out and sat panting for a moment on the ground, listening to the silence. Basketball wasn't a silent sport, and the irony of her often practicing in silence wasn't lost on her.

Kris and Scott stood, looking in the window at their sister and daughter. They had moved outside to the firepit to finish their conversation about what balancing the ranch and coaching would look like in the coming weeks and had lost track of the time. They were walking around the house to Kris's truck when he had noticed the lights on in the shop. When he had asked his father about them, Scott had shaken his head and nodded, walking over to one of the windows. Kris had followed and the two had watched in silence as she shot and moved on the floor.

"I had no idea," he said finally. Scott nodded.

"She prefers it that way. She's been doing this for over a year. Doesn't think any of us know," he said.

"And she won't go out? You're sure of it?" he asked.

Her father shook his head. "Alan doesn't seem to think so." He gestured in his younger daughter's direction. "But what do you think?"

Kris was still in disbelief at his sister. As far as he knew, she hadn't touched a ball in years. To see her out there, sinking threes and free throws and posting up, albeit without a defender, was shocking. "I don't know what to think," and he didn't. This was new territory for him.

His father nodded and clapped him on his back. "Well, Coach," he said, "sometimes you witness miracles. This may be your first."

The rest of the week flew by and soon Kennedy was in the back of her parents' vehicle with Grace, riding to Bridger for the semifinal football game.

It was a snowy Saturday, and they had left early enough to stop by one of the sporting goods stores in Billings for Grace to pick up the shoes she had ordered for basketball. She pulled them out excitedly in the car to show her friend.

"Ah, they are even better than I imagined!" she squealed.

Kennedy was suddenly sitting in the back of a different car while Jess switched out one of her shoes for Kennedy's. They had the same sized feet despite their height differences and Jess had come up with the idea to get the same shoes but in different colors and then to swap out one of each shoe for the year. It was her senior year so Kennedy had gone along with it, and she had to admit: what she thought was dorky had actually been pretty cool. The regional paper out of Billings had come out to do an interview with Jess and the team and had even mentioned their shoes in it. It had picked up traction around the state and several others had ended up doing it the next year.

"Kenna?" Grace said, tearing her friend back to reality.

Kennedy glanced at her friend's shoes again and nodded. They were cool, with black and a shiny gold on them. Her heart twisted as she thought about picking out shoes again. She had always loved participating in that tradition for the year.

The girls goofed off in the back row of the vehicle the rest of the drive. Kris was alone in the middle row, and he fell asleep as the left Billings. Kennedy pulled out her phone and snapped a few shots of him sleeping soundly in the car as her mother chided her. The girls laughed.

They watched the game bundled up in layers and blankets. A lot of people had made the drive out to support the boys, and the crowd was rowdy. Kennedy and Grace screamed on the sidelines for the team, rooting for them even as it became clear that they would not pull away with a win.

Six-man football was known for its running games, and the Bridger Scouts overtook the Pirates easily from the beginning with their plethora of people coming off the bench. Jack saw a lot of playing time in the loss, and Kennedy was proud to see how he had grown as a player during the year.

As the clock ran down, the Hysham crowd began clapping their hands and chanting "We are proud of you, say, we are proud of you" for the boys. The final buzzer sounded, sealing the game at 41-26, and the boys lined up to do the chant they did at the end of every game before going around to thank the fans. Jackson was crying, the black lines he had drawn under his eyes smearing as he fell into first his mother's arms and then his sister's. Her mother of course began to wail as well and Kennedy even fought off the tears. Paul, Grace and Kennedy's other classmate, came up, and she wrapped her arms around him. They weren't close, but the way in which he was sobbing broke her heart in two.

Eventually, the group wandered back to their car and headed home. Her mother's sniffs had quieted off by the time they got to Billings and made a stop the store to grab alcohol and food for the gathering that would take place in their garage that night.

Finally, they headed home. Kris and her father were visiting about basketball plays for a while, with practice starting on Monday, and Grace joined in, leaving Kennedy to her thoughts.

She had been wearing an older pair of shoes when she went out to the gym to shoot. She just couldn't bring herself to wear the pair she had gotten alongside her sister. It seemed wrong, to wear something that was meant to be worn with someone else. So, she wore her beaten up shoes from her freshman season instead, thought at this point they were beginning to fall apart. When she had run into the store with Grace, she had seen a pair that caught her eyes. All black high tops. They looked sharp, and she had stared at them for a moment before going to find her friend who was talking to an associate about the pair she had ordered the last time she was in. Kennedy had wanted to go and look at them closer, but she didn't want anyone asking questions. As far as anyone knew, she didn't play basketball anymore. It would be suspicious to look at a pair of basketball shoes if that was what she wanted everyone to believe.

But still, they lingered. She knew they would look good with both the home and away jerseys, and they would look amazing with the all-black warmups the team sported.

"It's too bad," Kennedy thought to herself. "Jess would have loved those."

In addition to her parents' party, the football team and the volleyball team ended up coming out to the Helland place that night. While the parents and adults in the community drank in the shop and pretended not to know where their kids were, the students of the high school huddled around a bonfire out at the edge of their property by the river, passing around what they had been given by their parents or had smuggled out of the house.

Kennedy drank slowly. She wasn't a heavy drinker because she tended to get emotional when she drank and everything she had witnessed with Kris also left her uncomfortable with drinking heavily and often. Besides: someone had to make sure no one was being a complete idiot. The group was most of the high school. Only a couple who didn't participate in sports were not out with them. Kennedy looked around and counted. There were only a little over twenty kids out tonight and a couple weren't even from Hysham; she remembered when her brothers would have forty or fifty people out for a celebration. Class sizes had shrunk rapidly the last few years. In May, her class would be the smallest to graduate since the first few years the school was opened, over a century ago.

Kennedy drifted from small group to small group, talking to her guests. While she generally hated playing the mini-version of host to her mother, she was alright with doing it amongst her peers. She was quiet but made sure everyone was doing okay. Things were starting to wind down when she heard the arguing.

Ellie's red-headed temper was coming out in full force. "No way in hell," she was telling a guy from Custer who was friends with Kennedy's younger brother. She thought his name may be Sam.

He shook his head, drinking his beer. "I swear, they are already talking about it," he was saying. Kennedy slid over. Jack was standing there awkwardly as the two went back and forth.

"You're making shit up." Ellie was slurring her words, and Kennedy stepped between her and the boy quickly. She wasn't sure how Ellie was going to react with alcohol in her.

She looked back and forth between them. "What's going on?" she asked, looking at Jack because she knew he would give an honest answer.

"He is saying we are going to have to co-op for sports next year," Ellie spat out. Kennedy looked at Jack, and he nodded in confirmation. Kennedy blinked in surprise. She had heard nothing about this before.

The boy was swaying slightly, and Kennedy could tell he had had as much to drink as Ellie had had that night. He was shaking his head. "Neither of us have enough for sports so they only way we can compete is if we come together," he was saying. "My grandpa is on the school board, and he told me it was going to happen, if we liked it or not."

Ellie went to move forward, and Kennedy quickly reached out to stop her. "Hey, hey, hey," she said. "Let's not worry about this tonight."

Ellie was pointing her finger at the Custer boy now. "Well my *dad* is on *our* school board, and he hasn't said shit. So, you're a liar," she spat at him.

The boy shook his head. "You'll find out soon enough," he answered.

Grace appeared at that moment. "Maybe we should all head back to the house," she said quickly.

Ellie stepped back from Kennedy, shaking her head still. The other sophomore girl came forward and wrapped her arms around Ellie, pulling her away and back toward the house.

"What the hell was that about?" asked Grace as Jack nudged the Custer boy toward the house as well, making sure there was a swath of space between him and Ellie.

Kennedy looked at her and shrugged. "He said they were going to co-op for sports next year," she answered.

Grace laughed. "With Custer? Our rivals? Sure," she said, shaking her head. "What an idiot."

Her friend shook her head in response. There hadn't been any discussion about this as far as she knew, so she was pretty sure that it wasn't true; however, the conversation she had had with both Grace and Mr. Davidson about there not being enough girls for a basketball team was lingering in her mind as well. Was the boy correct, perhaps? Was this really the last year they would be the Pirates?

Kennedy slid under her covers after washing her face of the smoke from the fire. Grace was already snoring on the other side of the bed, and everyone had cleared out or was camped out at various locations around her house until the morning when her mom would cook them all breakfast. Things had been calmer after they had made it back to the house, and Ellie seemed to have forgotten about the experience out in the trees, but Kennedy still had a feeling of uneasiness about her from the conversation. She was confused as to why she felt this way:

she wouldn't be here to play next year. But the idea of change and the loss of identity that came with a cooperative sports program lingered in her mind.

She had never seen it firsthand. But she remembered Jess telling her about the struggles when she was alive, about what her friends had gone through. How their town athletic programs had run dry, so they had to turn to the next town over, or even two other towns, just to field a team. How it was hard to know who you were anymore, if you were a Sugarbeeter or a Renegade or something else entirely. Living out in the country, Jess had also lamented how much it would suck to spend so much time in a bus every day, driving down the two-lane roads after a full day of school only to practice, come home, and do it all again the next day. "It would be hard," Kennedy remembered her saying. "I don't know how they do it." She had paused for a second. "Well, I do, actually. Because they love the game. But still," she continued, "it would be hard."

Kennedy stared at the ceiling for a while. She wasn't even tipsy now, and she felt the urge to move. Slowly, she slid out of bed to not wake Grace and pulled her shoes and basketball out from under her bed.

All of her parents' friends had gone home as well, so she slid across the parking lot in her shorts and hoodie, her shoes laced loosely on her feet. Her headphones were playing the warmup playlist her sister had made two years ago now: she had the song order memorized, and it was something comfortable to her.

Normally, when she came out here, she had somewhat of a routine she followed, starting with light shooting and then going to free-throws and then practicing spin moves under the basket. Sometimes she would run, as hard as she could, as if she was running the full length of the court, though obviously she had to modify it some. Then she would shoot by herself before sitting in the quiet, lying on the floor like she used to do with her sister at the end of an open gym or a summer scrimmage.

Tonight, though, she found herself stepping up to the free throw line first thing. She lined her right foot up with the small mark on the concrete floor. Gave the ball three solid bounces, readjusted her foot line up, eyed up the hoop, bent down, then shot with an extended follow through.

The ball bounced off the rim.

She frowned. "Free throws win games," she thought to herself as she jogged to retrieve the ball. She dribbled back over, doing a few cross over moves as she did so.

She came back to the line and began her routine again, falling into its familiar pattern. She eyed the hoop before she released the ball and as she did, the words seemed to appear out of nowhere: "If I make it, he likes me. If I miss, he doesn't."

Jess and Kennedy had tried to make the boring process of repeatedly shooting free throws more fun when they were practicing in the summer. This was one of Jess's creations. It took the childhood game of pulling petals off of a flower and upped the ante slightly. "If I make this," Jess would call out, lined up for the shot, "I'll get a full ride scholarship to Washington. If I miss," she continued, "I'll never be accepted anywhere." She would shoot, and the ball would fall through the hoop.

They both knew it was silly, that making a basket wouldn't decide their futures for them or if their crushes would like them back. But it gave shooting a free throw that edge, just like you would have in a game situation with ten seconds left on the line and you were down by one. It gave you an urge inside of you to really, really want to make a shot, just like you would need in a game situation.

Coach Davidson would make them run based on if they made their free throws or not at practice: that was enough to make them focus. But in the heat of the summer or when they were exhausted on a Sunday, sometimes they just needed a little bit more. So, Jess had started this little game to make her and her sister focus on their shots.

Kennedy hadn't had to concentrate on her free throws like this in a long time, not since her sister's death. There hadn't been something she needed in all that time: she knew that making a shot wouldn't bring her sister back, that this was a dumb way to gamble important decisions. But as she returned to the line, she felt herself racking her brain to try and decide what question she would ask herself. Should she ask if Adam would come back to her? If she would receive the scholarship she was hoping for from the state? If she would win prepared speech at her FFA contests this spring? She racked her brain, finally deciding on the prepared speech idea because it was something she had wanted for so long as an individual. But as she stepped to the line, the conversations from the night about a co-op and her conversations with Grace about basketball shoes came back to her.

She looked at the hoop, early that Sunday morning, while the rest of the word slept, and she stepped forward, lining up her toe to the mark at the center of the free-throw line. She bounced the ball three times hard, looked down at her toe and adjusted it slightly. She brought her head up, lining up eye contact with the hoop and bent down slightly. She shook her head and muttered under her breath "Well, Jess, now or never," and brought herself up, releasing the ball and following through.

It slid through the hoop, not even touching the net, and bounced before rolling away. Kennedy relaxed her body, still staring at the basket and nodded.

"Message received," she said simply.

17

Sunday passed by quickly. Kennedy helped her dad clean the shop from the night before and tried to get ahead on her reading for the week in English class. They were reading *Winter Wheat* at the moment, but they were also really cracking down on their term papers. She spent the afternoon locked away in her room trying to get some research done. Jess had written hers on gay rights in contemporary America, and Kennedy had enjoyed reading it and considered doing a similar topic, but she had found herself constantly being drawn back to the idea of women in sports. She hadn't realized there was such a discrepancy even in things like administration until something had come up on her Instagram, and she was glad Ms. O'Brien would let her run with it.

Her mom called her down for dinner around seven, and she begrudgingly left her research to go eat with her family. Jack was at the kitchen table and Kris was just taking his shoes off by the door when she came into the room. Her mother turned around and shook her head.

"Dining room tonight and no phones," she said. Jack groaned out loud, and her mother looked at him sharply. He quickly got up and sulked out of the room.

Normally, Kathy was quite lax about dinners since they all had such crazy schedules. It was a miracle to just get everyone home at the same time some days. But occasionally she would force them to have a proper, sit-down meal and actually conversate with one another. Kennedy wasn't too surprised she was doing this now: they had all been running around the last few weeks with tournaments and school and such. Things would get crazy again in a few weeks when basketball started again.

Guilt flooded Kennedy as she thought about basketball. She had woken up this morning and had immediately been brought back the free throw she had shot during the night and the question she had gambled with. How she felt like she had abused the game that Jess had made up by picking something she didn't actually want to focus on. How it made everything seem like a lie.

"If I make this," she had thought to herself, "I will go to practice tomorrow." And not only had she made it, but she had made it in a decisive way: that ball had gone through the hoop without a doubt. There was no bouncing off the rim or backboard. It was nothing but net, as Jess would say.

But now she felt guilty that she wasn't following through with it. It had all been a joke, just something she had done for… well, she didn't really have a good reason for why she had done it. But it meant nothing, nothing at all.

She helped her mom carry out a loaf of garlic bread and a bowl of salad out to the dining room where her father and brother were now talking about the first day of practice that was happening tomorrow, and Kennedy suddenly had an overwhelming rush of feelings. Her hands started to numb, and she knew she had an anxiety attack coming on, so she quickly excused herself to go upstairs to her bathroom before they ate. Her mom gave her a look as she rushed up the stairs.

She ran into her room and into the bathroom, closing the door firmly behind her and leaned back against the door. She put her hands on her face, and she could feel herself become shaky. She slowly slid down to the floor, her head still in her hands.

Kennedy knew her family would notice her red eyes from crying, so she tried to force the tears down even though she knew it would give her a headache. A few fell anyhow, and she hurriedly wiped them away and began telling herself to knock it off. This was why she wasn't playing basketball: because the idea of going out onto the court made her feel like this. This wasn't something she would get past.

"And besides," she thought to herself, "I don't even have shoes."

She shook her head and tried to breathe. There was no reason to have shoes: she wasn't going to be playing this year. She was done with sports. It was time to move on.

Yet, she couldn't help but wonder why her heart and head hurt so much if she was truly okay with this decision.

Kennedy finally got herself calmed down enough to go back downstairs. She could feel her mother's eyes on her as she sat down and began to dish herself up some food. Everyone else had already started eating.

She contributed to the conversation when she could, but she still felt like there was a giant weight pressing down on her chest. She couldn't wait to go back up to her room and be alone, though after she thought about it, being alone may be worse than being with her family and her mother's watchful eye.

She was just finishing picking at her meal when her mother began clearing the table. Her father and brothers were eagerly talking about basketball, and while Kennedy had managed to block a lot of it out, she needed to get away from the conversation. She went to stand up, hoping she could just put her plate in the sink and rush upstairs, when her mother cleared her throat.

"Mind helping me clean up?" she said pointedly, looking at her daughter. Kennedy felt herself deflate as she nodded and began clearing dishes. Her father tried to protest, telling his wife he would take care of washing and putting things away, but Kathy waved him off and told him to continue his conversation.

Kennedy carried in the first load of plates and began scraping them off. Her mother brought in the leftovers and began packaging them up for a meal the next day, when they all would be on slightly different schedules again. Kennedy finished her job and began wordlessly washing the plates, silverware, and glasses from the family's meal.

Her mother came up beside her and began loading the dishwasher. The two worked in silence, and Kennedy thought maybe she would not have to talk when her mother finally broke the silence.

"So, how are you doing?" she asked.

Kennedy shrugged in response.

Her mother sighed. "I wish you would just talk to me when you were upset."

Kennedy found herself scrubbing the plate she was holding extra hard. "I don't like talking to anyone when I am upset," she answered.

Her mother didn't respond for a moment as she began to lower the plates into the rack. "Have you thought at all about basketball this year? You know you have a therapy appointment on Wednesday, and we could get you shoes and things then if you needed them...."

Hot tears bounced back to Kennedy's eyes, and she scrubbed even harder at the plate. She didn't have the words to explain that yes, she thought about the game constantly, but she couldn't do it. She just couldn't bring herself to go out on the court again without Jess by her side. She felt like she had left a game unfinished, but she didn't know how to finish it.

"Kathy," her father's voice was rarely that sharp. Kennedy turned and so did her mother to look at him in the doorway. "Leave her be."

"But—" her father looked at his wife hard while Kennedy watched the exchange uncomfortably. After a moment of tense eye contact, he looked at his daughter.

"Go upstairs and work on your term paper," he said. She quickly set the plate down and rushed out of the room.

Her parents rarely fought, but she knew that they were likely having a tense discussion downstairs as she laid in her bed in silence. She should be working on her term paper, but she didn't really want to at the moment, and she felt like she had a solid start.

Instead, she pulled out her laptop and opened her side table drawer, digging though until she found the flash drive lying at the bottom.

As her computer booted up, she played with the drive, opening and closing it again and again. It was weird, how this little piece of storage held the memories of her sister.

Her hand-me-down computer finally came on, and she logged in hurriedly, plugging the drive into the port. She hadn't read any more of the writings from her sister since the first night she had the drive.

She opened the file and navigated to the document labeled "2."

I grew up on a ranch at the edge of southeastern Montana. It was kind of the middle of nowhere, but I never felt alone. I grew up with two older brothers, a younger sister, and eventually a younger brother. The land we grew up on was our kingdom... kind of like the kids from Narnia. We made do with what we had.

We grew up raising cattle and helping my dad in the fields we had during the summers. But the thing I remember the most from my childhood is the game of basketball.

Almost every memory I have is on the court or in the yard where my dad put up a hoop. Eventually, his shop would be where we played, but when I was young, it was out in the yard. I remember Kris teaching me how to shoot and Hunter arguing with him over if it was the right way or not. They fought a lot growing up. And I remember helping teach Kennedy to shoot, when she was just two or three and she couldn't even get it to the hoop.

We grew up playing ball against each other outside, no matter the weather. It was all we had. The town kids had pools and could ride bikes to the store for ice cream. We had wide open fields and a basketball. It was just how we were raised.

As I got older, I started spending time in the gym at school. Dad had grown up playing basketball, and he liked to help out Coach Davidson, who was in his early years then, when he could. So, he would bring me along to the girls' practices.

I got to know them all really well. I thought they were so cool. They would always say 'hi' to me when they saw me at games. I loved cheering them on. And at some point, I found a love for them and the community they gave me, the first family I had away from the ranch. That family is what sparked a love for being a part of a team for me, at this young age before I was in elementary.

Kennedy finished reading the draft and slowly closed the computer, setting it on her bed and lying back. It was weird to read the words of the dead, but it was even stranger to have her explain what she was feeling so well. To have her sister enunciate the feelings of why she missed basketball two years earlier made it seem so simple. Basketball had always been a part of their lives. It was where they found friendships and communities. That was why it was so difficult to let it go.

But it wasn't that simple. She wished she could find healing in the gym, like her brothers were. Jack even wore Jess's number, twelve, on the court. And Kris believed coaching would help him continue to heal. But she had grown up always on Jess's team, and she was scared all she would do when... if... she made it on the court, at least here, would be feel her absence, the missing piece of the puzzle.

"No," she decided. "I can't play." It just wouldn't be the same.

The knock at her door woke her up and her mother peeked into her room. "Honey, you have to get up, it's 7:30."

Kennedy bolted up. "What?" she gasped. She had fallen asleep in the clothes she had worn the day before. She didn't even remember drifting off. She quickly rolled out of bed, grabbing for her books and shoving them back into her backpack.

"Why didn't you wake me up sooner?" she gasped out, rushing to grab a clean pair of sweats out of her laundry basket.

"I thought you were up!" her mother answered. "But then Jack said he hadn't seen you yet today and was asking if you were giving him a ride or not—"

"Clearly not!" Kennedy answered, rushing into her bathroom and piling her hair on top of her head.

Her mother sighed. "I'll make you some toast," she said as she pulled the door shut.

Kennedy frantically ran around her room. She glanced into her bag and made sure her books were in there, quickly zipping it up and running downstairs. She was pulling it onto her shoulders as her mother handed her a paper plate with cinnamon and sugar toast on it. Kennedy grimaced at her as she rushed out the door.

It had finally gotten cool enough to frost overnight, and Kennedy was glad to see someone had started her car. Probably her father, she thought with a smile. She flung open the driver's door and went to throw her backpack across the seats when she noticed the shoes sitting there neatly. They were her ones from sophomore year she kept in her closet, the ones Jess had the opposite pair to, perched neatly on top of a pair of what appeared to be basketball shorts and a t-shirt. A folded-up piece of paper was stuck under one of them.

"Just in case," the note said. She looked up at the house, frustrated. But there wasn't time to go in and deal with it now, so she flung her backpack on them and headed for town.

She munched on a piece of toast as she drove. Hopefully Grace hadn't wanted to cruise that morning because Kennedy was going to be cutting it close making it to class on time.

Her friend may have gone in early to go shoot some hoops anyhow, she figured.

She cruised into the parking lot of the school with minutes to spare and hurriedly got out, pulling her bag with her. She was about to slam the door shut when she looked at the shoes and clothes and, before she could think about it, grabbed them and shoved them into her bag as well.

She didn't even stop at her locker: everything she needed for the period would be in her bag anyhow. She ran into Ms. O'Brien's room panting hard as the bell finished up ringing. Grace stared at her in confusion. Ms. O'Brien wasn't even in the room: Mr. M, a substitute and former teacher, was. Kennedy hurriedly found her seat as he began reading out the directions for the day in a monotone voice.

"What happened to you?" Grace asked.

"Woke up late," Kennedy whispered back between raspy breaths. She hadn't run that hard in a while. Conditioning had fallen off a bit toward the end of volleyball.

"Jeeze," Grace answered. "By the way, it's an open book quiz today."

Kennedy sighed. "Of course it is," she answered. She bent down to pull her book out and froze when she realized what Grace would see the moment she opened the bag. Why had she brought the shoes in anyway?

"Oh shoot," she said loudly. "I left my book at home when I woke up late. Mr. M, can I use a book off the back counter?" He looked at her and nodded.

She relaxed some as she went and grabbed a book off the bookcase that ran along the bottom of the north wall of the room.

Kennedy managed to shove her bag into her locker between periods and grabbed her pencil bag, along with her notebooks for class. She was glad she wouldn't need to open the bag again for the rest of the day and risk the items in it being seen. She didn't need anyone asking her what she had the shoes for.

The students in the high school were abuzz with excitement over the basketball season starting that day. It seemed to take the sting out of losing the football game a bit—the overlap between the seasons was a bit strange, but was just how things were working out now. The girls were talking excitedly when she sat her tray down at the end of the center table in the cafeteria over lunch.

Ellie looked up at Kennedy and blushed profusely as the senior sat down. She had texted her three different times apologizing for how she had acted on Saturday, but Kennedy didn't want her to worry so she smiled back at her when she caught her eye next.

"So, Kennedy," Rachel, one of the sophomores said, "is Kris excited to be coaching?"

Grace looked up sharply and seemed to want to say something, but Kennedy quickly answered. "Oh, yeah. He is super excited."

Rachel nodded back, her mid-length brown hair half up in a messy bun on top of her head. "I'm excited to have some new blood out there coaching us. At least he played in school; I swear Mary-Ann had no clue what she was doing out there.

Kennedy laughed along with the others but found herself tuning out as the conversation stayed on the topic of the game. She didn't have much to add since she didn't play with the girls. She found herself coming back into the conversation as they were discussing scheduling.

"I'm so annoyed we have late practice this week," Grace was saying. "I hate having to sit in the lobby for two hours before we even get into the gym."

Kennedy nodded along with the girls. She didn't know they had late practice first: she would plan on staying and getting her homework done with them right after school and then heading out when Jack did.

The rest of the day flew by quickly and soon she found herself sitting in the lobby with the rest of the girls who were going to play basketball, studying. Grace and Kennedy had a government test coming up, and since they were notoriously hard, Kennedy was pouring over their notes and past assignments. She could hear the whistle and buzzers going off inside the gym, and it made her a little anxious, so she tried to focus on the work in front of her.

Grace was not even trying to concentrate as she lounged in the orange chairs in the lobby of the school. Occasionally, she would make a comment or answer a question that Kennedy asked, but it was clear her head was already in practice mode. Kennedy shut her book with a sigh as the girls on the other end of the lobby began collecting their things to go change in the locker room. Grace didn't go with them.

She looked at her friend. "I didn't think I would be going in there alone today," she said. Kennedy didn't answer. "It was always supposed to be the two of us," she continued.

Kennedy nodded. "I know."

"Are you sure… absolutely sure…that you don't want to come in with me?" she asked. "I don't even care if you don't have clothes with you." Kennedy glanced at her bag quickly before looking back at her friend. "We can deal with that. I really want you in there with me."

Kennedy smiled sadly. "I'm sorry, Grace. I can't."

Grace nodded back and sighed. She reached out and squeezed her friend's hand as she rose. "Okay," she said. "Then I guess I should get to practice."

"You wouldn't want to be running suicides because the team captain was late the first day," Kennedy answered with a wink.

Grace nodded and gave her friend a half smile. "Guess not." She pulled her bag onto her shoulders and started toward the wooden doors. She turned as she got to them.

"Promise me you'll come to the games?" she asked.

Kennedy felt the knot in her stomach. "I'll try," she answered.

Grace didn't respond for a moment but then nodded and slipped inside the gym.

Kennedy sat in the silence. There was no reason for her to be sitting here now. She didn't need to give Jack a ride: nothing was holding her here. But she couldn't bring herself to leave.

Suddenly, Kris was walking down the steps across the space.

He didn't notice her sitting there, at a table in the corner, and she watched him go up to the framed jersey of Jess's. He stared at it for a moment before reaching out and touching the glass gently. He then turned and went down the other hallway toward the multi-purpose room.

Kennedy stood, leaving her books and bag at the table, and walked over to the memorial the school had put up for her sister. She stared at the jersey, wrinkle-free behind the glass. Then she slowly reached out and touched the glass separating them as well. She stayed there for a beat.

As her hand dropped back down to her side, the buzzer rang out on the other side of the door again. The boys would be pouring out of the gym any second now. She quickly went and pulled her things into a pile and hurried down the hallway to her locker, shoving them inside. She slammed it shut, the only noise in the silence of the nearly empty building. She walked down the silent, dark hallway. But as she got to the end, she couldn't bring herself to turn and go toward the doors. Instead, she just stood there, not sure what to do.

She could go out the door and into the cold and drive herself home and that would be that. It was so simple.

But the free throw and her question from the morning before were there still, haunting her. Another option. A chance she didn't think she would take again.

Allen Davidson stood in front of the girls, who were all sitting on the floor. His new assistant coach, Kris Helland, stood beside him.

The numbers were exactly what he had predicted at the beginning of the year. Three eighth graders, two exchange students (both of whom had played basketball in their home country of Germany, much to his relief), two freshman, two sophomores, and one senior. Kennedy Helland was nowhere to be seen: he wished she had changed her mind but knew he couldn't force her to come out. Still, ten girls was a manageable number, one he could work with throughout the season. It wasn't the worst he could have.

He looked out over his players and began walking them through rules and expectations that he had before launching into a recap of the last season and how he would like to improve for the year.

He knew that some of them weren't paying attention, but he needed to get through this before they could officially start practice. He heard the gym door open and close behind him, but he figured that it was just one of the boys coming out of the shower late.

He continued speaking, finally pausing at the end of his recap of how they lost out of the district tournament in two only to see that absolutely none of the girls were looking at him, including Grace Larkin, who looked like she was going to cry.

He felt his annoyance spike. "What on earth could you all be looking at right now instead of listening to me?" he asked.

Someone tapped him on the shoulder. He turned to look at Kris, who was white, his mouth slightly open.

"Uh," he said. He seemed to want to talk but nothing would come out. Finally, he nodded back at the gym doors.

Allen turned and felt his own mouth go slack and his arms drop to his sides, barely hanging on to his clipboard.

He blinked a few times, not sure how to proceed. Finally, he swallowed hard.

"You're late," he told Kennedy Helland, who was standing under the basket.

She nodded slowly. "I know. It won't happen again," she hesitated some before adding in, "Coach."

PART 2

18

"Your mother tells me that you decided to go out for basketball," Dr. Cameron said.

Kennedy slowly nodded her head up and down. "I guess I did."

"And why did you decide to do that?"

Kennedy shrugged.

She hated going to therapy. Losing her sister at a young age and so suddenly, plus having the added challenge of her being a teammate and friend, was something that would be hard for a lot of people to cope with. However, she did not like talking about her feelings and talking to a therapist seemed like torture. None of her brothers were seeing anyone as far as she knew, nor was her father, and her mother went willingly. She wasn't sure why everyone seemed to think that out of all the family, she was the one who desperately needed help.

Dr. Cameron sighed. "Kennedy, we have talked about the importance of us having a dialogue in these sessions. I don't want this to just be an hour of us sitting in silence while staring at each other."

Kennedy rolled her eyes. That was exactly what she wanted, but she knew Dr. Cameron wouldn't let her get away with it.

Her therapist began talking again. "Well, I think going out for basketball is a great idea. You parents spoke about how much you loved the sport growing up, and I'm sure your sister would be so proud—"

"How do you know that?" Kennedy asked.

Dr. Cameron blinked. "Know what?" she asked.

"Know that my sister would be proud of me," Kennedy answered. "You never met her."

Dr. Cameron paused for a moment. Her client was correct: she had never met her deceased older sister. Finally, she backtracked.

"You're right, I didn't know Jessica. But based on what you and your family members have told me over the years, I think she would be very happy to see you moving forward."

Kennedy rolled her eyes again, and Dr. Cameron made a few notes in the yellow legal pad she kept on her lap during their conversations.

Kennedy stared at her. She was always writing in that damn thing. She wondered what she was writing about. Dr. Cameron noticed her staring and looked up at her. Kennedy quickly looked away.

Dr. Cameron cleared her throat after a few minutes. "How is applying for schools going?" she asked.

Kennedy went to shrug again but stopped herself. Talking meant the hour would pass faster, if nothing else. "Okay, I guess," she answered. "I only applied to the U and got accepted right away."

"Well, that is exciting!" Dr. Cameron exclaimed. Kennedy flinched at her high-pitched voice. "What are you planning on studying?"

Kennedy wasn't fully sure on that front, to be completed honest. She had thought about going into teaching or even journalism, like Hunter, but she hadn't made any decisions yet. To be honest, she wasn't even sure if she wanted to go to Missoula: it seemed so far away from everyone at the moment, with Hunter moving to Denver at the end of the academic year.

"I'm not really sure yet," she admitted.

"Well," Dr. Cameron had a giant smile now, "whatever you decide on, I'm sure you will do great at. Now, let's talk about how managing your anxiety has been going lately."

Kennedy met her mom in the parking lot of the therapist's building.

"How was your appointment, honey?" she asked brightly.

Kennedy grunted in response.

Kathy had learned her daughter tended to be crabby after these appointments, so she quickly backed off. She drove with the satellite radio filling the car with noise while Kennedy was lost in her thoughts.

She had gone into the gym late, moving almost as if something else was guiding her. She had changed in the women's bathroom out by the front office and stared at herself in the mirror for a long time, surrounded by the light-yellow tile. She had slowly walked to the small sinks and splashed some water onto her face, breathing heavily. She hadn't been able to believe she was going to do this.

She had turned back to her backpack that was lying open on the floor. The shoes were still inside the bag, the ones that were the opposite of Jess's. She had stared at them for a moment, not quite knowing how to proceed. Then she looked at her Nike running shoes she had worn to school that day. She zipped up her bag and slid into her street shoes, making a note to pack her shoes from freshman year that night.

She had waited until the lobby was quiet again before she left the bathroom. She didn't want to run into one of the boys before she got wherever she was going; she didn't want to answer questions. She was scared if she saw anyone else before she got in there, that she wouldn't be able to convince herself to go in at all.

When the area was silent once more and the thick, steel doors at the front of the building had stopped slamming, Kennedy left bathroom. She walked past the front office and down the two steps to the lobby area. Her sister's jersey had overlooked her as she stopped outside the doors. "Beware, all ye who enter here," said the sign above the wooden doors. She had pulled one open and slipped inside.

Coach Davidson was talking to the team when she came in and a few of the girls glanced up. She walked slowly forward as they stared at her, each of them coming to the realization of what they were witnessing. Grace turned to look at one of them and nudged her, but the eighth grader, had shaken her head and continued to stare at the door. Grace looked up as well and brought a hand to her face. Kris was the next to turn, and she watched all the color drain from his face. She was starting to feel a little uncomfortable with everyone looking at her.

Soon they were all staring, and Allen seemed to have sensed that he had lost control of the floor. He looked up and asked them, "What on earth could you all be looking at right now instead of listening to me?"

Kris had tapped him on the shoulder. Kennedy couldn't hear if he said anything, but he nodded toward her. Coach Davidson had turned and stared at her for a moment, just like the others.

"You're late," he had said to her.

She had nodded back. "I know," she answered. "It won't happen again," it had taken her a moment to call him the name she had known him by for so long, "Coach."

They had started the practice by doing some drills. Kennedy knew all eyes were on her as she went for layups and shots, and she knew it was affecting her shooting. Nothing seemed to be able to make it through the basket and her ball handling was sloppy at best, but she was here and she was practicing.

After getting a short warm up in, Coach Davidson sent them out to shoot free throws. Ten at each basket, just like he always had. Grace immediately partnered up with Kennedy.

She bounced the ball to her, and Kennedy lined up. It was the first shot she made the entire practice.

Her friend still seemed to be in a state of shock over Kennedy being there, and she shook her head as Kennedy finished up her first ten shots. "I can't believe you are standing in front of me shooting right now," she muttered.

Kennedy went and grabbed her ball. She had made seven. Not bad, but also not the best. She passed it to Grace. "Can I be honest?" she asked. "So am I."

"Like," Grace bent down and shot. The ball bounced of the hoop, and Kennedy caught it. "Why didn't you tell me you weren't coming?"

Kennedy shook her head as she passed it to her. "I wasn't going to."

"Then why did you have clothes?" This shot bounced through the net and Kennedy whipped it back out to her friend.

Kennedy sighed. "My mom put them in my car sometime before I left this morning. I really didn't think I was going to be in here today, Grace," she answered.

Grace shook her head. "I just... I can't believe you're in here shooting with me again." She launched the ball and this one clunked off the backboard and in. Kennedy winced. Grace had never been a great free throw shooter.

"I can't believe it either," Kennedy concurred.

The girls chatted off and on as they continue around the gym, shooting ten shots at each basket. Everyone was partnered off in groups of two, minus the three eighth graders who were shooting together. It seemed so familiar to her, so comfortable, that for a while, Kennedy forgot that it had been nearly two years since she had stepped foot in the gym.

She finished the first round of free throws making 44 of the 60 she could have. It wasn't bad, but she was disappointed that it wasn't a higher number until she found out it was the highest on the team. Her heart sored a little bit, and Kris looked at her proudly.

The rest of the practice had been spent running drills. Blitz Drill, Jungle Ball, 2-on-3, a new drill that Davidson had yet to name... they crammed as many in as they could during their two-hour practice.

Finally, their coach told them to get on the end line. Everyone groaned. One-by-one, he called them out to the line and tossed them the ball. For every one a girl missed, the whole team would run what was non-affectionately called a "killer." The full length of the court and back, then to the free throw line of the opposite side of the court and back, then to the half court line, and finally the closer free throw line. Coach Davidson started with the eighth graders and worked his way up through the grades. By the time he got to Kennedy and Grace, they had run seven "killers" and all were breathing heavily. Kennedy thought she saw some black dots swimming in her eyes.

He passed the ball to Kennedy, and she caught it, hesitating. She dribbled out to where he stood. By the free throw line. She felt all the eyes on her again, and this time it made her heart race. She pulled into her routine, line up, three dribbles, realign toe, crouch down, eye up basket, and shoot. The ball bounced far to the right and flew off the rim.

She dropped her arm and her head simultaneously and shuffled back to the line as he grabbed her ball. He blew the whistle, and they ran once more. As she crossed the end line, she walked forward to the team, her back to Grace as she shot. Kennedy was covered in sweat and her t-shirt was sticking to her skin. She bunched it up by her hips and looked up, breathing through the pain and the tears that were mixing in with the sweat on her face. Her breath was haggard and shaky. She needed to get out of there.

There were claps and a few whoops at that moment, and she turned and looked. Everyone was surrounding Grace. She must have made the last shot. Coach Davidson was off to the side of the group with Kris. He nodded at her to come over to the group, and she slowly walked out to meet them.

"Sit down," he told the girls. They all did, and the older ones, minus Kennedy, began slipping of their shoes. Kennedy just brought her knees to her chest and folded her arms over them, resting her head on them. She was still trying to breathe.

Coach Davidson stood in the middle of the circle. He turned to look at each of his players as he spoke.

"This was our first practice of the year," he said. "There is a lot to improve upon." He paused for a moment. "But there also is a lot that I like to see. You all hustled the entire time today. The entire time. It doesn't matter how talented a team is if they don't work hard. If you girls keep working hard like you did today...." he paused again, and Kennedy looked up at him. He was starting straight at her. "You are going to make a lot of people very proud." She took another deep breath and maintained her eye contact with him. He had nodded and looked away, still turning. "This week is going to be a lot of conditioning. It's going to be a lot of running and sweating and hard times. But as we get closer to games," he added, "it's going to be more about coming together and playing as one. As a team." He smiled.

"Let's bring it in," he added. The girls stood up and Kennedy found herself uncurling from her ball when a hand appeared in her face. It was Ellie. The red-head's face seemed to match her hair, it was so flushed. Kennedy smiled and took her hand, and the sophomore pulled her up.

Everyone else had their arms up already, a collection of different skin tones that were slightly shiny from perspiration. Kennedy and Ellie added theirs to the group, and Grace called out, "Family on three. One, two, three!"

"Family!" They all chanted out.

Kennedy rushed out of the gym as the rest of the group collected their water bottles and headed toward the locker room at the other end. All of her stuff was out in the lobby still, but she rushed past it and back into the women's restroom.

Everything she had eaten that day looked back at her in the bowl moments later.

She leaned over the toilet, panting. She had thrown up a lot when she was younger, from nerves or excitement. She didn't do it often anymore; in fact, she couldn't remember the last time she had. But for whatever reason, that practice and missing that free throw had brought it out of her.

Kennedy sat back and leaned her head against the door of the stall. She was breathing easier now, at least. She tried to wipe at her eyes: she always cried while she was vomiting, which made the process so much worse to her. She hated crying.

Finally, she rose slowly. Her legs were shaky, from both running and being sick, and she flushed and made her way out of the stall and looked at herself in the mirror. Her bun from the morning had gone lopsided, nowhere near the top of her head. Her checks were rosy, and her face pale; it made her freckles stand out even more than normal. Her green eyes were vibrant, surrounded by the red from crying. She looked rough. Slowly, she undid her top knot, letting her long hair flow down. The top was soaked in sweat still, and the waves had kinks in them from her ponytail that had held the bun in place. She splashed some water on her face and took a few deep breaths leaning over the sink before she left the bathroom.

She flicked off the light switch as she left and went and gathered her things. It looked like everyone else had left—including Grace.

She was a little surprised her friend hadn't stuck around to chat after the practice, but she was glad at the same time. That had taken a lot out of her, both mentally and emotionally, and she needed a moment to think about what had transpired that day.

She walked into the chilly, late fall air in her practice clothes and started toward her car. Kris was leaning on it.

She stopped a few feet in front of him, letting her bag fall to the ground.

He nodded at her. "Are you feeling better?" he asked.

"I can't do this right now," she answered exhaustedly.

He nodded again. "I know," he said. He was still leaning against her car, and he didn't say anything else for a moment. "Mom called me in a panic, asking if I knew where you were," he said finally.

She looked away. She felt bad, not saying anything to her parents about being late. She knew she should have. She always tried to check in, after Jess, when she would be driving back to the ranch alone.

"I honestly haven't looked at my phone since after school. What did you tell her?" she asked.

"I told her you would talk to her when you got home in a little bit, but you may want to let her know you are, in fact, alright before you head home," he answered.

She looked at him now, in the dark parking lot, barely lit by the lights coming off the school and from one of the few working streetlights in the town.

"You didn't tell her where I was?" She was surprised he hadn't been honest with her.

He shook his head. "It wasn't my thing to tell."

She bit her lip, nodding. She appreciated he had let her come to her own conclusion about playing, but he was right. It was her news to share now, not his. No matter how much she didn't want to say it, it wouldn't be a secret for long.

She pulled her phone out of her bag and groaned as she saw the list of missed calls and text messages from her mother and even a few from her father.

She didn't even open them, instead simply typing out a group message that said "Leaving town now."

Kris finally pushed himself off her car and stood in front of her. He opened up one arm, and she fell into it.

"I am so proud of you," he said.

She smiled into his jacket as he squeezed her tight.

He let her go and began walking across the lot back to the front of the school where his pickup was warming up. She tossed her bag into the back seat and opened the front door when he called out to her.

She looked up.

He glanced up to the sky. "So is she," he said.

Kennedy smiled sadly at him and pulled herself into the car.

Her mother had been furious when she came into the kitchen, demanding to know where she was. Kennedy had shrugged her bag off and slid her shoes off, not answering for a moment.

He father came in and leaned against the door, looking weary.

She had stood, leaning again the refrigerator, looking at the floor. "I was at practice," she finally said.

"Practice?" Her mom had sounded confused. "You... you were at practice?" her voice had become more and more hopeful with each word.

Kennedy had looked up and nodded back at her, and suddenly her mother had her arms around her and she was crying. Kennedy didn't know how to respond at first, but slowly she brought an arm up and patted her mother on the back, still not saying anything.

She made eye contact with her father, and he nodded at her, slowly. She smiled a bit.

Her mother finally pulled away, still gripping Kennedy painfully. She looked at her husband. "I told you," she said, shaking a figure at him. "I told you she would do it."

Kennedy raised her eyebrows at her father, and he slowly drawled out "I never said she wouldn't."

Her mother went off on a tangent, telling her that they would need to get her shoes on Wednesday after her counseling appointment in town and she probably would need some other things as well, like socks and basketball shorts. She insisted that Kennedy sit down to eat dinner, but Kennedy shook her off, telling her she was tired.

"Oh, of course of course," her mother said. She was nearly over the top with excitement. She quickly made up a plate and handed it off to her daughter. "Go lie down and eat in your room," she said.

Kennedy raised her eyebrows. Kathy hated when she had food in her room. Her mother waved her hand at her daughter. "Enjoy," she said.

Kennedy had glanced at her father and slipped upstairs to her room. She nibbled at the things on the plate and knew she should be eating more, but it was hard after she had been sick.

When she brought her plate downstairs to throw away what she hadn't gotten to, her father was the only one in the kitchen. He nodded at her, and she scraped her food off into the garbage can before rinsing her plate and dropping it into the dishwasher. When she turned around, he was taking a long sip of his beer.

She had hesitated a moment before sitting down at the table with him.

He had nodded at her, looking down at his label. "How was practice?"

"It was fine," she answered. "Just running and drills and stuff mostly."

He had nodded, setting his beer down and looking up at her. "And how are you?"

Now, she looked away, down at the blue checkered table cloth her mother kept on the kitchen table. "I'm okay," she said.

The two sat in silence for a long time. Finally, her father pushed his chair back and stood up. She looked up at him. "What you did, by going out," he said. "I know it took a lot out of you." Kennedy looked away. She was scared if she made eye contact with him she would start to cry. "I know you didn't want to be there. But I'm glad you went. And I'm glad it was your choice to do so."

She had swallowed hard, not able to answer him. She heard him begin to leave the room, when he stopped by the door. "Did the shoes fit you still?" he asked.

Kennedy looked up at him. He hadn't turned around when he asked, just stopped right before the door.

"I didn't try them," she replied honestly. He had leaned back slightly, onto his heels.

"Your mom will get you a new pair on Wednesday," he answered as he walked out the door.

Kennedy stared after him. She had been convinced it was her mother who had done it, put the shoes in the car, as a last-ditch attempt in order to get her to go to practice today. When her mother had acted so surprised, she had thought she was faking it, at least a little. But now she realized her surprise had been real. She really hadn't thought that Kennedy would go out.

Kennedy was brought out of her thoughts as her mother parked the car in front of Scheels. It had been two days since then, and she had survived another practice and a morning lifting session that day. She had thrown up the night before, again from nerves, but had made it through the lifting session okay. It also didn't take place in the gym, which helped some.

They walked inside the store, to the women's shoes section, where Kennedy pulled the all-black Nikes down off the shelf and an associate fetched her size for her. She stood up, looking at them in the little mirrors they had so you could see just your feet. They looked just like she thought they would, and they were comfortable on her feet.

Her mother teared up again at the store and went off about how proud she was of her daughter to the sale associate, and Kennedy found herself turning bright red. Her mother had done her grocery run during her counseling appointment so they could get back in time for practice that Wednesday. Wednesdays were family night, so both teams practiced right after school, splitting their time in the gym and multi-purpose room so they could all be out by 6:00 p.m. on the dot.

They drove home in silence, Kennedy occasionally checking her phone but not saying much. They had just passed Custer and were entering the Hysham Hills when her mother finally spoke.

"So," she said. Kennedy looked at her, knowing a conversation she probably didn't want to have was about to happen. "What made you decide to play this year?" her mother asked.

Kennedy sighed. She knew this conversation was going to come up eventually, but she didn't want to have it still.

The truth was, she wasn't sure what had made her decide to go back into the bathroom and slip into the clothes her father had apparently put into her car. She wasn't sure what inside of her made her go out into the gym and made her stay the entire practice or what made her go back the next day. And she didn't know what to tell the people who asked her, like Grace or her mother or anyone else, as the news had spread that she was playing the day before.

"I don't know," she finally said. And it wasn't just a way to avoid the question. She really didn't know.

She didn't know what compelled her to go back into the bathroom and slide into her practice clothes, just like she had done hundreds of times before. What had made her walk to the gym doors and pull them open and step out to the court. She couldn't explain it. She just knew she had to do it.

19

When she came into band class that afternoon, right before the bell rang to dismiss them, the room seemed to be in a somber mood. People were grouped around talking to each other in hushed whispers; they barely looked up at her when she walked in.

Grace was playing the piano. Kennedy went and stood next to her as she finished the song she had memorized the previous year for the music festival the school attended each year. The final chords of the piece drifted out over the small gathering of high school and junior high students in the room.

"Who died?" Kennedy asked, before realizing what she had said.

Grace looked at her in confusion for a moment, and Kennedy let out a nervous giggle. Her friend finally shook her head.

"Your brother's friend—Sam?—from Custer?" she said. "He's right. We're co-oping for sports next year. Well, not 'we.' 'They,' I guess. We won't be here."

Kennedy blinked, unsure if she had heard her friend correctly. "What?" she finally said.

Grace nodded. "Mr. Johnson had called all of the junior high and high school, minus Paul and me, in for a meeting at lunch." She cocked her head slightly, a glimmer in her eye. "I sweet-talked Evelyn and went and sat on the other side of the library door going into the office so I could hear whatever he was telling them," she said with a grin. Slowly, though, it melted from her face.

"Yeah, the board is going ahead with it" she sighed. "I can't believe they didn't ask anyone for our input though," she added, "before deciding on it."

"Well, our opinion wouldn't count for much anyhow," Kennedy pointed out. "We're done here in May."

Grace shook her head. "I know. But still," she nodded out over the underclassmen in the room, "they had a right to be involved in the process."

Allen Davidson looked out over the eleven girls on his basketball team. Next year he only knew of seven of them that would be playing, if they all stayed here and no one moved or transferred to Forsyth, a town over. The two exchange students and his senior girls would be gone. The prospects for anything in the grade below didn't look good either. There were only four boys in the seventh-grade class at the moment, so none of them would be joining the team.

The mood had been off the entirety of practice. He could feel the girls just didn't have their hearts in it at the moment. After the news had broken during lunch about the co-op that had been approved at a meeting between the two school districts the night before in Custer, he couldn't blame them.

It wasn't like it had been a secret. The schools had been meeting about it off and on all summer. There had been notices posted around the town, just like they were supposed to be. The teachers and administrators had all known about it. But still, it had come as a surprise to the students.

"They're teenagers, Greg," Allen had said exasperatedly after the meeting at lunch, which had not gone as well as the principal seemed to have hoped. "You can't think they would have known about this if they weren't given the information straight on."

Greg Johnson had shaken his head. "I told the board we should wait and hear from them, but it just wasn't happening. They had their minds made up. Final vote at the meeting with Custer was 5-1 yesterday. There's no stopping it now."

Allen had sighed exasperatedly, throwing his hands into the air as he walked out. He wasn't necessarily upset with the co-oping for sports: he knew that was going to happen years ago as he watched the numbers dwindle each season, but he was upset that the students seemed to have had their democratic process snuffed out. Where was their voice in this? How was he supposed to teach about them using their voices if no one even cared to let them?

Now, at practice, he knew he had to address the elephant in the room, if only because no one else was going to.

The girls were sitting in a circle around him, breathing heavily in the gym. Today had been a hard conditioning day for them: short practices made it an excellent excuse to get some running in instead of trying to cram in multiple drills. Kris was standing outside the group, looking at him expectantly.

He was nodding as he stood in the center of them. "Good job today, ladies," he said. "I know you all had some news dropped on you somewhat suddenly this afternoon. And I won't lie, it sucks." Several of the heads that had been looking at the floor shot their heads up at this comment. "It sucks that we don't have the numbers anymore. It sucks that your voices weren't heard in this decision. It sucks because, well, it just sucks." He looked around at the girls sitting on the gym floor. "I know next year is going to look very different to you all who will be here. But we aren't there yet. This season hasn't even officially started yet." He gave them a sad smile. "So, let's focus on the next three months and on how we can make this last season as Pirates be a great one. Okay?"

There wasn't much of a response from anyone. He nodded once again. "Alright, everyone up and bring it in."

The girls slowly rose and came together, their arms held up toward the sky. "Family on three," Allen said, counting them off.

"Family," the girls said. There was less force behind the chant today.

Kennedy rode home with Jackson that night since her mother had just dropped her off in town after they had gotten back from Billings. He didn't say much either, and she wondered what was going through his mind at the moment and how he felt about the news.

When they got to the house, she went to get out, but he didn't move after turning the car off and pulling out the key. She stood outside for a moment, staring at him, before crawling back into his little pickup.

"You okay?" she asked. He shrugged in response, and she felt her heart break a little. "So, no," she answered.

"It's just weird," he replied, staring out the front windshield.

Kennedy nodded, looking away from him. "That's fair," she answered. "I don't know how I would feel if I was in your shoes right now."

He didn't reply, clipping and unclipping his lanyard a few times.

She sat beside him, not knowing what to say or if she should just sit here, like she did with Kris after Jess's death. The silence with Kris was comfortable, though, and this wasn't. She felt the need to fill it.

"I mean, you're friends with Sam, so it could be fun to play on the same as him?" she tentatively threw out into the air.

He shrugged again but still didn't answer.

Kennedy tilted her head at him and then leaned back in the seat. She didn't know what else to say to him.

Finally, he reached over and opened the door to the pickup. She watched him slide out of his seat, and she opened her door and did the same. When they got inside, he didn't even stop to give Otis a pat or slide off his shoes. Instead, he just continued through the kitchen to the stairs and up to his room.

Kenney stared after him, but she didn't try and stop him. She slid off her shoes and went to sit at the table, pulling her reading assignment out of her bag. They had moved on to *Hamlet* in English, and she was struggling to understand some of the language.

She sat in the kitchen until her parents came in a while later. They had told her they were going to dinner with the Davidsons and Kris that night, and she expected her mother would have heard the news there about the cooperative, if she hadn't already after dropping Kennedy off at school.

"And who exactly does that Jodie Smith think she is, not even telling the rest of the group that her husband was pro-cooperative?" Her mother was in the middle of a rant as she came in the door, carrying the takeout she had brought for her kids from the Brunswick. She noticed Kennedy at the table and turned to her. "Did anyone tell you that this was going on?"

Kennedy shook her head as her mother dropped the white plastic bag containing her and her brother's food onto the table. She threw her arms up in disgust. "Exactly! We knew it was a possibility, and we knew they were discussing it, but to just go ahead and decide it with little fanfare just seems so shady to me."

She hadn't seen her mother this fired up in a long time. Not since Hunter was in high school and he had had been fouled hard shooting a three that the ref didn't call with seconds left in the game. Of course, she had held her tongue there as well until she got home. The family had listened to her complain for weeks, and Jess and Kennedy had even been forced to read several letters of complaint addressed to the officials' association until she had finally calmed down. She would never say these things to the board members' faces, of course, but she would let them have it in the comfort of her own kitchen. She made eye contact with her father, and he shook his head, giving her a resigned look as he walked out of the room.

Kennedy sat at the table with her mother storming around the kitchen as she went off, letting her take out as much anger as she needed to. Finally, she sat down in a huff, and Kennedy pulled her chicken strips over and began to eat. Her mother continued to stew, making comments under her breath and even pulling out a pen and paper and jotting a few of her thoughts down.

Finally, she leaned back with a sigh.

"Where's your brother?" she asked.

Kennedy covered her mouth with her hand. "His room," she said.

Her mother sighed. "How did he seem to be taking this?"

Kennedy hesitated, not sure what to say. She finished chewing and swallowed, taking her time. Finally, she answered. "I'm not really sure," she admitted.

Her mother sighed again. "Well, that's fair. Because I'm not sure how I feel either."

She reached her hand out and took Kennedy's. Kennedy fought the urge to yank it away and made eye contact with her mother.

"I get the need for the co-op, I really do," she said. She squeezed her daughter's hand once before pulling away. "I was hoping you all would be out of school when it finally happened, but it doesn't appear that will be the case." She sighed again. "If it means we can have teams and compete, then I'm all for it. But how this came about... it just feels wrong."

Kennedy nodded. "I get it," she answered. "And I would be lying if I said that I wasn't relieved not to have to deal with it because it sounds like those first few years are hard."

Her mother was looking at her intently now. "But," she said, "if it means that the girls in the elementary will get to grow up watching their cousins and neighbors play or if it means that Ellie doesn't have to drive to another school and play under a host or if it means the eighth graders can actually play their junior high season and have a program and we can build and grow," she shrugged here, "then I guess it means this will all be worth it someday."

Her mother looked at her for another moment before shaking her head. "When did you get so wise?" she asked.

Kennedy knocked lightly on Jack's door. He didn't answer, but she pushed it open anyhow. He was lying in bed staring at the ceiling. She didn't go in but leaned against the doorframe.

"Your food is in the fridge," she said.

"Not hungry," he answered, not even looking at her.

She stared at him for a moment, hoping he would turn to look at her, but he didn't. So, she slowly left and pulled the door shut behind her. Her hand fell away from the handle.

She couldn't count the number of times he had knocked on her door over the last two years and she had done the exact same thing. Not really responded, if she even bothered to at all. Refusing to participate in whatever he was wanting her to do. Having it done to her hurt more than she thought it would.

By Friday, morale had shifted back up some at the high school, and Allen could feel the difference at the conclusion of practice that afternoon. He had decided to have a team meal at his house that night and give the girls Saturday off since they would end up with more than the state-mandated ten practices by the time their opening game rolled around, so after he talked to them and thanked them for a good start to the season, they had packed into cars and headed to his house just outside of town.

Marty Davidson and Kathy Helland had been cooking most of the afternoon, and the girls came in to the smell of taco meat. They all sprawled out around his kitchen and living room, laughing and filling the house with noise. It had been too quiet since MacKenzie had left for school that fall, and he was thankful to have the sounds of girls playing cards games and shrieking again.

Everyone ate until they were full and then overate when Kathy brought out her "famous" caramel brownies and some ice cream from one of the local shops in Billings. Scott had shown up at that point and spent time talking to Kris and Allen about how the week had gone. By this point, the girls had moved out onto his back porch and were sitting around the fire.

Kennedy was talking to one of the eighth graders and Grace was visiting with Ellie and Jo, the freshman, arguing about football it appeared. He smiled.

It wasn't just about having a team. It was about building a team as well.

20

Kennedy woke up with confusion on Saturday afternoon. She hadn't set her alarm the night before because she didn't have practice, but she still was a little surprised to see it was nearly two in the afternoon when she finally woke up.

She dragged herself out of bed, her body achy from the week of practice. She hadn't run like that in a long time, and she was paying for it now.

She shuffled to her bedroom door and pulled it open and started downstairs.

The house was quiet, with no one in the kitchen or living room. Jackson had had practice that morning, so she figured he had stayed in town after to hang out with some of his friends. He still was being distant after the news about the co-op had spread, and she hadn't seen him much over the past few days. Still, it was odd that her parents were gone and that they hadn't said anything to her.

She looked in the fridge and the pantry, but nothing sounded good to her, so she went back up to her room and began to work on her term paper again.

She was in the middle of reading an article about the decline in women's sports participation as they aged when she heard a vehicle pulling back into the yard. She got out of bed and peeked out her bedroom window and saw her parents getting out of one of her father's smaller work vehicles and coming into the house.

She waited for a while and finished reading her article before she went back downstairs. Her father was leaning over the kitchen sink when she came into the room.

"Where did you guys go?" she asked. He turned to look at her. It was clear he had been crying.

"Oh," he answered, "out to Jess's grave."

Kennedy looked at him, not quite sure how to respond. Her father went out there pretty often, but he wasn't usually so emotional afterwards. She cocked her head in confusion.

Her father looked at her, realization dawning on him. "Kennedy," he said softly. "It's her birthday."

Everything rushed out of her, and she leaned against the counter. "Oh," she responded. She wasn't quite sure what to say.

Jess's favorite time of year was her birthday. She loved having people celebrating her. It was always the first week of basketball season when she was in high school, so she would invite the team out for a big dinner either the weekend before or after and then they would all come out to the ranch and spend the night staying up and bonding with each other.

She wasn't a big fan of cake, but she loved pie, so her mother would stay up the night before baking a variety of flavors. The morning of her birthday, she would eat a piece with a candle stuck in it, and when the team came out to celebrate, there was always a spread of options to choose from.

Her last birthday, her mother had managed to surprise her by inviting the team to an outing in Billings. She had walked into the restaurant on Saturday afternoon to find a small crowd waiting for her, and she had actually fallen over in surprise as she walked into the room. They had gone bowling before heading home and continuing the celebration there. Jess had been all smiles all day, laughing and giggling with her teammates she knew well and those she didn't know as well. Her mother had cried during the party because she knew it was likely the last birthday she would have gotten to spend with her daughter at home; she never could have known how true that would have been.

Kennedy crawled back into bed, suddenly feeling defeated and exhausted. She couldn't believe that she hadn't realized the date.

Her mother had gone straight to her room when they came back from visiting her grave. Her father, though, had sat at the kitchen table with her for a few minutes, reminiscing and drinking coffee.

"When you're a parent," he had said heavily, "you never even imagine what it would be like to bury your own child, because it is inhumane. If we really thought about it, it would destroy us: we would never let them leave the house. But we do, because we put faith in the world that it will protect them and so that they can learn." He had looked at Kennedy here. "I didn't want you kids to be afraid, growing up. Because our fears can hold us back. It's why I never left the ranch, you know. I went to school for one semester and came back and said it wasn't happening again. I didn't want you kids to have that. I wanted you to know the world was at your fingertips."

"But," he continued, "now I have to watch you leave and grow and not come back. Even knowing this, I thought I would always get to talk to you, that you would call and visit us when you could. That eventually one of you would come back by choice, after exploring the world, and stay with us and raise your own family here. I never thought that one day I would say goodbye and that would be it, that I would have to keep living without you." He had sighed heavily here. "That's my fear. And it's a fear I have to live with every day for the rest of my life, thinking about how she died.

"She should be here; it's not fair that she isn't. And I miss her every day. But on days like today or Christmas or when all of you kids are home and under one roof... I miss her a little more, and it's like she is going to come walking back into the room at any second." He shook his head and wiped at his eyes, and Kennedy wiped hers too. She hadn't even realized that she had started to cry.

"I have wanted you guys to always follow your hearts and dreams, and I was so excited to follow along in the passenger seat," he continued, his voice shaky. "And it destroys me that her story ended so young because she had so much more to give. She had so much more life left to live. I hope she knows how proud I am…I was… of her." He looked at his younger daughter now. "And I hope you know how proud I am of you."

Kennedy had been openly trying not to sob now. The two sat in silence for a few minutes, trying to collect themselves. She had finally gotten up and walked over to him, sliding her arms around her father.

"I love you, Dad," she whispered.

He patted her arm. "I love you, too, Kennedy," he answered, still choked up.

Alone in her bedroom, she let the sobs echo through her body. She always felt bad when she forgot something about her sister. In the beginning, it was her physically: how tall she was or the way her freckles appeared in the summer, a smattering of brown paint against her pale skin. Now however, it seemed like it was more and more of who she was. It was her favorite smells and the things that made her laugh.

Kennedy knew she shouldn't feel this awful. She barely even knew what day of the week it was with how busy she had been. But still, to forget your sister's birthday… it felt wrong.

Kennedy took a few deep breaths, trying to calm herself down some. She rolled over, so she was staring at the wall she shared the Jessica's room.

"Happy birthday, Jess," she whispered.

A gentle knock woke her up from her nap and she sat up in bed. Kris was in her door. He nodded toward the stairs.

"Come on," he said.

She shuffled out of bed, wincing again. On top of her body aching, her head was now screaming at her as well from crying. She shuffled downstairs and into the kitchen.

Her mother had on an apron that was covered in flour. Jack was dropping toppings onto his pizza and her father was setting his own completed pie down onto the firestone her mother was opening the oven for. Kris went and began stretching out his own dough, and Kennedy followed him over to where her own lump sat on the table.

They talked and laughed and cried over the next two hours as they sat in the living room to watch TV. After everyone had finished their pizza, her mother went and brought out the pie she had made the night before. There were no candles in it, when there should have been twenty, but even so, as Kennedy sat on her living room floor with most of her family and they laughed over stories of her sister she would have blushed at from embarrassment, it seemed like she may have been there anyway.

21

The first few weeks of basketball blurred into one long week, it seemed. Even with Thanksgiving break, it felt like Kennedy had no time to catch her breath and think about what she was doing, being back in the gym.

Hunter had come home for Thanksgiving, but Adam didn't tag along with him, much to Kennedy's relief. She didn't think that she would have been able to handle it at this point. They hadn't spoken since he had texted her the day they had lost out of volleyball, nearly a month ago now. She still wanted to reach out to him, but there was too much hurt there at the moment, so she didn't.

Hunter had rolled back onto the ranch late Wednesday night. Kennedy had been at the table with Kris, who was waiting for his brother to make his appearance. Hunter had conned him into going back into town, to the only bar that was open, to have some drinks with the past graduates. A Thanksgiving-eve tradition: to finally party at the bar they all wanted to drink at and then end up in someone's garage anyhow.

He came in with the same duffle bag that he had used in high school, hair and hoodie lightly dusted with the snow that was finally starting to fall. Kennedy hadn't talked to him much either in recent weeks and she threw her arms around him into a full-on hug when he came in.

"Whoa, there," he said. "That's not how a Helland hugs." Kennedy had rolled her eyes but let go and stepped back, watching Kris shake his hand and clap him on the back. Jackson had gone to Forsyth with some of the guys in the high school for an evening, and Grace was on her way out to the ranch now for a much-needed girls' night. Her mother came into the kitchen and threw her arms around Hunter before calling out for her husband to come in and say hello as well.

Soon, the boys left, and Grace arrived and the two locked themselves away into Kennedy's room for the night. They talked, laughed, and watched all of their favorite romantic comedies. It had long been tradition for Grace to stay the night at the ranch the night before Thanksgiving. It was weird to think that this could be their last time doing this. Next year, they could probably be served at the bar if they really wanted to be.

The girls had Thanksgiving off from practice but were back into the swing of things on Friday morning. Kennedy and Grace had gone black Friday shopping with Grace's stepmom that afternoon, and Ellie's family had hosted them for dinner that Saturday after practice. Sunday was the day before Hunter left, so Kennedy stuck around the ranch, wanting to spend time with him before he did.

When she came downstairs that afternoon, he was nowhere to be found. Jack, who had locked himself back into his room most of the weekend, didn't know where he was. Kennedy had all but given up hope to find him when she noticed that the shop light was on out the kitchen window.

She trekked out slowly and pulled the door open. The old music system her dad had rewired was blaring; she had heard it halfway across the parking area between the buildings.

She stood, staring at him for a moment.

Hunter had always been the most athletic of the boys in her family and even many in the town. He was strong and graceful and had the talent to back up what bite he dished out. He was the leading scorer on the boys' team in Hysham for three years and had been named All-State his junior and senior seasons in football, basketball, and track. In the summers, he had played baseball. That was his true love, the one that made him want to go into sports writing.

Even after he had started college, he had continued to work out regularly. She was a little surprised that he hadn't even tried to walk on for a sport, but he seemed as burned out as Jessica did during her senior year once he finally put up his bat and glove that summer, just days before he left for school.

He had been much closer to Jess than he was his other siblings. And she knew he had taken her death hard: harder than he would ever let on.

He was shooting and running for his own rebounds for a few minutes before he noticed her. He plodded over and picked up the remote for the stereo system, turning it off.

"Yeah?" he said.

She had shrugged her shoulder, crossing her arms over her chest. He bounced the ball a few times, crossing it between his legs.

"Want to play a game?" he asked. She shrugged again, and he whipped the ball to her. She untangled her arms and caught it haphazardly. "Don't do that. It makes you look bored," he said. She dribbled to the top of the key, and he crouched down into a defensive stance. She went to go forward without bringing her arm up to protect the ball, and he swatted it away and shot past her to collect it.

"Mine now," he said.

She tried to protest, arguing that she was a post player, a "4" or a "5" in small town lingo, but he had shaken his head. "The best players can play anywhere on the court."

She wanted to say she wasn't the best player, but he took off before she could say anything, easily sliding into a layup. He caught the ball as it came through the net and whipped it back out to her. Now she was getting mad.

They lost track of time, running play after play against each other. Later, as they laid on the floor panting, Hunter had rolled over to look at her. His hair was wet with sweat. "How long have you been practicing for?" he asked.

She had been staring at the ceiling, but she turned her head to look at him. "Season started two weeks ago," she answered.

He had propped himself up on his elbows and looked at her hard. "I'm not stupid, Kennedy," he said. "No one takes two years off from the sport and comes back that fluid and with so little rust. I mean, you can see it here and there, but your shot is still solid, and you have moves I don't remember you using down below before."

She had looked back up to the ceiling and closed her eyes for a moment. "Since the summer after she died," she answered. It was the first time she had told anyone. "I came out here and there was just a ball, sitting over there by the couch. I picked it up and... I shot. And then I cried. I cried a lot," she had laughed slightly. "And then I just kept coming out here, when I needed to clear my head." She had paused here, for a moment. "It makes me feel closer to her," she finally said.

Hunter had nodded, lying back down beside her. "I get it," he answered.

They stayed that way for a while until he finally sat up and began to rise. He told her he was going to go shower and was on his way out when she called out to him.

"Hunter?" she was still on her back, staring at the ceiling.

He turned back to her. "Yeah?"

"Were you playing with a girl's ball when I came in because you knew I would come out here?"

He had nodded a little, giving her a half smile she couldn't fully see. "You were always pretty intuitive," he answered.

Allen watched them run through their plays. They had started with simple ones: motion, isolation, five out. But he had thrown in a few others today as well, letting the girls pick out their names. So now they had Reba and Usher as well. They like to stick with a theme each year: this year was musicians, apparently. It was going to be a light practice, nothing too challenging. He wanted them to save their legs for the opening tournament in Broadview-Lavina.

Kris was talking to them about the teams they would play that weekend. First up was Reed Point-Rapelje Renegades, who had made a run for the state championship last year before ultimately coming in third thanks to an upset their first game. They would be returning all of their starters from the previous year and were going to be tough again this season. On Saturday, they would take on the Broadview-Lavina Lady Pirates. They would have a more even match-up as they were a younger, less experienced team, but still nothing to scoff at.

Grace went in for a layup, easily driving past one of the eighth graders, Jill. At practice, everything seemed to be going according to plan. They could run the plays and score baskets with ease. Allen knew this was not going to be the case this weekend, when they matched up against one of the top teams in the state.

Kennedy sat on the bench in the locker room, feeling totally defeated. The first game on Friday had been horrible: the game today had been just as bad if not worse.

The Renegades had won the tip off and basically every moment of the game from that point on the night before. They ran Grace ragged, putting her into a box one defense and forcing her to the sidelines to double team and trap her. Kennedy couldn't get physical enough with their post player on defense, and when they finally started pulling Julia, the exchange student, back to front her while Kennedy tried to get defend her from behind. It worked for a few minutes, but soon they just started shooting threes. And more threes. And then some more. Kennedy didn't know what their shooting percentage was, but it had to have been a ridiculous number. They had ended up losing 70-26.

The team had been disappointed with its performance, but the girls also knew it was going to be a tough game. They had watched the Broadview-Lavina games earlier that afternoon, and the match-up seemed to be even, so they had spent the rest of the night preparing to face the other Pirates in Broadview the next day.

But, everything fell apart the next game. Kennedy had actually won the tipoff, and their first few times up and down the court were successful. The post player Kennedy was defending wasn't quite as physical as the Reed Point-Rapelje girl had been, so Kennedy took advantage of the situation and bodied up to her each chance she got. The junior was clearly getting frustrated, and their coach pulled her out near the end of the first quarter. Coach Davidson moved them into a 2-3 zone to give them a breather. That's when things began to go downhill.

Their fouls ticked up quickly in the second quarter as their point guard began blowing past them, and Kennedy and Ellie, who was at the bottom of the key alongside her, began fouling instead of trying to stop her. The lead the Hysham Pirates had quickly dwindled until halftime, where they only led by five.

Davidson had expressed his frustrations in the locker room, telling them they were moving back into a one-on-one. While there were technically eleven girls out, their bench didn't really have any depth to it, with a freshman, the three eight graders, and one of exchange students who hadn't played much before behind their sixth men of Hannah and Jo.

Things just kept spiraling after halftime.

First, Grace had the ball stolen from her. She had busted down the court, her speed allowing her to overtake her opponent. She had firmly planted herself under the basket, and her opponent plowed her over. However, the referee called a foul on her for a block. Grace had gotten up absolutely fuming and tried to argue with the ref, and Kennedy quickly pulled her back. Another foul on the Hysham Pirates.

The rest of the game, the fouls continued to grow and grow for their team, and their frustrations with the game and with each other grew. Grace began to go into shut-down mode, where she was arguing with everyone and everything. No one could do anything right, so she was going to be the one to take the ball down the court and try and score every time. At one point, Kennedy was wide open under the basket, jumping up and down and clapping her hands for the ball, but still, Grace tried to take it to the basket and turned it over in the process. Kennedy found herself throwing her arms up in the air in exasperation at Grace as she jogged back down the court to take the ball out. Halfway through the fourth quarter, Grace fouled out, and Julia took over the ball handling. She was more open to passing, but it seemed like too little too late. Kennedy took the ball to the hoop and was fouled several times in the process, taking her to the free throw line, where she shot well. However, the team still lost by eleven points.

Grace had been sitting down dejectedly on the folding seats off the court after the final buzzer sounded, her head covered with a towel. She didn't say anything in the huddle and had gone over to her father in tears after the game. Kennedy was frustrated as well, but she kept her emotions more in check. She went and thanked the fans who were in the crowd before heading back into the locker room, where now she sat and waited.

The girls had trickled in slowly, peeling off their shoes and braces and tapings. Grace came in right before Allen did, looking even more upset now.

Coach Davidson had nodded a bit, looking around the room, making eye contact with each player at least for a moment. He stared at Grace until she finally flipped her head up and made stoic eye contact with him.

"We should have won that," he said. He shook head and slid his hands into his pocket. "We should have won that," he said again, matter-of-factly. "Why didn't we win that?" he asked.

No one answered him. He was right: there was no reason they shouldn't have won that game. It was an even match up. Talent-wise, they may have even had more skills than their opponents.

"Think about it," he said, turning and walking out of the locker room. Allen Davidson had never been much of a yeller: his disappointment and limited words stung just as much, if not more, sometimes. He was clearly upset. Not upset enough to yell, but upset, nonetheless.

The girls hadn't spoken much as they showered and changed into sweatpants and hoodies. They watched the boys' game in silence, clapping along when something good happened but not providing much support other than that.

The bus ride home was silent as well, and Kennedy drifted off to sleep until they made it to Billings and stopped to eat.

Grace had gotten her food last, even after the boys, and found a small table that only fit two away from the team. Kennedy had stared at her in concern, but Allen had beaten her over to the table.

He had talked to her for a few minutes while she stared at her food. Finally, he stood and said something to her. She looked up at him and had nodded before turning back to her food, finally picking up her burger and nibbling at it.

Kennedy had finished her own food, so she stood and went to stand by Grace's table. "Hey," she said.

Grace was absentmindedly playing with a fry. She looked up. "Hey," she answered.

"You okay?" Kennedy asked, tucking her hands into her sweats.

Grace had looked away; "Yeah, I'm fine," she said.

Kennedy didn't respond, bobbing her head a little. "Okay, then," she answered. She took a few steps back. "There's room over there with us," she nodded toward where the girls' team was sitting, "if you want to come sit with us."

"Thanks," the other senior nodded. She didn't move.

Kennedy had slowly backed up before turning and heading back to where her seat was. The boys' team was just finishing up their meals, and they would be leaving in a moment. She made eye contact with Allen, and he had nodded at her, but she had looked away. Kennedy didn't know what had happened while he was talking to Grace, but it was clear something had.

The girls didn't talk the rest of the drive home. Kennedy helped the younger girls unpack the bus of their water bottles and jerseys and snacks that their parents had provided for the weekend. It wasn't expected of her to help out, but she remembered what it was like when she was younger on the court—in fact, the last time she had been on a trip, she was still borderline expected to help out with packing and unpacking the uniforms and water bottles. She looked around for Grace when she was done, but her friend was nowhere to be found.

She went over to Kris's pick up. He had driven her and Jackson to town today—there was no point in them hauling three vehicles in to go to the same place. She threw her stuff in the backseat of his pickup, where Jackson's already was and climbed into the vehicle Kris had left running. He was talking to Allen and the boys' coaches: Martin and Lawrence.

She leaned forward to the front seat where Jack was. "Did you see where Grace went?" she asked.

"Yeah, Kris told her he could give her a ride, but she said she was fine walking," he said, scrolling through the music.

Kennedy leaned back and pulled her seatbelt across her body and sat in the dark until Kris finally came back and got into the driver's seat.

They drove home mostly in silence, listening to the playlist that her younger brother was putting on.

When they got to the house, Kris got out to pull his siblings' bags out. Jack grabbed his and went inside, but Kennedy hesitated. Kris had just opened his door to get back inside his vehicle when Kennedy stopped him with a "Hey."

He turned to look at her, half inside the truck. "Yeah?" he asked.

"What did Allen say to Grace?" she asked.

Kris hesitated a moment before turning to face her. "Did she say something?" he asked.

Kennedy shook her head. She hadn't said a word, which is what was concerning.

Kris sighed. "Grace is just having a tough time transitioning to being a leader on the court right now," he answered. "The two of them got into it after she fouled out. She had tried to argue when she was coming off the court, and he had had it after the last foul she gave up. There wasn't even a point to it: the girl wouldn't have been a threat that far out on the court." He shrugged. "That's why she was upset after the game. He went to get her to bring her into the locker room, and she started arguing again, and he told her he didn't want to hear it right now and to go sit down."

"What about when we were eating?" she asked.

He had shaken his head. "I don't know what he said to her there. But he wasn't happy with how she was acting the rest of the night."

Kennedy had nodded. It was weird, how distant Grace had been from the team the bus ride home, even after a loss like that.

Kris smiled at her. "How did you think the games went this weekend?" he asked.

Kennedy had paused for a moment, thinking about what she wanted to say. "I think they could have gone better," she said slowly. "But, it's also the opening weekend. We have a lot of season left."

Kris had nodded here. "That's true," he said. They had both stood there for a moment until Kennedy pulled her bag up and thanked her brother for driving them. She was just heading up the porch stairs when he asked, "How did it go for you?"

She had frozen on the steps. She knew what he was asking. "It went well," she said.

Her hands had been sweating uncontrollably and she wiped them hurriedly before she slid her fingers into Ellie's and Grace's prior to the game. It was a tradition, to grab hands and have a moment in silence and focus like this before the game.

Kennedy thought her heart was going to beat out of her chest as she huddled in silence with the ten other girls. Eventually, Grace began talking.

"Let us play this game with strength and protect us from injuries. Keep us safe and help us succeed on the court." The girls squeezed hands around the circle as she spoke. Silence settled across them again. Finally, she broke it with a "Family on three." The all let go of the hands around them and brought them into a huddle. "One, two, three—"

"Family!" they shouted back, heading out to the court.

Kennedy lingered in the locker room for a moment, taking a few breaths. She only had a second, while someone ran to get balls to warm up with.

She looked up at the ceiling and closed her eyes. "Help me get through this," she whispered before she jogged out onto the court as well.

Her anxiety grew and grew throughout her body during their warm-ups. It spread through her body, coating every inch of her. By the time the players were announced, she felt numb to the world around her. But she blindly stumbled over to the seats to be introduced. She had the highest number of the starters with thirty-three; it had been the only number left when she finally got to pick a jersey out in the fifth grade, and she had just kept it through the years—she wasn't a fan of change, and she liked the tie in it had with her home being the country seat of County Thirty-Three. She would be called last. She felt each of her teammates leave her side as their names, grades, and numbers were called out. Soon it was just her on the bench.

Kris had reached out to her and squeezed her shoulder hard as Rachel had had her name announced. She had reached up and squeezed his hand, suddenly feeling sick. She wasn't sure if she could move.

But then her name crackled over the loud speaker, the way she thought it would two years ago. And suddenly her feet were moving her forward, out of the girls that lined both sides and over to the opposite bench, where she shook the Renegades' coach's hand. He had squeezed it hard, and she had made eye contact with him. Like her coach, he had been on the sideline for a while and she recognized him instantly even two years later. "Good luck," he said. "And welcome back." She had given him a slight smile before pulling back and giving each of the three refs a first bump and jogging out to meet her team.

As they began swaying, she felt herself becoming more and more grounded again as her body found a rhythm in the motion and her mind focused on the yelling they were doing in their huddle in the center of the court. As they rose and cheered "Pirates" and the starters found their spots, she continued to move as if she wasn't the one in control, but in a different way: it was like she had always done this. As the other girls shook their hands of the opponents around the court, Kennedy reached her hand out to the girl she would be guarding. She gave her an enthusiastic shake, and the ref stepped up beside them.

"Ready, ladies?" he asked. Kennedy turned and looked at him and nodded; out of her peripherals she could she her opponent do the same. He crouched down and tossed the ball into the air and she felt her nerves lift away as the ball slid off his fingertips.

22

They were back in the gym early Monday morning for lifting. Kennedy felt some lingering frustrations within her at her friend. Grace was acting like nothing had happened over the weekend and brushed her off as she spotted Kennedy in power lifts. "It was nothing," she said, quickly changing the subject to a test they were having in Ms. O'Brien's class that day.

Kennedy was annoyed and took up her own code of silence the rest of the morning, but that wasn't very different than how she normally acted so no one questioned it. She would have liked to have remained quiet the rest of the day but found herself being pulled out of her shell.

Her teachers were all enthused that she was back on the court, and they asked her each class period how the weekend had gone. A couple pulled her aside and told her how proud they were of her in quiet moments before or after class, whispering how they knew how hard it had been for her. Even though they hadn't won, they seemed to know she had conquered a very large mountain.

As they talked to her, Grace seemed to become more and more agitated again, and Kennedy's annoyance levels shot up. By the time they made it to government, Grace was refusing to even look at Kennedy. Coach Davidson noticed the tension and quickly told them to ignore the lesson plans he had meticulously written on the board earlier that morning and that they were going to work individually on some other projects instead.

As the bell ring and the two packed up their things, Kennedy noticed how he was looking hard at Grace. Her friend rushed out of the room before he said anything to her. Kennedy moved more slowly: Mrs. Jean had a sub, and she doubted that they would notice if she came in late.

"Coach?" she asked, standing by his door. Allen had looked up at her and just shook his head slightly. "Not now," he answered.

Band class had been turned into a study hall since their director was gone for the day. Kennedy got permission from the sub to go to Ms. O'Brien's room to work. When she asked Grace, her friend had shaken her head and gone to sit at the piano. Kennedy felt her temper flare some and quickly left the room.

She popped into Ms. O'Brien's room. All of the team was currently in band, so there were just the two juniors who didn't play basketball in the room. Ms. O'Brien had looked up as she came into the room, and Kennedy had held up her the slip from the substitute teacher. "We were having study hall today," she explained.

Ms. O'Brien nodded her head and turned back to her grading. Kennedy sat down at the computer, sliding her backpack to the floor. She logged in and was about to open her web browser to go to the yearbook editing website, but then stopped and reached back down to her bag.

She hadn't read much of her sister's self-penned life story since before the season had started. She felt like she had barely had time to sit down and catch her breath, let alone read anything since she had walked into the gym. She pulled the flash drive out from the small zippered pocket at the front of her bag and plugged it into the computer.

She sorted through the files again, opening up the life story her sister had begun. It was a little surreal, reading this, when she would be starting her own writing of her story in just a few months. The next chapter labeled was simply titled "Before I Was, There Was..."

Kennedy skimmed through the section. Most of the information was things she already knew. Some history about the ranch, how her maternal grandparents had ended up moving to Hysham, and how her parents had met in late junior high and fallen in love. She quickly exited the document and opened up the fourth part, titled "The Early Years."

My first memory is my older brother Kris playing hide-and-seek with me and Hunter in the yard. Kris had picked me up and tucked me into the lilac bushes that ran around the yard, separating it from the rugged terrain around the ranch. I was giggling and he kept telling me to be quiet, but I didn't listen and Hunter found me right away. He told me I wasn't very good at the game and that I couldn't play anymore; it frustrated me. I think that's where my competitive nature began. I wanted to keep up with the boys, to be the best. Even today, all these days later, I'm the best at hide-and-seek, I swear. I can sit still for hours and people will walk by me over and over, having no idea that I am there. It all started in that front yard when I was three or four.

Kennedy smiled. She had forgotten how much Jess liked playing hide-and-seek. And she was right—she was really good at it. She once spent several hours folded up inside the back of the tool storage in a ranch pickup and was only ousted when her father had tried to drive off with her still in the back.

It's funny how those moments come together to shape you into who you are today. I remember starting kindergarten and how the bigger kids played sports. My brothers were both playing football on the playground when we were out together. I wanted to play too. But they told me I was too small and sent me away. The other girls were playing house and pretending to be mothers with the dolls they brought from home, but that didn't fit me either. So instead, I went to the basketball hoops. I couldn't make it the first few months. They were taller than the one my dad had set up for us in the garage when we were learning to play. The ball wouldn't even come close to the net. But slowly, my stubbornness paid off and I would get closer and closer to the hoop. I remember that now, when I am working at something and trying to accomplish a goal. What it felt like to stand on the concrete with no one around me, throwing a ball into the air and praying that it would go in. Working to make it go through the hoop, day in and day out, until finally it did.

Jess's determination was also something Kennedy remembered quite well. It was what had driven her to relearn how to drive to the paint after she had the wind knocked out of her during her freshman year of basketball. The fear of failure could not keep her down. And she really was stubborn has hell, too.

"Watcha reading?" Grace slid her chair over next to Kennedy, and Kennedy quickly clicked out of the page, pulling the flash drive out as she did so. Kennedy looked at her friend, feeling frustration bubble up again.

"Nothing," she answered. Grace turned away slightly and muttered "Right" under her breath.

Kennedy bit the inside of her lip hard. It was a habit she had had since she was little, chewing on her lip when she didn't know what to say. She was also a little worried about pulling the drive straight from the computer, but she wasn't going to plug it back in now.

"What are you doing here?" she asked as she dropped the drive into her backpack.

Grace shrugged and pulled her phone out. "It was boring in the music room," she answered. "Figured I would see what you were doing on the yearbook, but you're not even working on that."

Kennedy pulled a webpage up and logged onto the design platform they used for their annual. She began clicking through photos from the fall, trying to sort them into folders that would make it easier to place them later.

Grace sat next to her in a stony silence, not speaking or helping at all.

Grace didn't speak to Kennedy while the two dressed out for their practice that day. She held back as they changed in silence, their team-mates around them chattering away, in hopes that Kennedy would leave before she did.

Her plan worked, and her friend and co-captain left the room before Grace did to head to the library to watch film. Grace hung back, taking her time filling up her water bottle with ice from the ice machine and at the water fountain. She wasn't just avoiding her friend: she was avoiding the entire team and especially her coach.

She had never had a coach rip into her the way that Allen Davidson had let her have it on Saturday. She knew that she had thrown away her final foul and that she hadn't played her best game. But she didn't expect him to come down so hard on her on the bench.

Everyone had been making errors during that game. It wasn't just her. And it wasn't fair that he was putting so much pressure on her. And for the next two hours, she was going to get to relive every little mistake that she had made through a recording of the game.

It wasn't just the game that was bugging her though.

She was happy that Kenna had decided to go out for the team—she had been the one begging her to go out all last year and all of volleyball season, it was true. But now that Kennedy was out on the court with her, though, it was weird.

Grace had spent the last season proving herself on the court, earning the role she had been given as a starter and as a leader. Kennedy had come back and had all this praise thrust upon her from the start. Where was that when Grace was trying last year? And this year, why was Allen being so hard on her but letting Kenna get away with errors and travels? It didn't seem fair, and it felt like they were being held to such different standards.

Normally, Kennedy would fall into Grace's shadow; Grace was louder and more outgoing, so it was easy to focus on her in the spotlight. But now, it felt like the roles had shifted, at least for the weekend, and Grace wasn't sure how to handle it.

She slowly made her way out of the ice room and through the gym where the boys were warming up for their own practice. A couple of them said "hello" to her as she slowly walked through the gym, dragging her feet. She stopped a few times and collected balls that had bounced off the rim and out of bounds, passing them back to the team.

Finally, though, she was at the doors to the lobby and couldn't put it off anymore.

The walk down the hallway seemed especially daunting today. She remembered how scary it was when she was in elementary school, to walk down past the classrooms filled with high school students and how old they seemed compared to her. There were a lot more people back then too—even their class had had twenty students when they started kindergarten. They had since dwindled down to the three of them: Kenna, Paul, and herself. It was funny because walking down the hallway, she wasn't scared anymore. But now the world beyond the school was what scared her. She didn't know what was coming in the next few months of her life, with graduation coming faster and faster each day, let alone where she would be in just a few years. She didn't even know how this practice was going to go.

She slinked into the library just as 4:00 p.m. hit and quickly found a seat in one of the chairs that someone had pulled over in front of the TV in the room. She was toward the edge of the group, with underclassmen next to her. Ellie looked away from the conversation she was having with one of the freshmen and smiled at her, but Grace looked away.

Coach Davidson came into the room talking quietly to Kris and put the DVD from the first game into the TV. Grace leaned back into her chair, not knowing what to do or where to look.

Davidson cleared his throat and she looked up. Kris was standing next to him holding a stack of papers.

"We will plan on doing film each Monday either before or after practice for the rest of the season," he said. "Coach Helland had the idea to have you guys keep track of your own thoughts about the games throughout the season, so we can see where we start and how we can improve as the year goes on." He nodded at Kris, who began to hand out the papers. "You don't need to share these with anyone else, these are going to be between you, me, and Coach," he continued. "I just want you all to keep track of your own thoughts and ideas, and maybe we will share some things that you are proud of at the end of the season with the group."

Ellie handed a paper to Grace and Kris began passing out pens. Grace glanced over the typed sheet as Kris moved among the rows, handing out pens. It was pretty straightforward: five things that she thought others did well; three things she thought she did well; two things the team could work on; and two things she herself could work on. At the bottom of the page, there was a space for additional comments.

A pen suddenly came into her view and she looked up at Kris, who was holding it out to her. She slowly reached up and took it, maintaining eye contact with him for a moment before looking back down. She would need to remember something to write on the next week for this.

Davidson began the tape, and the team fell quiet.

Allen paused the film clips every few minutes to rewind and point out things that the girls were doing well and things they needed to change. He tried to emphasize the good and, while he would point out the bad, not overwhelm them with mistakes that had been made during the game. Tearing down his teams would do nothing to help them in the long run.

The first game was okay. There were a lot of promising moments on the film, even with what the score showed, and he tried to stress to the girls that it was just the first week and some of these things would come with time. He tried to point out at least one good thing that each member of the team that made it on the court had done for each thing that he thought could use more work.

This became increasingly challenging he switched the DVD and the Broadview-Lavina game came on.

The girls seemed aware that he was pulling at straws, especially as the fourth quarter came onto the screen and all hell seemed to break loose. He finally fell into a resigned silence, and the girls watched the game quickly get away from them. He looked over at Grace as her fifth foul flashed up on the board, and she looked at the floor in shame, not even watching what happened. Kennedy was sitting a row back and a few sets over, and it looked as though she was going to reach out and over to her friend, but she did not. Everyone averted their eyes from Grace and the screen.

The game finished, and Grace could feel her face burning. Allen had called her reactions embarrassing when he talked to her when she was eating—she could see now that he was right. That wasn't the way a leader would act, but her emotions had just gotten away from her that night. As soon as he dismissed the girls to go start warming up, she had run out of the room and gone to the bathroom at the end of the hall. She could hear the other girls talking as they headed to the gym behind her, but she just needed a minute.

She looked down at the sheet Kris had given her at the beginning of film, now a crumpled, sweaty mess. She had been writing along during the two games they had watched. It was easy to point out the things that the team needed to improve upon. They weren't cohesive on the court. Their passes had been soft and sloppy. They had thrown away too many fouls. She could see some good though. They had run a few nice plays during the beginning of the game against Broadview-Lavina, at least. It was looking at herself and her own mistakes that she was struggling with on the sheet.

She knew Coach Davidson was right; it wasn't him she had frustrations with. It was herself and her actions and how now she had gotten to a point in her mind that they just kept swirling around and around her brain. She couldn't escape them.

She didn't know why she was crying in the bathroom. The tears were just coming out now and she couldn't stop them. They were hot and she was blinking fast, trying to get them to stop. She grabbed the sink and leaned over it, the hot liquid spilling from her eyes. She was trying to breathe but was struggling to take in long breaths of air.

Kennedy stood in the doorway of the bathroom, looking at the shaking body of her friend. Just a few weeks ago, she had been in such a similar position. She didn't know how she would have reacted if Grace had come and found her in the bathroom then. Probably not well.

But now, something pulled her through the frame. It didn't matter if they were fighting and things were tense. She would be there for her friend, even when times weren't going well. She came up behind her and tapped her on her shoulder. Grace turned and looked up at her longtime friend, and her face crumbled as she fell into her.

Allen watched the two seniors come into the gym as the last few seconds on the clock for warmups ticked down. He had let Kennedy go find Grace. Normally, this wasn't something he would do, but he felt like this was a moment bigger than basketball between the two.

The rest of the girls put up their balls as the two girls walked to Allen and Kris. Grace held out a shaky hand with her paper crumbled in her palm, and Kris gingerly took it from her. Allen could see it wasn't fully filled out, and Kennedy made eye contact with him with a tight-lipped, slight smile.

Allen nodded at the court. "Get to layups," he said, and the two girls nodded and hustled back onto the court.

He could tell Grace was still shaken as they went through practice. He knew she was under quite a bit of stress at the moment, with trying to figure out what she was going to do once she graduated in the spring, and that she had taken on a drastically different role as a leader in the past few months. But still, something just seemed off about her the last few days.

He wondered if he should grab her and ask her what was up. She seemed to be trying to figure it out as well, at the end of practice, as the girls shuffled to the locker room, but she hung back a bit. Kennedy waited as well, clearly unsure as to how she should proceed as Allen began pushing the balls toward the boy's locker room.

Grace looked as though she was going to cry again, and he simply shook his head at her. "We'll try again tomorrow," he said. His voice was heavy.

Grace blinked a little, her face pinching, and nodded. She went back to Kennedy, who reached out and pulled her in for a little hug as the two began walking back to change and go home.

23

Kennedy perched in the last seat of the bus, slightly nervous. She had curled her hair for their games this time and all the girls had decided to wear all dresses to match with each other. They were on their way to Ekalaka for their first conference game of the season.

The boys had already yelled at them twice to turn off their "crappy" music, so Kennedy had finally turned off the Bluetooth speaker and put in her headphones. The sounds of heavy rock blasted into her ears, reminding her of riding along the backroads with Hunter and Jess as they helped their dad irrigate in the summer in an old ranch pickup, a chord ran through the tape player so they could listen to their own music and not what the radio chose.

They were going to stay the night in Baker since they played in Plevna the next morning. It made no sense to drive all the way back just to go to basically the same place a few hours later. So, her duffle was extra full and wedged down onto the floor with her feet on top of it.

Rachel was sitting in front of her, and the sophomore turned around and smiled. Kennedy nodded back at her. She had been spending a lot of time trying to talk to Kenna, and she was pretty sure it was because of her younger brother, Jackson. She had asked about coming out to the ranch a few times over the last few weeks to shoot around on Sundays, though Kennedy had quickly turned her down, running a gambit of excuses. Jackson didn't seem to be interested, and Kennedy didn't want to get involved. She had watched the mess of Jess being very involved in Hunter's relationships growing up and didn't want to go through that as well.

Kennedy leaned back in her seat and against the window, closing her eyes. The song had clicked to a country song, now, and she sighed. This was Adam's genre of choice.

She wasn't sure why she missed him so much. They hadn't spoken in weeks now, but when you go from knowing everything about someone to them being a stranger, it was hard to let go of the memories. He kept coming up in her dreams, and she would wake up frustrated, unable to go back to bed for fear he would return.

She had been going through the motions of the week in a daze because of it. Now, she was exhausted and knew that it was going to affect the game that night. The drive to Ekalaka was a long one, so she tried to get comfortable and let her mind wander at the least, if she couldn't sleep.

Grace shook her awake as they pulled into town. She had finally drifted off somewhere near Miles City, and exhaustion had overtaken her, meaning no dreams to keep her awake on the bus. She sat up and stretched, thankful to have gotten at least some sleep on the long drive.

The boys filtered off the bus as it parked in front of the school's doors. The girls followed and the eighth-graders and freshman began pulling the bins of jersey and water bottles out the back door as the upperclassmen filed inside and behind the bleachers to their locker room.

The boys shoved their things inside and then quickly left so the girls could start getting ready for their game. Jackson told his older sister "Good luck" as he finally left, always a straggler, and Kennedy smiled and pushed the door closed.

The girls had their pregame tradition down to a science. It started with Kennedy or Grace plugging in their speaker and putting on some of the newest songs, as well as some older ones that they all knew the lyrics to. The girls would dance and laugh, letting off some steam before the ones who needed their ankles taped would venture out to find Allen or Kris to have that done on them. After everyone was dressed, one of the freshmen or eighth graders would go once again venture out to find their coaches and bring them back in, and the girls would put their socks and shoes on and talk with their coaches about the game ahead.

Allen would neatly write their starting players names and numbers on the board and point out where they would be on the court. He would talk about the players they knew were going to be threats from previous years and the buzz he got through the eastern Montana coaching community.

Ekalaka was going to be a younger team, similar to the Pirates. The Bulldogs competed in six-man football as well and had smaller class sizes, though they were larger than Hysham and had significantly more girls. While they could compete a JV squad for the girls, the boys only had eight out for the season. It should be a competitive evening for both sides.

Once Allen stopped talking, he would leave the girls for a few minutes to get their things together. Their warmups were on and they came together, putting their right feet into the circle their bodies formed. Clasping hands, they would whisper the prayer they all knew by heart and then Grace would ask that they all remained safe and healthy during the game as the girls squeezed each other's hands and intertwined fingers. They would break and go out to the court, where the pep band was starting to warm up under the large mural painted on the home side of the bleachers. Twenty minutes were on the clock, but it hadn't started yet. The girls formed a huddle under the basket, waiting for the timer to flick the switch that would begin the countdown on their warmups.

The Ekalaka girls came out and formed their own huddle at the end of the court. The scorekeeper flicked the switch, and the timer began as the Bulldogs began their chant and swaying. As they broke, the Pirates began their own and soon they were going through their warmups.

Coach Davidson was shaking the hand of the refs as Kennedy came back and touched half court from her first layup. The Bulldogs' coach was there as well, and Kennedy watched him wave for his captains to come over. She got back into line, and Grace trotted by her for the captain's meeting. She had been the one to do it last weekend, so when she heard a sharp "Kennedy!" come from her coach, she had turned around confused as he beckoned her over. She jogged over, and he nodded at the small huddle in front of the scorer's table. "Captains' meeting," he said. She looked at him curiously but went over, shaking the hands of the two girls and the coaches from the other team with Grace, who seemed a bit saddened but unsurprised.

The refs went over their guidelines, reminding the girls to make sure they didn't have bobby pins in their hair and that they had all their jewelry out. They broke by shaking each other's hands again and saying "good luck" before rejoining the line for warmups as the trumpets from the pep band blared overwhelmingly from the bleachers.

As the last few minutes ticked down, the younger girls went to put the balls they had gotten out for warmups back into the metal basket. As the older girls began to line up on the baseline, the home team's school song was playing, led by cheers from the parents in the crowd as there were no cheerleaders for either team. The girls lined up for the national anthem, putting their right hands across their bodies and linking it with the teammate behind them on their shoulder before sliding their left hand up onto the shoulder of the player in front of them as the band played for them and then returned to their bench for the starting lineup.

Getting onto the court this time was even easier on Kenna as her teammates ran out to the center of the court. She was eager, still slightly anxious but ready to go. As Grace left her side (Ekalaka announced by grade-level, starting with the youngest starter and moving up numerically), she looked up at the ceiling and closed her eyes again. Kris squeezed her shoulder as her name was called out and the claps echoed around the gym as she jogged out, shaking hands with the opposing assistant coach and first bumping the refs before falling in with her team.

The group huddled around Allen after they cheered out "Pirates" in the center circle, and he turned his clipboard around so they could read it. Kennedy found her name and saw she had been paired up to guard one of the captains, a senior, on the other team. Allen threw out a few more commentaries about things to watch and reminded them they were starting in man-to-man and picking them up at three-quarters of the court in a partial press. He stood up from where he had been crouching in front of the starters, and Kris rejoined the group from shaking the Ekalaka girls' hands in place of the head coach. "Family on three," Allen said, holding up his arm.

The girls put their arms up as well and chanted "One, two, three: Family!" and the starters made their way onto the court to shake their opponents' hands.

They sat in the locker room, dejected, as Allen rocked back and forth on his heels and sighed. There had been so many good things that happened during that game, but they just couldn't finish it off.

He shook his head, not sure where to begin. They had been down by three in the last few moments of the game. Kennedy had connected a long court shot down to Ellie, who had hit the three with ease as they had left the younger girl wide open. Tied game, 47-47.

Kyle Johnstone, the Ekalaka coach, had called a time out quickly and rehuddled his girls, and Allen had done the same.

"Don't foul unless it's the freshmen," he had repeated again and again. The freshmen girls on the court had struggled the entire game to sink anything if they got fouled and went to the line. "Don't let the O'Connell girl drive, but don't foul her. Foul the freshmen. Trap at the corners."

The starters for his team were all still on the court. There was substantially less foul trouble this game, and he had only thrown fresh legs in occasionally to give the girls a breather. The Bulldogs had struggled a bit more to keep their starting five on the floor, and one of the captains had fouled out early in the fourth quarter, but they had a deeper bench they could pull from.

They broke and went back to the court, now in a full-court press. Allen was nervous—they hadn't practiced the full court press often, so he was hoping they would be able to keep the movements up in the 1-2-1-1 press.

He watched Grace get in front of the girl taking the ball out and Ellie and Rachel line up. Julia, the exchange student, stood on the ten-foot line at the other end of the court and put her hands on her knees, waiting to trap anyone she could or drop back to help Kennedy cover.

The ball had been passed to the Bulldogs from the ref, and Grace dug in, trying to intimidate the younger girl sending it in. The O'Connell girl danced in and out of the area trying to break free but ultimately the girl got called for a five-second violation: Pirates' ball.

Allen had clapped his hands enthusiastically, and Kris had jumped up from the bench holding his hand into a four, signaling them to run the out-of-bounds play Swift. The girls had gotten into position, with Kennedy moving up the key to set a screen for Grace just to get the ball onto the court. She planted her feet and crossed her arms, set up to block the girl. But as Grace moved and the ball was thrown in by Rachel, the Bulldog player pushed through and Kennedy fell over, the girl toppling on top of her.

The whistle blew and Kennedy rolled away from the girl as Ellie came to help her up. Grace's indignant "What?" echoed across the court as the Ekalaka crowd roared. Kennedy looked around as Ellie pulled her up, confused. Grace was holding the ball in one hand, looking toward the scorer's table with bug eyes. Kennedy turned and faced the table as well, where Allen was getting in the ref's face, yelling, as Kris tried to pull him back to the bench. Allen didn't get upset like this often, but it was clear he didn't agree with something that had been called. Kennedy blinked and looked at Ellie, who also looked a bit shocked.

"She plowed her over!" Grace snapped from behind her. "She didn't push her down."

Kennedy finally looked up and saw her number flash across the board, with a "3" behind it signaling it was her third foul. She looked over to the bench in disbelief, where Allen was still in the ref's face.

The ref brought his hands up and blew his whistle, making a "T" with his hands. Kris finally pulled Allen back.

"Go to your benches, girls" one of the other refs said, and both teams quickly separated. Allen stood near the end of the bench, positively fuming and shaking his head as the girls on the court huddled around him. "That was wrong," he kept muttering as they grabbed drinks of water. "Kenna," he said. She looked over at him. "You did nothing wrong there. Absolutely nothing." He shook his head and clapped his hands. "Okay," he said, "they are going to shoot and then they are going to get the ball again. Twenty seconds is a lot of time. Once they take it out, let the freshman get it and then foul her. They are going to have a bonus. We don't have any more time outs so listen closely. She will shoot. Get the rebound and get it down the court," he said, as the buzzer went off, telling them to get back on the court.

"Just drive," he said. "Drive hard, whoever gets the ball. Let them foul you."

He put his hand up again and the starters did too. "Pirates on three," he said. They counted down. "Pirates!"

He had watched the junior, O'Connell, miss her first free throw and sink the second. Grace had come out to foul the freshman, just as he had told her to, when they threw the ball in, only to have her quickly pass the ball along to their post as Kennedy was set up with a hard screen she couldn't get by and the refs call nothing. The girl easily moved the hoop and the ball slid through the basket. Down by three again, Kennedy had taken the ball out and gotten it in to Grace as the final few moments ticked down. Grace had dribbled hard and launched the ball from just beyond half court as the buzzer went off. Final score: 50-47, Bulldogs.

Back in the locker room, Allen didn't know what to say. That game could have—should have—ended differently. He finally sighed again and began to speak what was on his mind.

"I'm sorry about the technical foul," he said. The girls were looking up at him. "That wasn't fair to you, at all. I threw away one of those points. But the call was wrong, and I will make that very clear to anyone who asks me."

He looked over his team, still shaking his head. "I don't have much else to say. That was a strong showing, and I'm proud of you all." He paused for a few seconds. Well," he finally said, "if the sun doesn't come up tomorrow, we're all screwed anyhow."

Kennedy snorted. She had missed his one liners when she wasn't playing last year.

"Get something to eat," he added, putting his hand up. The girls rose from their various locations on the floor and benches in the room and joined him. "Family on three," he said. "One, two, three... family."

The girls sat together after they showered and changed and watched the boys play. The game was easily in the Pirates' hands from the first shot on, and the boys defeated the Bulldogs soundly. After the game, the parents from Ekalaka had cooked for the team, and the group went to eat the lasagna the moms had prepared.

Kennedy went and found her parents to say goodbye before joining the team in the school's cafeteria. Her mom was still fired up over the foul from the game before and was complaining to Kris about it when she walked up. Her father pulled her in for a side hug and told her "Good game" before her mother laid in about how ridiculous it was that they had lost.

Kris looked annoyed by the conversation, and Kennedy quickly tried to change the subject, asking them when they would be coming up the next morning to meet them in Plevna.

Her mother began talking about how they were going to head home and that they would be stopping in Miles City the next day to do some grocery shopping and that Kennedy and Jackson would need to text her if they wanted anything specific. Jackson appeared just as she was finishing her commentary, and her mother pulled him in for a big hug, telling him what a good game he had.

Kennedy made eye contact with her oldest brother, and he nodded back toward the cafeteria. She nodded and hugged her father and said a quick "Bye, Mom," before walking with Kris back out to their team.

The two grabbed plates of the lasagna and salad and went to sit down. Kennedy found a seat next to Grace, and Kris went and sat with Allen, who was eating with the coaches from Ekalaka. Grace was staring at her phone and quickly flipped it over as she made eye contact with Kennedy.

"How are your parents?" she asked.

Kennedy shrugged back and began twirling food onto her fork. Her appetite had come back more and more over the last few weeks, and she found herself starving now that the game was done and her jitters had calmed down some.

"I can't believe we lost that," Grace continued on with a sigh. "We were RIGHT THERE."

Kennedy looked up at her friend. Grace, the one who always had an appetite, was picking at her food. Kennedy lowered her fork. "It's still early in the season," she answered.

Grace shook her head. "That shouldn't matter, these games are really important and can influence our ranking down the road," she answered.

That was something the two girls always disagreed on, no matter the sport. Kennedy took the view that this was all a preseason and that districts was the real season, where everyone was even. This was all just preparation for the end. Yes, records did matter, but it was a whole new time at districts. Anything could happen. Grace, meanwhile, took a completely different view on the topic. To her, the traditional season was the end-all, be-all and what was going to help them be a team that made it to divisionals for the first time in over twenty years.

Kennedy sighed. She didn't want to fight about it tonight. She was tired and wanted to make it to Baker and go to bed. "Whatever you say," she finally got out, stabbing the pasta back onto her fork.

Allen laid down on his bed with a sigh. While technically the coaches could have their own rooms, he and Kris had decided to share to save the school and program a bit of money. It wasn't like they were in the Bellagio in Baker—but he figured a little went a long way in their community. Kris was just getting into the shower—Allen could hear the water running through the paper-thin walls. They had been so close that night to defeating the Bulldogs, but it had slipped right through their fingers yet again.

It was hard not to think about what could have been different at times like these. Jessica Helland had been what held them together that last good run they had, two years ago. He had been coaching for over twenty years now, and they hadn't made it to divisionals in that time. Any other place, any bigger city, and he would have been canned years ago. But not in Hysham: every year the town had the suspended belief that this year would be different.

He did it all right. He brought the program from the ground up. He worked with the young students every chance he got: he had raised daughters that went through the program. Yet, while everyone else seemed to believe they would make it someday, he himself didn't really believe it anymore. It felt like the Fates were against him every time he almost made it. He dropped his feet over the edge of the bed sat up before leaning forward and propping his head in his hands. He knew it was a single game, early in the season: but right now was one of the days he wanted to throw in the towel.

Looming above him was the decision as to what he would do the next year, especially now that the co-op with Custer was imminent. Sure, he could come and see if two towns, rivals since even his wife had been in school, could be united. But his girls were getting older. His older girl, Courtney, was graduating college soon. It wouldn't surprise him if she found someone and got engaged—as long as she and Hunter stayed away from each other—and then came grandkids. Did he really want to miss the moments like he missed out on so many of his own kids' firsts as a young coach?

His phone started buzzing, and he looked over. His younger daughter's name flashed across the screen.

"Hey, honey," he said.

"Hey, Coach," Mac answered. She had called him that when they talked about sports since she was just a kid. "How was the game?"

Allen heaved a sigh out and stood up, sighing slightly. "Not our best," he answered.

"Well," she replied. "The sun will come up in the morning," she replied.

He chuckled. He would sometimes throw this comment out in the locker room after a particularly stinging loss. "And if it doesn't, we're all screwed anyhow."

Kris could hear that Allen was on the phone, so he stayed in the bathroom longer than he needed to. Finally, he heard him hang up with his daughter with a "Love you, bye" and Kris came out. Allen had set up the video camera they used to film the game and was just settling in as his assistant coach came into the room. Kris climbed onto his own bed as Allen started the film and the two watched intently in silence as the game unfolded before them.

He could feel Allen's frustrations rise as the game continued. "Dumb turnover," he muttered a few times. A couple of times his frustrations came out with the refs. "Travel!" he called out. Kris watched in silence.

It was well after 1:00 a.m. when the game concluded on the screen and the feed cut off. Allen had moved from sitting near the pillows, like Kris still did, to the bottom of the bed leaning forward more and more, almost like he could change the outcome of the game the closer he got to the screen.

The two men sat in silence for a moment, before Kris finally cleared his throat. "I think I'm going to go to bed," he said finally, the first words he had spoken since the rewatching had started. Allen waved over his shoulder at him and Kris slid under the covers, turning away from the head coach and his father's best friend. He laid awake for a while, waiting for the other man to get up or turn off the light, but nothing happened. Finally, in the silence, he drifted off, not even hearing Allen begin the game over again with the television set muted.

Kenna had been quiet the entire night, shut down since they made it back to the hotel. The two seniors had bunked up with Ellie and Rachel, the team's sophomores, and Grace and Kennedy were sharing a bed like they always did. Kennedy had gotten into bed as soon as they made it back to the hotel the night before and rolled away so she was facing the wall. Grace had looked at her and over at the sophomores, who looked concerned. "Is she okay?" mouthed Ellie.

Grace had waved them away, telling them to go get ice from the machine outside. As the younger two left the room, she tried to get her friend to talk, but Kennedy hadn't answered, just staring at the wall. Grace had finally given up, pulling her phone out and playing a game on it as the younger two emerged, giggling.

"They locked Tim out of his room in a towel," they told the senior between giggle fits. Grace had rolled her eyes. The upperclassmen guys could be jerks to the underclassmen. The girls were better, with no initiations, but they had their own moments. However, they knew that neither Kenna nor Grace would put up with anyone locking someone else out of their room in just a towel.

The three of them had stayed up and chatted for a while. The sophomores wanted to hear all about Grace's plans for the next year, after graduation. While she knew what she wanted to study, she didn't know much else, so she made off-hand comments about looking at a few schools. A couple of the coaches had reached out to her based on her initial contact points about sports too, so she had been emailing them back and forth. It sounded like the coach from the smaller private school in Billings would be coming to one of her games in the next few weeks, squeezing in another scouting around their own schedule. She was familiar with them both having gone to their camps growing up and talking with them at Big Sky State Games. A few of the other coaches from around the state had also followed up with her, but she was hoping to stay close to home. The coaches from the community colleges to the east had actually already given her offers but she wasn't loving either one of them and was hoping to find a more stable place where she wouldn't have to transfer after two years.

She asked the other two how things were going with school and FFA since they were in the chapter too. The chatted for a while on their projects as they finished getting ready for bed. Kenna still hadn't moved, but Grace could tell she was still awake. Finally, the other two stopped chattering and Grace flicked the lights off. The sophomores' breathing became even and soft. She could feel Kenna was awake still, but she didn't say anything. She kept facing away from her, but reached back and found her friends' arm under the blankets. She squeezed it gently before pulling it back and curling up on her own side of the bed.

Neither one of them spoke again.

Kennedy was better in the morning, playing music and singing along with the girls as they got ready for the day in their little motel room. She never knew when one of her moods would hit her, where she shut down, but something had managed to set her off the night before. One of the boy's moms had packed breakfast foods for them to eat, and the girls ate bagels and fruit as they curled their hair. Grace was even able to convince Kennedy to let her do her hair and makeup.

She got her sat on the bed and began painting her face. Kennedy rarely wore makeup—even less since Jess's death. Her sister had always been the one who showed her how to put these creams and gels and powders on her face. She hadn't attempted to learn to wear much of it since her sister had died.

"Okay," Grace said, holding the liquid eyeliner applier. "Close your eyes."

Kennedy pulled back slightly, squinting. "What are you going to do?" she asked.

Grace rolled her eyes. "Just close them, it's for a cat eye," she answered.

Kennedy hesitated slightly and then sighed, leaning forward. Grace continued calling out commands to her friend as she kept adding things to her face. Finally, she sat back on the other bed and looked at her friend, tilting her head.

"Okay," she said, clapping her hands together. "That's it. Go look."

Kennedy stood up and walked to the bathroom.

Very rarely did she look like her sister. While she was tall and favored her dad with his darker hair, Jessica had been short and blonde. Really, the only similarity they had had appearance wise was the smattering of freckles all the Helland children had and their deep green eye color.

However, now, with whatever magic Grace had worked, she could see Jess's eyes and little hints of her on her face. It actually took her back a little when she first looked into the mirror.

Grace had braided her hair after curling it into a style that she could play in. Loose waves framed her face and the thick braid fell over her shoulder, tied off at the end into a loop. She hadn't done the typical "senior girl chop" like most the girls did after senior photos, cutting off as much hair as they could as a nod to fresh beginnings. Kennedy turned a few times in the mirror, still fixated on her face and the little glimmers of her sister she kept finding. Grace came and poked her head in a few minutes later and knocked lightly on the door. Kennedy hadn't realized she was starting to tear up until she heard the knock and she quickly looked up and started blinking.

"Do you like it?" Grace asked softly. Kennedy looked at her friend in the mirror and pulled her lips into a thin line, nodding quickly. "Yeah, I do," she said.

Grace slid into the room and wrapped her arms around her friend. "Good, because you look beautiful," she said. "Go get dressed and we will take a picture and we will post it and make all the men jealous," she said.

Kennedy laughed, feeling her heart relax some and her tears ease back into her eyes. "Yeah, okay, sure," she said.

Kennedy looked at her phone, scrolling through the few photos that Grace and her had snapped in the bathroom mirror. She rarely posted on social media, and she didn't really know what to say. Grace was the one comfortable with coming up with witty captions.

Eventually, she picked one of the images and typed out "Dressed to the 9s" as the caption, tagging Grace in the photo.

Finally, they headed out to the bus to head to Plevna for the second games of the weekend. There wouldn't be JV again since Plevna struggled to suit both boys' and girls' teams—there were fewer than fifteen of them out between the two teams—so it would be an earlier night home for them than normal with later afternoon games instead of night ones.

Kennedy made it to her seat and sat down. The boys got the back of the bus for this portion of the trip, so she and Grace were across from each other near the middle of the bus. The coaches came out and got on just minutes before they were set to leave. Kris stood up to count the girls, starting with the ones closest to him. His eyes tracked up each seat, counting quietly. When he made it to the seniors, though, he froze and some of the color fell from his face. Kennedy locked eyes with him and once again felt a lump grow in her throat. She looked away quickly, but he kept staring at her and she felt his eyes on her until he finally slid down in his seat. She glanced toward the front of the bus to see him leaning with his back against the window now, rubbing his face. Grace was talking, but she couldn't really process what she was saying.

She looked away from her brother and kind of laughed. "Yeah, right," she said back, hoping that would be sufficient.

The girls easily outran the Cougars. Kennedy felt good and like she had her legs under her this game. They didn't put much pressure on her in the first quarter, focusing on Grace instead, and she felt more confident with her moves. Her friend would lob it to her and she would quickly convert it and score as the post. Their turnovers were lower, and they seemed to be more cohesive on the floor. All the bench got in and scored as well, which was amazing.

Coach didn't say much in the locker room after the game, just offering them a few praises before huddling them together and having them say one last "family." Kris, however, stayed back and tilted his head toward the door after making eye contact with Kennedy. She followed him out into the hallway in her sweaty socks and untucked jersey. He stopped just before they would go into view of the bleachers in the gym and turned and looked at her.

He opened his arms and she melted into them, ignoring the normal side-hug her family would give each other. The two of them were the same height, with him shorter and broader than her other two brothers. She buried her face into his shoulder before remembering her makeup and pulling back quickly. There was definitely some foundation on his grey polo.

She laughed softly. "Sorry," she said, wiping her eyes that were starting to get teary again. He squeezed her shoulder tightly. "It'll wash out," he answered.

"You played well," he said after a moment. She finally looked at him and smiled. Kris had always been the more encouraging between her older two brothers, but his compliments still meant a lot to her.

She nodded a few times: "I felt better," she finally answered.

"I know no one thinks you two look alike," he began, and she felt her face crumple. "No, no, no," he said, pulling her in for a side hug, "listen to me." His voice was shaky too. "I know a lot of people think you're different, but when you got on the bus today, I had to do a double take, and tonight, when you were on the court—you had a few drives like she would have had—I swear it was like she was back out there."

He pulled back from Kennedy and held her at arm's length until she finally looked up at him. "Thank you for coming out this season," he said simply.

She knew she couldn't speak without crying, so she nodded some more at him, and he gave her a smile before dropping his arms and walking out the door back to the court.

Most the team fell asleep on the way home that night, even though they were earlier games than they normally had. The girls groggily marched off the bus in Miles City at the gas station, ordering their meals and sitting down to eat together. Kennedy pulled out her phone as she sipped on her drink. She hadn't checked it since before the game.

About twenty people had liked the image she had posted online. She clicked on the list of names and began scrolling through to see who had liked it. Most of the double taps had come from the other girls on the team and few of the guys. A couple of her friends she knew from sports and FFA had liked it too. At the bottom, though, a name stood out to her. Adam had liked her photo.

She stared at the screen for a moment before turning her phone over and setting it down again. Her appetite was suddenly gone.

She remembered the first time they had kissed. Adam and Hunter were back at the ranch helping with irrigating the small amount of land her father did harvest each year. They had been back a few other times, to help with spring brandings throughout the county, but Kennedy and Adam talked more than she did with Hunter when the two were gone.

It was early in the morning, and the two of them had been assigned to go out and check the irrigation water. Or rather, she had, and he had volunteered to come along and help.

The radio in the old work truck was playing softly. Adam had told her to wait in the truck, that he would check this last field for her. She watched him slowly make his way out to the pipe, looking it over. He made his way back through the mud and climbed back in the pickup. "This one will be fine for a bit longer too," he said. "Hunter can deal with it then."

She had nodded back at him. "Okay," she got out. Her stomach had been in knots all afternoon and even now she had to focus on her breathing. She wasn't sure why she was suddenly so nervous around him, she had never felt like this before.

She had been tasked to check the water the day before. He had volunteered to go with her to help out immediately. Hunter had made a comment about her getting out of doing work "again," and her father had quickly shot him a look. "I don't mind," Adam had said, his voice deep and slow. Her heart had leapt a bit in her chest.

All day she was a nervous wreck as she helped her mom out with chores around the house. And when everyone finally went to bed that evening, she laid awake and stared at the ceiling.

Normally, she would wear her pajamas out to check water, but she felt the need to do something different. Instead of sleeping, she wandered into the bathroom she had shared with Jessica. Her hair was a frizzy mess, and she didn't know what to do to fix it. She slipped a ballcap on and pulled her hair through it before securing it into a messy bun. She pulled open the drawers and looked at the makeup in them. She didn't have much, nothing like what Jess had on her side of the vanity, but she felt uncomfortable using it.

Finally, she pulled out her mascara and flicked it onto her eyelashes. She didn't know what else to do, so she tossed the tube back into the drawer and made her way into her room. She pulled on some leggings and slid on a sports bra—should she wear a real bra? No, that was dumb, she was checking water not going on a date with Adam—a date with Adam made her heart flutter again, and she froze for a second. "You need to get a grip," she thought to herself. "You are checking water with this man. Nothing more, nothing less."

She pulled on one of the hoodies from the previous season's volleyball tournaments out and pulled it on, looking at herself in her full-length mirror. It hid everything about her body, which normally she was fine with, but tonight she just didn't want. Instead, she went and dug through her drawers, finally finding a cut-off T-shirt from a volleyball camp. It was tighter on her and showed off the muscles she had from working on the family's land the last few months. She pulled a flannel on as well and posed a few times in her mirror. She still hadn't been fully happy with the outfit but finally walked away and laid down in bed. She glanced at her phone. 11:11 p.m. "Make a wish," she had whispered.

Her alarm finally went off at 2:40, and she quickly sat up in bed. She hadn't slept at all, but at least now she could go downstairs. He was in the kitchen when she came in, the coffee pot just finishing up. The smell greeted her as she came into the room.

He picked up the pot and had looked at her. "Want a cup?" he asked. "Sure," she answered, her stomach turning again.

They had ridden out in silence mainly, the radio station out of Forsyth playing the day's hits quietly. Adam occasionally asked her for directions, and she would let him know when to turn and when to not. She had a death grip on her coffee thermos the entire time, just so she would have something to hold onto.

Now, on the way back to the ranch house, they drove in total silence. Adam pulled into a spot and parked the truck, and they both started back to the house from the shop, when Kennedy had glanced up at the sky.

"Big Dipper is out," she said, stopping to look up at it. He had stopped too and looked up.

"Where is that?" he asked.

She looked at him, knowing her face was saying a lot. "You don't know where the Big Dipper is?"

He looked at her. "No?"

She pursed her lips together and walked over to him. He watched her the entire time, not breaking eye contact. She looked away, down at the ground and took a quick breath before looking back at him. She pointed up to the sky and looked at her finger, pointing out the constellation in the sky. She felt him look away too, to where she was pointing, and she began to describe the shape to him.

Her hand fell down slowly and she looked back at him, finally realizing how close the two were standing to each other. "Now you know the Big Dipper," she said.

"You know a lot about stars," he said.

Immediately, she felt the color rush to her face, and she began talking quickly. "I like mythology and a lot of constellations have ties to that. My favorite is Orion, but you can't see him right now, just during the winter. That's the first one Mom taught me how to find. I don't know I just think the constellations are so cool and sometimes you can see the Milky Way, it's just so dark out here that it makes it easy and—" she stopped herself and looked at him, suddenly realizing his hand was on her back.

He leaned forward slowly and so did she, until their lips softly met in the middle. They stayed like that for a moment before she pulled back.

"I should go back to bed," she said, her heart beating in her throat. He seemed a little surprised but nodded back at her. She quickly walked inside and ran up the stairs to her room, shutting the door behind her. She slid down the door so that she was sitting on the floor. Her heart was pounding. "What the hell was that?" she thought to herself. She stayed on the floor until the knock came.

She looked around. Should she answer? "One second," she finally got out. She pulled herself up and tried to straighten her outfit. She pulled the door open.

Adam had changed back into his pajamas. "Just... wanted to say good night," he said.

She nodded, trying to stay calm. "Good night," she answered.

He rocked on the balls of his feet and looked at the ground. She sat and looked at him for a moment, neither one speaking.

"I'm sorry," he finally said, looking at her. "I shouldn't have done that."

Kennedy didn't answer Adam for a moment. She had a ball in the pit of her stomach. "It's fine," she answered. "We were just... caught up in the moment."

He started chewing on his lip a little, not answering for a moment. "Well, I'm sorry," he said again. "I'll see you tomorrow."

He turned and began to move back down the hallway to Kris's old room, where he would stay when he was there. Something pulled at her heart as he retreated and suddenly a "Wait!" came out of her mouth.

His hands were in his short's pockets when he turned and looked back at her. She didn't know what to say for a minute and struggled to know what to say. Finally, she pulled the door open a bit more. "Do you want to come in for a bit?" she asked.

He smiled crookedly and nodded, moving back to her.

The entire ride home, she couldn't get him out of her mind. For over a year, they had kept what they had a secret, not telling anyone. That had been on her. He would sometimes like her posts on social media, but this time felt different. Maybe Grace was right—posting it had caught his attention.

There were a lot of things about their... she hesitated to call it a relationship but didn't know what else to label it... situation that confused her. But the one thing she was certain about was that she missed him and missed talking to him. Even now, as she sat alone in the dark and silence, listening to the sound groans and sighs of the bus, she would do a lot of things to call him, to hear his voice, to talk things out.

But something held her back. It was a two-way street, after all. He wasn't calling either. And she wasn't fully sure she wanted him to. She still didn't know what had drawn him to her in the first place.

24

It was home opener weekend in Hysham the third week in December, and the girls were ready. They were full of holiday cookies from the end-of-the-year party the school had hosted that day and were now huddled at the baseline of the gym under their basket, waiting for the water bottles and towels to be sat down on the bench by the younger teammates. Kennedy and Grace had balls tucked under their arms once again for warmups.

The pep band was starting to play. The school's speaker system was lackluster on its best days, so warmups and halftimes still consisted of a traditional pep band at the school. Most of the girls would end up playing in the group during the boys' game, and currently the boys' team was playing for them. Everyone pulled double duty in a small town to help game days happen. The junior class would run the concessions, and the junior high students would help with the halftime pop toss for student council. It was just how it went.

Kennedy's palms were sweaty as the other girls finally arrived in their huddle. Her nerves that had calmed down the last two weeks were suddenly back with a vengeance; the only thing she had heard about all day at school was the opening home games against the St. Labre Braves and the next day, the Terry Terriers. Adam, who was from Terry, had younger sisters who played, so she was sure his parents would be there as well. It sent her stomach into fits to think about, so she was just trying to get through the game at hand.

Finally, everyone was there. The clock runner, Mr. M, who had retired from teaching about a decade earlier but still substitute taught and helped at games, flicked the switch to start the twenty-minute countdown on the clock. Kenney held her arm up into the air, and the rest of the team followed. "Pirates on three," Grace said. "One, two, three, Pirates!" they all chanted back, breaking and getting into their warmup lines.

It was mass hysteria in the locker room when Kennedy had finally made her way in after thanking the fans at the end of the game. It had taken her much longer than the other girls—it seemed everyone in town had wanted to tell her how proud of her they were and how great it was to see her back on the court. She couldn't catch her breath, and it felt like her heart was going to pound out of her chest.

As she came in, Kris immediately threw his arm around her. "Wow," he said. "Just, wow." She blushed. It had been a good game, that was for sure.

Something had just come alive in her when the ball was tossed into the air by the ref. There was a fire in her that she normally didn't have on the basketball court, and it seemed to have made all the difference. If the last weekend had allowed her to get her feet back under her, then this weekend had been the time she learned to run.

She couldn't miss in the first quarter. No matter where she was, the ball connected with the hoop time and time again. After her eighth point of the first eight minutes, the Braves' coach had quickly switched tactics on her. "Smith," he yelled. "Get on her NOW." The next time down the court, Alli Smith was stuck to her like glue. Kennedy remembered playing against this girl years ago, her freshman year of school. She had been a force to reckon with then, as well, quick and light on her toes. However, Kennedy stood taller than her by at least a head and quickly began calling for lob passes down below. She would take the moves her brothers had taught her as a post growing up and take a powerful bounce of the ball before squaring up, easily laying the bunny in. She pulled a few fouls as well, with her opponent slapping at her arms as she became more frustrated.

As the buzzer went off for the end of the first quarter, the girls hustled to their bench. The Braves' coach was visible agitated—Smith, his star, had pulled two fouls in the first quarter. The crowd on this side of the gym small gym was riled up as well, yelling as the girls came into the huddle.

Allen crouched down in front of his bench, complimenting the girls as they sipped on their waters. He hadn't subbed anyone yet, but now he looked around and called to Anna, the junior exchange student, and Hannah, one of their freshmen, to sub into the game. "Rachel, Julia... take a breather," he said. The fresh legs quickly ran and checked in with Allen's wife, the bookkeeper, and the other two girls stood up so that their peers could take their seats.

"Okay," he said, as they two subs rejoined the group. "We're switching things up." Quickly, he explained that they would now be running a high post-low post with Hannah and Kennedy and that Maddy would be their runner, shifting from the "motion" plays they had been running the first quarter. They broke their huddle with a "team." He grabbed Kennedy as the other girls made their way out to the court. "Kennedy," he said, his hand wrapping around her arm. She looked at him. "Keep this up."

The second quarter and second half were just as successful as the first for Kennedy. Smith was still on her, sticking to her like glue. She was struggling to guard her, though, in the post still. Kennedy kept driving and pulled another foul from the other senior. Quickly, her coach took her out. From there, it was Kennedy's game.

She wasn't keeping track of the points she was scoring—she had never been one to do that. But she knew she was feeling hot that day, and Grace and her teammates seemed to sense it as well. Whenever they could, the ball would be passed to her, and she would try and connect it. Coach Davidson didn't take her out at all. She didn't think she had ever played a whole game in her life before, but at one point he looked at her and said, "If you're good, I'll keep you in." She nodded. "Keep me in," she answered. She was sure that she would be finishing out that game.

So, she stayed in. She blocked some shots and even gathered a couple of steals. As the full-court pressure from the Braves became more intense the second half, she felt herself stepping up and taking a role in bringing the ball up the court. It wasn't that she made every shot or never turned the ball over. Her number flashed a three behind it late in the third half, signaling three fouls, and she fumbled the ball as well as missed shots. But something just seemed different this game.

Now, in the locker room, Kris was beaming at her and her heart felt full. Allen huddled the girls up.

"I'll be honest, ladies," he said. It was clear he was trying to have a moment but was feeling a little overwhelmed. "We shouldn't have won that. You all know this. This is a state-ranked team, a team that is transitioning back to Class B at the end of the year. They have a depth of bench we could only dream of." He paused for a second and brought his arm up. "But what happened out there wasn't a miracle. That was hard work, blood, and sweat and tears." He nodded up and down. "It wasn't a perfect game, but what happened out there lets me know that we're on the right path." He sighed. "There's a lot more I could say to you all, but we'll save it for another day. Get some rest tonight and eat well, we have the Terriers tomorrow."

They huddled together one last time. "Family on three," he said. "One, two, three," he counted and the girls enthusiastically answered, "FAMILY!"

Kris got up early and drove to town the next morning. Something inside of him had told him he needed to. He parked at the convenience store and waited for the paper delivery out of Billings to arrive. It was thirty minutes later that the truck appeared and the stacks of papers were handed off to the local delivery person and a few more were left at the Friendly Corner to sell.

He went inside and bought a cup of coffee, taking as long as he could to pour the cup before making his way up to the counter. He nodded at the cashier and then looked at the small pile of papers. "I'll take one of those, too," he said. She gestured at him to grab one and rang him up on the old cash register. It still beeped as it added the numbers together. He pulled out a few crumpled bills and handed them over to her, and she passed back a few coins in return.

He barely made it into the truck before he was opening the paper and flipping through to the sports section. He turned it to the prep section and looked at the stats from the night before first.

He had been shocked when he saw the numbers the previous night too. Kennedy had never had a game like that—hell, Hunter had never had a game like that, and he was the most athletic of them all. But something had been different about her that night.

Some poor college student had stayed up late the night before typing in all this information, so he wasn't surprised to see that her last name was spelled wrong in the statistics from the game. But there it was, staring back at him:

Kennedy Hellend – 34

He shook his head. "Damn," he muttered, sipping his coffee. He flipped the page over and saw the bold heading of the section he was looking for: Thirty Point Club.

The papers around the state collected the names of anyone who scored thirty (or, as seemed to be more common now, more than thirty) points in a game. None of the other Helland kids had ever made it. Not even Hunter, much to his annoyance. Yet, there was his younger sister's name, typed correctly this time, with the previous day's date.

He drove home with the radio playing quietly. The sun was just starting to come up as he reached the curve with the memorial for Jessica on it and pulled over. He made his way across the road, where the decorations still sat that honored her. There was the small white cross that the state had put up, and then the larger, metal cross that had her name pressed into it. He made his way to the metal one and stared at it for a while. His hands were shoved into his pockets.

Jessica had been the spitfire, the one whose laugh would roll around you and pull you in. He missed her a lot, but mainly he missed her talking about life and what was happening around her. He hadn't been as close with her or any of his siblings when he left for school, being so much older, and not reconnecting with her when he got back was something he regretted every day. He was trying not to lose Kennedy too, but it was so long since he had seen a fire in her like he had seen the night before. While the two of them spent a lot of time together, he still felt like he didn't know her a lot of the time.

But now... he wondered what was changing. When he had seen her on the bus the weekend before and when he saw her play the last two weekends, something had been different. Sure, Jess had appeared when she put on the makeup, but it was more than that. She was suddenly a woman and not the kid he had grown up babysitting anymore. She could take care of herself and she was learning who she was. And watching her discover that and come back to life was amazing to see. But he still wondered when and if Jess had ever gotten that chance.

He rocked on his feet for a minute, looking around where his sister had taken her last few moments of life in, alone. They still didn't know where she was going or why she had left the house after getting home from that game; they probably never would. The questions of not knowing haunted him nearly every day when he drove past this spot. But he knew that she wouldn't want him or anyone else dwelling on it.

If Jessica knew anything from her short time in life, she knew how to live in the present and take it all in. Couple that with her unstoppable positivity and she had always been a force, one of those people you were always attracted to. One of the few things he remembered from the night they had celebrated her life was one of his classmates stumbling up to him and hugging him and telling him all about his sister and their interactions. "She was just... she was magic, Kris," she had said, hugging him again. "She just had this quality about her that I've never seen before."

That quote had stuck with him through the years. Jess had been magic. Even now, her magic lingered in the house when they were all together and in the gym when Kennedy was playing. It couldn't be diminished or dulled. It was always there, even when it wasn't as strong. It was certainly there last night, pushing Kennedy. He could feel it and see it. It was all Kennedy on the court, but there was something else flowing in her as well.

He stopped rocking and nodded his head a few times. "Let's go make some magic, then," he said, heading back to his truck.

Hunter watched from the doorway of the gym as they announced the starters. It was surreal to see Kennedy out on the court again. He truly never thought that this day would come, even after practicing with her in the shop. Yet there she was, doing a handshake with Grace on the court before huddling up with the rest of the team and doing their chanting.

Adam came up beside him, and he turned and looked at his friend. Getting him to come to the game with him had been like pulling teeth, even though his sisters and parents were there. He had wanted to just keep going and surprise his parents at home, but somewhere in the hills outside of town, Hunter had finally convinced him to stop. He was stony faced, looking out at the court.

Hunter had never pried. But he could tell something had happened between Kennedy and Adam. They had been close, he suspected closer than they should have been, and were always in contact. Yet now, it seemed to be nothing. Adam didn't even want to go out to the ranch at all while they were back, and normally that was his favorite activity to do.

The girls were lining up now, shaking hands. Kennedy was walking back to her spot on the court for the tip off when she looked up at the door. Her face broke into a smile when she saw Hunter. He hadn't told anyone he was coming and made it sound like he would be there a few days later on his own Christmas break. She reached her hand up to wave at him and then froze.

He felt Adam tense up next to him, and he watched Kennedy's face fall. She seemed disoriented, looking around the gym as she made it to the center court line once again. Hunter turned to look at his friend, but he was gone.

Allen looked out over the girls in the locker room. Coming off such a big win the night before and then having another tough loss was rough.

Kennedy was not the same player she had been the night before. It wasn't surprising to him—he didn't expect her to put up numbers like she had previously. But it was like she was an entirely different person the whole night. Basically, every time she came off the court, she looked like she had seen a ghost.

Even now, she was wide-eyed and tearful looking. Grace was frustrated and had taken her annoyance out on her friend several times on the court, but the other senior's actions had started before the game even began.

She had been cool, calm, and confident going out onto the court. She was sure of herself in the locker room and had been laughing with the girls on the court just before tip-off. It was that moment the ball went up that everything seemed to change.

"Well," he said, finally. They all looked at him. "I'm not sure what happened out there," he finally admitted. "The key to a successful season is consistency. Not a high-low-high-low roller-coaster. We're still working on finding our consistency."

He knew he should say something, but he was drained. There was nothing else he could say currently.

"Uh," he looked around the girls. He couldn't pull any more words out. "Practice on Monday, Tuesday, and Wednesday this week at 10:00 a.m. each day. Then you'll all get the weekend off to rest and spend time with your families and then we will get back to it after the holidays." He looked around nodding. "Go watch the boys," he finally said, leavening the room.

Grace was fuming by the time Allen and Kris left the room. "Kennedy, what the hell happened out there?" she asked.

Her friend looked at her but couldn't seem to bring herself out to say anything.

Grace held eye contact with her co-captain. "Well?" she asked.

Kennedy didn't answer. A few of the girls were still in the room, but for the first time Grace didn't care if they saw her picking a fight.

"Talk to me." She stepped in front of her friend, who was moving toward her bag.

"Please let me go," Kennedy said softly, but Grace held her ground.

"No." Grace crossed her arms. "Tell me what's wrong."

Suddenly Kennedy seemed to find her voice. "You don't get to bully me into telling you what my thoughts and feelings are every time I'm upset," Kennedy snapped.

Grace blinked a few times and felt the eyes of the other girls on them. She shoved past her friend and walked out of the locker room, grabbing her flute off the bench as she did so.

Her friend sat down, feeling heavier than she had in a long time.

Kennedy didn't want to ride home with any of her family members but decided that Kris would probably be the best to deal with out of all of them. She was sitting in his pickup when he finally came out of the school.

He didn't say anything to her as they started on the two-lane out of town, driving on the roads that the snow was just now starting to stick on. She stared out the window, tears silently streaming down her face.

Finally, he spoke. "So, what happened tonight?" he asked her.

She didn't answer, the soft sounds of the radio filling the cab.

"Kennedy," he said. She didn't turn to look at him for fear he would see her crying.

He didn't speak to her again.

She went straight to her room when she got home, not even thanking Kris for the ride. She curled up under the covers on her bed, still fully clothed, staring at the wall in the dark. She hadn't expected seeing him to hurt her like this.

She lost track of time and may have dozed off when there was a knock at her door. She didn't say anything, but she heard it softly open and felt the hallway light spill in and hit her bed.

"Hey," Hunter said.

She didn't answer him.

"I'm sorry, I should have told you I—we—were coming today," he said from the doorway. Silence.

"Sounds like your game on Friday was incredible. I'm sorry I missed it," he continued to speak into the darkness.

Still, she didn't reply.

"All right," he said finally. "I love you, Kenna." He waited for a moment for her to answer, but still she remained quiet and still. He finally pulled the door shut.

"Love you, too," she whispered.

She had been spending all her free time working on her senior paper, but now that was over and turned in for the holidays and she was off from school, she suddenly had a lot of free time on her hands. Mrs. O'Brien had given her a few books to read over the break, but instead she pulled out *Blind Your Ponies* again.

It just summed up her time in a small town and playing sports so well. There was the undying hope that this would be the year that things finally happened; the small town, family drama that impacts everyone and everything; some romance. It truly had it all and its familiarity soothed her.

It had taken her a while to get over the shock of seeing Adam. She felt like she was just going through the motions at practice each day, floating aimlessly from her house to the gym and through chores with her dad and then back to her room where she would lay in bed until dinner. Hunter kept trying to talk to her, but she felt a weird disconnect from him and would leave the room when he came in.

Finally, Christmas Eve had rolled around, and she couldn't get out of avoiding Hunter anymore. Most of her parents' siblings were staying at the ranch, spread out between Kris's house, her grandparents' house in town, and her family's house. Jessica's room was off limits, but other than that it seemed like if someone could sleep in a location, it was taken up.

After dinner that evening, Kennedy had found herself sitting on the stairs—near enough to the family that her mom wouldn't yell at her later, but far enough away that she could catch her breath some. She was watching some of her younger cousins run around the dining room from her perch when Hunter appeared at the bottom of the steps.

She moved over to let him go upstairs, but instead, he came and sat next to her. She wasn't sure what to do or say. Getting up seemed rude but sitting next to him made her uncomfortable and she wasn't sure why.

The two sat in silence for a moment, watching their younger relatives, before Hunter spoke. "You've been avoiding me," he said, charging head on into the moment. He was never one to shy away from conflict— neither was Jess. They had certainly been the ones who fought the most out of the family, even more than Kennedy and Kathy did now.

She was startled for a moment. "No, I haven't," she said. "Just been tired and stuff."

Hunter looked at her. "You leave the room any time I come in. This is the most time we've spent together since I got home." He was always direct and to the point.

She didn't answer, looking back over her family. "I just... it was surprising to see you ...and Adam...at the game," she answered.

He didn't say anything back to her for a long time. It felt like hours later when he finally spoke. "I don't know what happened, and I'm pretty sure I don't want to know what happened. One of you dating my best friend was enough." Kennedy tensed up here, the urge to run increasing inside of her. "But both of you dating him is… well, I won't lie, it's weird. And neither you or him will talk about it with me, so I'm not sure where to go from here," he said.

"We never dated," she answered. That part was true at least. There was never a label attached.

"But you talked all day every day and neither one of you has been fine since I heard you arguing upstairs the night we were celebrating you all making it to divisionals—"

"You heard that?" she cut him off and he looked at her.

"Yeah, I heard that," he answered. She pursed her lips into a thin line and turned away quickly.

"Look—he asked me some questions that night about relationships and stuff. I didn't know why then, and I'm not going to ask you why either. But I was here with Courtney, and I shouldn't have been, but I was. And I know we shouldn't be together—both of us know that and we always have. But something keeps bringing us together when we are around each other. If you ask her, it's the universe. But honestly, neither one of us is good together. We're good people, but not good for each other. It's comfort—it's knowing that that other person was around when you were going through some hard shit. But us being together and holding on to the past isn't going to let us grow."

Kennedy was looking away still.

"I love her, you know." She looked at him and he saw her eyes were tearing up. "I told her I loved her all the time when we were together. I didn't then—or I didn't realize it anyhow. I thought I was just going through the motions. But I love her. And I want to see her be happy and meet her goals and even fall in love. I want that for her because she deserves it. She's been there for me through a lot, and I've been there for her. But even though I love her, I can't be with her because if I'm with her, that's it. This is it for both of us."

Kennedy was rubbing at her face now, wiping away her tears. Suddenly, his arms were around her, pulling her in. It was so unlike him that she wasn't sure how to react.

"It fucking hurts," he said. She crumpled into his chest. "But sometimes you have to let go to grow."

She could tell he knew she was crying, and he held her for a long time as she silently let the tears fall from her face, trying to even out her breathing. They stayed that way for a long time, until she finally pulled away, rubbing at her eyes.

He looked at her. "Go upstairs. I'll deal with Mom. Cry about it all you want. But come down tomorrow and hold your head high because that's the only way you'll ever get past this."

She nodded and got up, turning to head up the stairs. She only made it a few steps before he said her name.

She turned and looked at her brother. "I'm sorry. I should have told you he was coming."

She rubbed her eyes again. "It's okay," she said.

"It's not. If you all had surprised me with Courtney at anything—I would have blown a gasket. Honestly probably would have made the damn 50-point club and taken my aggression out on the court. But you don't do that. You retreat. I'm sorry, it wasn't fair to you. It won't happen again."

She pursed her lips again and felt the hot tears coming in full force. "Okay," she answered. "Thank you."

She let herself cry it out in the shower, just like he told her she should go do. She sat on the floor and let the water wash over her and just sobbed. She knew no one would hear her with everything going on downstairs.

She let her emotions and frustrations rush out of her and just tried to feel them all. There was sadness, heartbreak, anger, frustration. She was good at keeping them pushed down and away from everyone else, but it felt good to just feel for a second. To feel everything and not have it be shameful or something to hide away.

She finally got out of the shower and looked in the mirror. Her eyes were swollen and red, her skin blotchy and pink. Her hair was what her mom would call a rat's nest, with knots and tangles throughout. She pulled out her hairbrush and began to brush it out slowly, working out the snarls as she went, sitting down on her toilet seat and wrapped in her towel.

She stared at the floor as she did, trying to cope with the swirling of feelings that now took up her thoughts and sat heavily on her heart. It took a long time to finally get the brush all the way through, but she finally did it and set it on the counter. She went to stand and pushed herself up, suddenly feeling weak.

She sat back down and took a few deep breaths. It hurt when all the emotions came out of her. It exhausted her. But it also felt good and refreshing.

She gave herself a few minutes before she tried to stand again and found her footing this time. She made her way to her bed slowly, pulling one her old t-shirt and shorts and crawling in, pulling herself into the fetal position. She had no tears left in her to cry, but she really wanted to try again. But instead, she tried to level out her breathing and remain calm.

For the first time in a long time, she fell asleep deeply and calmly and without even trying to at all.

25

There was something different about Kennedy the last few weeks, but Grace couldn't put her finger on it. She was just... different.

It had taken them a while to make up this time around, after their fight in the locker room. She had seen how out of it her friend had been for the days leading up to Christmas, but when they came back together to practice on Monday, it was like she was a different person, joking and laughing with the other girls again.

She could sense that things had still been strained between the two of them though. They were talking and interacting less both in the gym and outside. Normally, Grace would go out and go sledding with the Hellands for Christmas Day in the afternoon, being pulled behind the four-wheeler on a tractor tire. But nothing was said to her, so she didn't go out.

It was nearly New Year's Eve when Kennedy grabbed her after practice. "Hey," she said, rushing to catch up with Grace as she was leaving the gym, both of them wearing basketball shorts and slide on shoes with hoodies. "Do you want to come out for New Years?" she asked. "I think some of the other girls are too."

Grace didn't even hesitate—she missed her friend. "Yes, of course," she answered.

Kennedy had smiled back at her. "Great," she answered.

From that moment on, things had improved between them, but still, something about Kennedy was new and strange. The girls went shopping for winter formal dresses on New Year's Day, and Kennedy didn't even seem upset when Grace told her that she had asked someone to go and that it wouldn't be the two of them going stag as originally planned. She had curiously asked about the guy, someone from Custer, and Grace had even gotten up the nerve to ask her if she would take his friend finally.

She had fully expected her to say no—even before she knew about Adam, Kennedy had never said "Yes" to going out on dates with her. So, it nearly floored her when her friend agreed.

It had surprised Kennedy when she had agreed to take him too; Grace hadn't done a good job at hiding her surprise, and Kennedy had quickly wandered off for a minute, pulling dresses around the racks. By the time she came back over, Grace had assembled his phone number for her. "Josh is so excited he doesn't have to come alone," she said, quickly adding Austin's contact to her phone. "I already told him that your dress was black," she added, "just so he knows what to wear."

Kennedy nodded and smiled at her phone. She kind of knew of Austin from sports and from FFA, but they had never spoken before. She didn't know if she should text him or not, so she slid her phone into her purse and helped Grace continue to look for her own dress.

School started again that Wednesday and soon they were on the road for two more games. On Friday, they made the trek to Wibaux near the North Dakota border. It was their second longest trip of the year, and they left school early to head out to take on the Longhorns. The girls were tough with six seniors who had been playing together since elementary school. Their cohesiveness was evident, and they easily took control of the court. Kennedy did notice, though, that they seemed to be sticking on her a bit more, catching them a few times saying "She's crossing, she's crossing," or snapping "Helen, she's by you!" The few times Kennedy was able to get the ball, she tried to make it count.

The ending score was 63-31 for the Longhorns. Allen talked to them for a bit in the locker room before finishing out with "It's hard when they have that closeness" as he and Kris wandered out of the visitor locker room.

Kennedy was a bit disappointed: it was the only time they would get to play this team until tournaments. That was part of the issue of being in such a large conference. The opportunity to play or even advance come tournament time was so small that it was hard to break through. Of course, add in the fact that something always seemed to go wrong for the Pirates during tournaments and it had been over twenty years since they had made it out of the conference, at least on the girls' side. If they got to face Wibaux again, it wouldn't be until February in Miles City. This had its pros and cons, but she felt like they would have a better chance at keeping up with them if they were to meet up again before the end of the season.

Jordan went better the next day, though not at first. The girls were tired as they made their way onto the court. It was clear, especially in the first half that they were dragging their feet. It was a slow start, with the game dragging out. Allen was not happy in the locker room.

"I know it was a late night and we have spent another day on the bus, but you all need to get it together," he threw out as he came into the room. "Thirteen turnovers, we can't make a shot to save our lives, and what the hell is that defense?" He looked at Kennedy and Grace, who were seated on the floor. "Pick it up, you two are seniors. I expect more from you."

Kennedy blinked at him, and she felt Grace tense up beside her, but her friend held her tongue.

The second half was different. Grace came out fired up and quickly converted two steals into points, first off the ball-in and then another off a press. Jordan's coach called a time out on her third steal after one of his players fouled her.

"That's what I'm saying," Allen said, clapping Grace on the back as she came off the court.

From there, it was the Pirates' game. Kennedy found her feet near the end of the third quarter and converted some points for them, and

Ellie had a solid game all-around. When Grace went out near the beginning of the fourth quarter, when it was clear that the game was in their hands, she even ran point and had some solid drives.

Coach Davidson was waiting for them in the locker room after they finished thanking the fans for coming. He waited until each of them was seated before he went around the room, giving them each a high five. "That's what I'm talking about!" he said. "Do you see how one of you can change the game for everyone." He looked at Grace.

"Grace went out there in the second half absolutely pissed at me." Everyone laughed and he let out a chuckle as well. Grace immediately started arguing that she wasn't upset, but he waved at her until she stopped talking. "She took that energy, and she left it out on the court for everyone to see. She made a statement and channeled it into the court, but when she did that? The rest of you followed. The rest of you stepped up to meet the energy level and look how it paid off.

"Did you all have a game like Grace did? No. But you all sensed your roles out on the court and filled them. I think sometimes it's easy to get caught up on who had the best night or who is the best player—but that's not what our goal is here. That's not what our goal has ever been here, in this program.

"Our goal has been to help you become strong, confident young women. To take the emotions you have and learn how to channel them into something. To be leaders.

"You'll statistically not play basketball for the rest of your life. But I hope you can take the lessons you learn here and use them in your job or in future relationships. I hope you can learn to communicate better and differently with the people around you who may be very different but work alongside you. I hope you can look back on this season with a sense of pride and see how much you've grown. Because all of you have grown in some way this year and we're only halfway through the season.

"I'm proud of what I saw out there tonight. I'm proud to call you all my team. Let's take this momentum under us for the rest of the season and see what we can do," he finished.

"Let's make magic happen," Kris chimed in. Kennedy looked at him. He never spoke in these moments, and he was blushing.

But Allen looked at him and nodded a few times. "Yeah, let's make magic happen. Bring it in," he said. The girls gathered around their coaches, extending their hands to the sky. "Magic on three," Allen said.

Kennedy stayed in the shower longer than her teammates, letting the lukewarm water run through her long, wavy hair.

The things Allen had said during their huddle were sticking with her now. She found it curious this message about communicating and growing was coming at her from two different points in her life—both Hunter and Allen had brought it up and it was making her think. She and Grace certainly played better together when they were communicating and open about their thoughts and feelings, and Kennedy had been closed off these last few weeks.

The other girls had left the locker room by the time she came out in her towel to get dressed; all of them, that was, except Grace. She was sitting down, scrolling through her phone when Kennedy emerged from the showers.

"There you are," she said. "I'm starving, can we get a pretzel or something?"

Kennedy nodded. She would tell her it all, she resolved, but not now.

She quickly pulled a brush through her hair and slid on her hoodie and sweatpants. The two were just leaving the room when she realized she didn't have her phone.

"Shoot," she said. "Sorry, give me a second."

She went back and pulled her phone out of her bag. A few texts from her mom, some notifications from her social media—the things she usually found after a game. Then, however, she noticed the message from someone named "Austin."

"Grace," she called out. Her friend poked her head from around the door. "Did you give Austin my number?"

"No," she answered. "I gave you his so you could talk to him before the dance. Why?" She seemed confused.

Kennedy held up her phone. "He just texted me."

"Okay..." Grace answered. "And?"

"I never texted him," she answered. "So, how'd he get my number?"

Grace rolled her eyes. "Chill," she said. "Text him back!"

"And say what?!" she answered.

"....Hello?" Grace said with an eye roll. "Come on, I'm hungry."

Kennedy waited for the bus ride home to finally text Austin back. "Hey," she answered. Immediately the little chat bubbles on his side of the screen popped up.

"What are you doing?" he typed.

She found herself answering him each time they made it back to into service on the road to Miles City. It was small conversations, little tidbits about their lives. It was very different from her conversations with Adam, where they had already known each other for so long that they never needed to talk about the small, minute details of their lives.

By the time they got back to the ranch, it was nearly two in the morning, and he was still up chatting with her. It was nice: to have something so innocent and new. They messaged for a while longer, mainly about their plans for college, until he told her that he needed to go to bed. She was a little sad when she saw that flash across the screen, but quickly pushed the feelings away, telling him good night. She went to bed too and thought that would be it, when her phone lit up once again. She reached over and held it up to her face.

"Talk tomorrow?" she set it back down without answering. But she hoped they would talk tomorrow.

Their schedule for the week was a little odd. Instead of a traditional Friday and Saturday night game, they were playing on Tuesday and Thursday since Rosebud and Custer were just up the road from them. It meant that they could have a Friday and Saturday off from the games and that they could have their Snowball dance in January instead of in December on a weeknight.

The Tuesday game in Rosebud was uneventful, with the teams getting in and out quickly. The Thursday game, meanwhile, had the teams fired up. The formation of the co-op with Custer was still fresh in the minds of the Pirates, and they took it out on the court, running up the score aggressively during both games. However, things already seemed to be softening between the two towns, with the younger girls coming and sitting with the Pirate players during the boys' halftime and chatting with the girls some.

Unbothered by the co-op with their upcoming graduation, Kennedy and Austin had chatted themselves throughout the week, and she found herself waiting for his name to appear. She had never spoken to him in person, so she was excited to meet him officially on Thursday after the game.

She was waiting in the main hallway in Custer with Grace after the boys' game had concluded. She suddenly had butterflies, and she wasn't sure why. Grace was poking fun at her though, telling her that she was getting red in the face. Every time she spoke, Kennedy blushed more. She feared by the time he finished changing her face would be permanently red.

Finally, the two boys emerged from the gym.

He was taller than her. "Thank God," she thought, because she had bought a pair of heels to wear to the dance. He smiled when he saw her, and she thought her heart melted a little. He had really nice teeth.

"Hi," he said.

"Hi," she answered. She was a little out of breath. "Get a grip," she thought. "You barely even know the guy."

They chatted about the games as Josh and Grace laughed beside them. Kennedy watched Grace and how she flipped her hair around her shoulders and lightly touched him on the arm when she spoke. She had never done anything like that with Adam.

She suddenly realized that Austin had asked her a question, and she had completed missed it. "Oh," she said. "I'm sorry, I'm tired from the game. What was that?"

"Have you applied for schools yet?"

She nodded. "Yeah, I've been accepted to the U so I'll head there in the fall," she said. One of Josh's teammates had come up to talk to him, and he now had his arm around Grace's shoulders. She was smiling and looking at him. She was just so natural at this.

"Nice," he answered. "I'm finishing up my applications right now. I was planning on going to Mountain College, but the coach from Yellowstone reached out to me about a football scholarship today."

"Oh my gosh, that's amazing!" Kennedy answered. She had tried to put some of Grace's perkiness into her words but seemed to have missed the mark, and it came off a little aggressive.

He blinked at her for a second. "Yeah…" he answered. "Have you talked to any coaches?"

Kennedy was startled. "About what?"

"Playing," he said simply.

Kennedy laughed hard, then realized he wasn't joking.

"Uh," she finally answered. "No, I haven't. Grace is the one talking to them."

He cocked his head at her. "You don't want to play in college?"

Kennedy shrugged. The boys' team was finishing showering and heading out to the bus now. She pulled her bag up on her shoulder. "No one would want a former bench warmer who didn't play her junior season," she said with a laugh.

"I disagree," he answered. He made eye contact with her and held it. "My cousin plays in Billings. She was at the game tonight, and I was sitting with her when you were playing. She had a lot of good things to say," he said.

Kennedy took a long pause and looked at him. "I have to get on the bus," she said finally. "I'll see you on Saturday." She turned to go when he said her name.

She turned and looked at him. "Can... can we hug?" he asked. She bit her lip and nodded, and he stepped forward and wrapped his arms around her.

He smelled nice.

Allen Davidson had once again been talked into chaperoning the high school dance along with Denise O'Brien. They were standing in the multi-purpose room in the school, watching their students sway around to a slow song that he was pretty sure had been popular when he was in school.

Denise took a sip of her tea and looked at her colleague.

"So, how's the season going?"

He nodded a few times, looking out over the students. "You know, it's going," he answered. "Not really where we want to be at ranking wise, but there is still time to do some shifting. As long as we don't end up in the toilet bowl game, I think we will do okay."

Denise nodded, taking another drink. "It's been nice to see her out again," she said. "Kennedy."

Allen nodded as well. "I'm still a little shocked every time I walk into the gym and she's in there," he admitted.

"I'm not," the high school English teacher said.

Now he looked at her. "You're not?"

"I could see how much it hurt her not being on the court last year during paper and annual. She was always volunteering to help out with photos for the yearbook. And she wrote about it in her journal once—how much she missed being out there." She smiled. "I think they think I don't actually read what they write."

Allen shook his head. "They also think that we don't see them texting in class."

After the dance, they all went out to the ranch. Grace and Kennedy drove back out of town together with a small caravan following them.

Kathy had taken her hosting to the extreme as usual. She had a spread of pizza and chips and all the drinks they could want—minus alcohol.

Grace immediately curled up next to Josh out by the firepit off the side porch. Kennedy looked at her friend and sat by herself. She still wasn't sure about this whole PDA thing. Austin came and sat next to her, and they started chatting.

He was so nice. And it was nice to be able to bring him home and for him to shake her dad's hand. But now that she had been around him, she wasn't sure how to feel. He was so nice, but it wasn't that familiarity she felt with Adam. And she knew this wasn't fair and she knew that Hunter would tell her that would be okay, but she was just conflicted. Wasn't it supposed to feel natural?

Jackson came outside a bit later with Ellie. Kennedy smiled at her. She was glad she had finally gotten the courage to ask her brother to the dance (and it had kept Rachel at bay some the last few weeks too).

"You guys want to play cards?" he asked.

Kennedy looked at Austin. "Whatever you want to do," he answered.

Adam would have answered for her. She looked at her younger brother. "Sure," she answered.

They were mostly home the next two weekends and did decently in the standings. They clinched their first season sweep over the Plevna Cougars and the Rosebud Wranglers as well as winning against the Melstone Broncs. The only loss they faced came at the hands of the Northern Cheyenne Eagles on the other team's home court. Soon, they were back on the bus and traveling to St. Labre's school and Terry. Both games resulted in losses for the girls, and they found themselves solidly ranked sixth in the rankings as they came upon tournament season. This meant they wouldn't be a part of the dreaded "toilet bowl game," where four teams would face off in a single elimination game to see who would take the 7th and 8th spots of the tournament (or, as the 11th-place team in the conference would be hit with, not playing in the post-season at all) the week of the tournament at the community college in Miles City.

The final week of the season would be home, and that meant senior night was coming quickly. Kennedy had a lot of emotions about this: she remembered walking out onto the court with her family two years prior, without the senior they should have been honoring. She remembered how numb she had been at that point, how she had stood in the gym by a casket just a week prior in the same spot. It was a lot to take in.

She was trying to feel her feelings more: her therapist was continuing to remind her that it was okay to feel emotions and let them show. She remembered how Grace had taken her emotions onto the court and had played so well in Jordan: she was trying to do the same thing.

It seemed to be working. She would hold onto her emotions and then let them come out on the court, trying to channel them into something productive. She was feeling a connection and grounding herself in the game, and she knew that it was paying off in unexpected ways. She had been putting up good numbers each game, and it was getting noticed. Grace had had a few coaches from a few schools in the state come to watch her play in the past few weeks, and both of them had chased down Kennedy as well.

"We were so sorry to hear about your sister, she was a tremendous player," they would begin, before asking her if she had thought about continuing on with her basketball career.

"Oh," she would say, glancing at Grace, who had been working so hard to make this something she could do after high school. "No, I'm not interested."

Her friend would always be distant after this. Kennedy had finally grabbed her a few days after the second set of coaches had spoken to her and they had had a few rocky games between the two, asking her if she was upset.

"Of course I'm upset," Grace had snapped. "I've worked my ass off the last four years to get to this place only to have my best friend have it handed to her on a silver platter without even trying."

Kennedy was hurt, but she understood. She didn't want to talk to these coaches, they just kept coming up to her.

Austin wasn't exactly helping the situation either. He had asked if he could give her number to his cousin who played in Billings, and she had politely declined. However, he kept dropping hints she would be coming to the senior night games in Hysham when the Cougars and the Pirates faced off once again.

Her nerves had calmed down a lot during her time getting back into the swing of basketball that season. Yet, the morning of her senior day, she felt sick to her stomach all day. She went and helped her father feed cows in the morning before coming back to a spread that her mother had put together for her, Jack, and Kris. Kennedy had picked at her food because she was truly afraid that she would vomit if she ate anything before the game.

She had then gone upstairs and started getting ready. She brushed her hair out and pulled out her curling iron from under the sink, staring at it. Finally, she went and opened the drawers where Jess had kept her things and pulled out a wand that seemed a little easier to use. She took her time wrapping her hair around the hot tool and then pulled out her sister's makeup that she still didn't really know how to use either.

She pulled on one of her knit dresses and a pair of leggings with boots. Her letterman's jacket was the next thing to slide on and then she grabbed her bag, packed with her shoes and everything she needed for the game.

Her mother pulled her in for a hug as she went to get in Kris's pickup with Jackson. "I am so proud of you," she whispered. When Kennedy pulled back, she could see that Kathy was crying. The younger daughter quickly looked away and went to leave again when she stopped, her hand on the doorhandle.

"Hey, Mom?" she asked.

Kathy was fanning her face. "Yes, honey?"

"Can... can you bring Jess's senior photo with you for tonight?" Her mom's face crumpled, and Kennedy immediately felt a pang of guilt.

Finally, her mother nodded. "Of course, of course," she answered.

Kris let his youngest siblings into the gym early. Technically, this wasn't supposed to be happening, but if it didn't happen here, it was just going to happen in his father's shop.

Kenna and Jack grabbed their respective balls from the ball rack and began shooting. Kennedy had kicked off her boots and was shooting free throws in her socks. He caught each one and would whip the ball back out to her. If there was anything she was dependable on out on the court, it was making free throws.

Eventually, he left her to just do some of her own shooting in the dimly lit gym. It felt like just yesterday he had been the one walking out on senior night, but now it was the second youngest's turn. Life went by fast.

Today was a big day for Kennedy, even if she didn't know it. Allen had told him who was coming that evening, and it was a little staggering.

The head coach from University of Billings had called earlier that week, explaining that one of his women's players from had been at the game in Custer and saw something in Kennedy. The player had known Jessica, as the Montana basketball community was small despite the size of the state, and she had even helped try and recruit her back when she was still considering playing college ball.

Kris hadn't known what to say when Allen had told him the coach was coming. Finally, he had gotten out a "She didn't even play last year," to Allen.

Allen had shrugged. "Doesn't seem to matter to him, said it's no different than a season-ending injury. What matters to him is that she's back out there right now. Says that's the kind of player he wants in his program."

Kris had shook his head. The two of them were standing in the gym after practice. "Shit," he finally said.

Allen looked hard at his assistant coach. "You can't tell her."

Kris started. "What?"

Allen shook his head. "Not a word. She can't know. I know she's already turned down even talking to the other schools, but I think this could be good for her."

"So, you're just not going to tell her a coach, one that likely she will not want to play for based on the fact she doesn't want to play at all, is coming to scout her."

"You saw how she reacted when Hunter showed up," he answered. "She won't know who he is more than likely. Just... let him see her play."

Kris had agreed begrudgingly to let this happen and hadn't told anyone. Not Hunter, not Kennedy, not his parents—no one knew.

Now he watched her grab her own rebound and go up for a quick layup. She had been putting up big numbers and had had some really key plays in the last few weeks. The fact that these colleges wanted to take a chance on her—it validated what he knew. Something magical was happening on the court.

Kennedy pulled her uniform on for the last time in the locker room she had grown up in. Grace had already made her take what seemed like a thousand photos, and she had taken a few with her parents as well. Hunter had rolled in a few minutes before she had gone to get dressed —alone, thankfully—and had given her a hug. She was excited to have everyone here to cheer her on during her last night on the court.

A smattering of aunts and uncles, cousins, and grandparents were likely filing into the gym now, finding their seats on the brown metal bleachers. She would have to go out and try and warm up as best as she could without letting her nerves and anxiety get the best of her. She was more nervous now than she had been during her volleyball senior night, and she had no idea why.

Grace was already crying by the time the two of them went out to line up with their families. Grace walked out first, accompanied by both her parents and her stepparents, and Greg Johnson read her senior biography. When he got to the portion about her signing to play basketball at Yellowstone College, a decision she had finally made earlier on in the week, the crowd cheered loudly, and Kennedy felt her heart swell. She was so proud of her friend.

Next, Kennedy walked out, her mother holding her hand and her arm linked through her father's. Her brothers surrounded them, Hunter carrying the picture of Jess her mother had brought into town. Kennedy had been surprised to see it was the one from her bedroom and not the one from the living room, and she had gotten a little weepy herself. Her parents had brought her flowers, as had her extended family, and Ellie came out and brought her the small bouquet from the school as well as a bag of goodies for her. She had wrapped the underclassmen up in her arms, smiling as she took the bag.

She missed most of what her principal had read out about her, but she tuned back in for the part where he was reading the people she was thanking. "Kenna would like to thank her best friend, Grace, for being by her side every step of the way the last thirteen years and her teammates for supporting her, even when she wasn't on the court." She looked over at Grace who was still crying and smiled and then back at her teammates. Ellie was crying now too.

She looked back over the crowd as he continued. She made eye contact with her relatives and some of the members of the community as Mr. Johnson thanked them for her. She smiled at Ms. O'Brien as she thanked her teachers for all their support as she prepared for the next step in her life. Finally, she heard him begin to thank her family.

"To my parents, thank you for being by my side every step of the way and helping me up when I fall. To Kris, Hunter, and Jackson, thank you for being my best friends and my protectors. The bond we share is special, and I wouldn't trade it for anything in the world. For Jess—"

Greg suddenly stopped talking and seemed to struggle to get the rest out. "—what I wouldn't do for you to be here today. I miss you and I miss playing with you. But every time I come into this gym, I can feel your spirit here. Thank you for everything. I love you." Greg took another long pause before saying: "Good luck to the boys the rest of their season, and ladies: let's make magic happen."

Kathy was very clearly crying when Kennedy turned to hug her and her father and brothers seemed a little misty-eyed too. She didn't mean to get them riled up, but she felt wrong leaving her sister out of the equation.

She parted ways from her family and met Grace for a hug at center court. Their teammates surrounded them, pulling them in for hugs as well. As they trotted back to the bench, she made eye contact with Austin, who waved at her. A young woman and an older man were sitting with him in the bleachers on the guest side of the gym; she didn't recognize either one of them. She gave him a quick wave back before joining the huddle.

After the game, where the Lady Pirates completed another season sweep, the girls wandered down to the annual "Soup Supper" the booster club put on in the multi-purpose room. The event was held on every senior night, and the cooks of the community made homemade soups and desserts as its annual fundraiser. The girls quickly ate and headed back out to the gym to watch the boys play and Paul's senior ceremony.

She saw that the unidentified people from earlier were sitting with Austin's parents now (she hadn't met them, but he looked nearly identical to his dad): they had to be relatives of his of some kind. Suddenly, she saw Allen wander across the gym and shake hands with the man before talking to the young woman next to him. He looked a little familiar, though Kennedy couldn't place why and she tried to turn her attention back to the game.

It was a weird dynamic, watching it unfold. While Jackson may be playing against these boys this year, next year they would be teammates. He and his friend Sam were guarding each other and chatted casually between plays. A few times, he would make a comment to Austin as well. After the Pirates won the game, Sam and Jack even went and found each other for another handshake on the court before going their separate ways.

She waited for Austin to come out of the locker room. Grace had already ended things with Josh, so she jetted off to go eat dinner with her parents at the only restaurant in the town before it closed for the evening.

She smiled politely when he came out of the guest locker room. He was carrying a small bouquet of flowers. "For you," he said, handing them to her. Sunflowers—her sister's favorite. Adam would often buy her those too... but she had never told Austin that Jess loved them—he must have gotten them because he thought she would like them.

She felt herself blushing. "Thank you," she said, taking them from him. "Good game," she said as we pulled her in for a hug. He smelled nice this time too.

"You too," he answered. "Wish it would have ended differently for us, but there's always tournaments."

"It is a whole different season," she agreed.

She sat in the pickup, waiting for Kris and Hunter. Finally, Kris came out and got in and shifted the pickup. She looked at her older brother. "No Jackson?"

"He's getting a ride with Hunter," he answered.

"Oh," Kennedy answered.

The two started driving back out to the ranch in silence. Kennedy was staring out the window. When the curve came up, she suddenly tensed up. "Stop," she said.

Kris looked at her. "What?"

"STOP," she snapped. He did and pulled over.

She threw the door open and looked around before crossing the road. Someone had put solar powered lights up the year before, and they guided her to the spot.

She collapsed at the base of the iron cross, the sobs echoing around her. She may have put up a front for the night, but there was no fighting it now. She had outlived her older sister.

She knew the snow was melting under her and soaking her clothes, but she didn't care.

She let the emotions flow out of her and echo around her in the darkness of a rural Montana night.

Suddenly, a hand was on her shoulder.

"Hey," Kris whispered. "It's okay, it's okay."

"I shouldn't be older than her," Kennedy wailed back to him. "She should be here."

He crouched down next to his sister, his own tears coming to his eyes. "I know," he whispered back. "I know. Come on, Kenna, let's stand up."

She pushed him away and fell over, still sobbing uncontrollably. Once again, he reached out to her and tipped her upright and then pulled her to her feet. She was shaking from the tears and the cold as he began to lead her away, and she leaned onto him, her body suddenly too heavy for her to hold up.

He helped her into his pickup and shut the door, cranking the heat as he got into his own seat a moment later. However, he just sat there and waited for her to speak.

"I've outlived my older sister, Kris," she finally said, her head too heavy to hold up and leaning against the window. "It's wrong."

Kris didn't answer for a moment. "I know," he finally replied. "I'm sorry. It is wrong. But you can't get upset like this every time. I understand this time, because it's a big one. And graduation and going to college are big ones too. But you can't get pulled into this place every time something new happens she didn't get to experience, because if you did that then you died tonight too. You would never live again."

She looked at her brother. Tears were still streaming down her face.

He turned and looked at her too. "I'm sorry, Kennedy. I am. And maybe this sounds shitty of me, but if it helps you move on then well... then fuck it." Her eyes widened at this. While Hunter and Jack cussed regularly much to her mother's annoyance, Kris never did. "Instead of thinking of it as something you never got to see her do, think of it as you carving your own path. There's no more 'Jess did this' or 'Jess did that.' Everything from here forward is your own journey and path and that's exciting. She would be excited for you. And I know it still sucks, but maybe that will help it hurt a little less. Can you try that for me?"

She didn't answer for a moment and then finally nodded. "Yes."

He switched the car into drive and pulled on the road. "Good," he answered.

They drove in silence until they made it to the ranch. He pulled her bag out of the backseat and handed it to her. She pulled it onto her shoulder, and she put her arms around him. They hugged for a minute, until he clapped her back. "Alright," he said. "Enough of that. Go inside and get some rest. It's a busy week."

She pulled away and started to head to the house. She turned around as he opened his door. "Kris?"

"Yeah?" He stopped and looked at her.

"You're going to make a really good head coach someday if you keep up speeches like that," she said as she opened the door and snuck inside.

He sat there for a while, shedding a few tears of his own.

26

Tournament season was every high school athlete's favorite season. There was just something about the hustle and bustle and unknowing that added to the excitement of it all.

The locker hallway was decorated by the Hysham Booster Club, and the pep club hosted sign and t-shirt decorating contests. The boys were ranked third and were likely to make it to divisionals. The girls, meanwhile, were solidly in sixth. But, as Allen kept telling his team (and Kennedy had been saying all year): the past three months didn't matter. What happened now did. Anything could happen in the post-season.

Grace was annoyed with their placement, but Kenna was trying to have a more optimistic view. "It's really hard to beat a team three times," she reminded her. The Terriers had beat them twice, but both games were close.

"But they still beat us twice," she answered. Kennedy sighed. There was no changing her mind.

"Well, at least we aren't in the toilet bowl," she reminded her as the kept working on their poster for the Miles City gym that said "Pirates Rule the 4Cs," a clever play on words for their conference: the 4C.

They played silly games at the Wednesday morning pep rally, and both Kennedy and Grace spoke for the girls' team while Paul spoke for the boys. Then, the girls made their way out to the bus that had been decorated, and little goodie bags had been left on each seat. Most of the rest of the high school and junior high filed onto the band bus behind them. Allen and Kris came onto the bus with their arms loaded down with the warmups they had gotten specifically for tournaments. The girls wore the same ones for the regular season year-to-year but got ones specially made for tournaments.

The coaches moved around the bus as they left town, handing them out to the girls. Kennedy unwrapped hers—the front said "Magic Is Happening" with a starry design. When she flipped it over, though, she had to catch her breath.

She had always been "K. Helland" on the back of her warmups, and Jessica had always been "J. Helland." Even after her sister's death, Kennedy had had the "K" on all her volleyball warmups. They had had the same basketball ones for years, so there was no issue there—it had been "K. Helland" since her freshman year. This one though... this one just said "Helland."

Grief was a funny thing. You never knew when it would hit you one day. She felt herself start to withdraw as the girls around them held up their own warmups and laughed and smiled over them.

"Kennedy?" Grace said. "Are you okay?"

Kennedy looked at her friend. She felt like she was in a fog. But Kris's commentary the other night snuck up on her, and she finally nodded. "Yeah," she answered. "I'm fine."

Allen paced back and forth outside the locker room door, waiting for one of the girls to come and get him. Kris was looking over the stats from the last time they had played the team from Terry. "So," he said, "the Lewis girl is the biggest threat, I think."

Allen nodded. "She's definitely a threat in the paint," he answered. "Kennedy is going to have to take her head on today and be a force on defense, but we need her to show up offensively, too."

Kris flipped through the rest of the stats, and Allen made comments about which girl to put on the opponent's other starters.

Finally, one of the eighth graders came out and opened the door, and Allen took a deep breath in. It was show time.

He stood in front of the girls. They were perched around him on their side of the locker room. They were playing the last game of the day, and the St. Labre team had already vacated its side of the room.

"Alright, ladies," he said. "We're here."

"We're all 0-0 right now. What has happened up until now doesn't matter anymore. What matters is what happens here, on this court." He looked at the girls. "I am so proud of all of you and everything we have accomplished this season. And I truly believe the ranking we got—sixth—doesn't reflect the talent that we have here. Each of you has the ability to contribute on the court, and I expect you to do that the next few days. It's our time to shine." He looked at his assistant coach. "It's our time to make magic happen.

"I want you to forget about everything that is happening off the court. None of that matters out there. You can worry about that stuff after the game, after Saturday night. Until then, it's time to be a Pirate and show them what that means. It's the last time you get to say that—that you're a Pirate. So, let's show them what that means. Let's be courageous and work together as a unit. Let's show them our strength and not worry about our weaknesses." He looked at Kris now. "Coach, tell them who is matched up with who."

Kris went down the lineup, reading off their names and the numbers they would be guarding. Allen threw in comments about each player as he did and what he would like to see his girls do out on the court: "Rachel, make her go to the left when she gets the ball, she has no left hand" and "Julia, we need you to be big down in the paint, we may need you to front the Lewis girl."

He kept throwing out comments until finally, he seemed to run out of steam. He looked around at the team in front of him. "Girls: I am damn proud of us so far. Now it's time to let everyone else see what I see. Let's bring it in."

They surrounded him and took each other's hands and sat in the silence for a moment before he began to speak again. said. "Let's be safe.

Let's be healthy. Let's make some magic," he said. "This, right here, this is our time. Let's go get it. Amen."

"Amen," the girls answered back.

They held their hands up in the circle. "Family on three," their coach said. "One, two, three—"

"FAMILY!" The girls screamed in their end of game huddle. Kennedy looked at Grace as the broke up the huddle. "I told you," she said. "It's hard to beat a team three times."

Grace rolled her eyes. "Yeah, okay," she answered. "But you can't blame me for being surprised with a 6th-placed team beating a 3rd-placed team."

Kennedy made her way up the bleacher to her parents. Her mom wrapped her in a hug, and her father pulled her in as well. "Great game," he whispered to her. She gave him a little squeeze before they pulled away.

"So, it looks like you all will play on Friday at 3:00 p.m. against Labre," her mother was saying. "And you've already beat them once!"

Kennedy nodded. "Yeah, it should be interesting," she answered.

Suddenly, someone tapped her on her shoulder, and she turned around. Austin was standing there. She blinked a few times while he smiled at her.

"Hi," she finally got out and took a step down on the bleachers to hug him. "What are you doing here?"

"We had an early morning practice so we could come play pep band for the girls this morning," he explained. He looked at her parents. "Hi, Mr. and Mrs. Helland," he said.

Her mother immediately began gushing. "Oh, Austin, you don't need to call us that," she said. She looked at Kennedy. "It's so sweet you stayed to watch her play!" she said.

Kennedy looked at him. "Yeah," she answered. "Thank you."

"Of course," he smiled at her. "We have to get on the road, though. We head back up here tomorrow morning."

"Oh," she answered. "Okay, yeah. We'll probably be around for that game since you're playing—"

"You guys," he finished for her. "Yeah." He suddenly got a little awkward. "Hey, uh—could we take a picture together? To post?"

Her face immediately flushed. "Uh," she answered. Her mother chimed in with a "I'll take it!" and herded them down to the court. She eagerly took Austin's phone and began snapping photos. "There," she said, beaming. She stood there a minute until she seemed to realize she was lurking a little.

"Okay, then," she said. "Kennedy, we will see you at home."

"Thanks," she answered. Her mother made her way over to her husband and took her bag back from him. It was clear she was gushing over Austin, even from hallway across the gym.

Kennedy looked back at him. "Uh, thanks again for staying," she said.

He beamed. "Of course."

She looked over at the locker room. She needed to go change so they could go to dinner. "I should—"

"–Can I kiss you?" he blurted out.

She blinked at him. "—go shower," she finished.

"Right," now he seemed flustered. "Sorry, for holding you up," he shoved his hands into his letterman's jacket and turned to go. Her heart jumped in her chest a bit.

"Austin?" she said. He stopped and turned.

She hesitated then walked over to him and kissed him on the cheek. "I'll talk to you soon," she said. He was smiling again as he walked away, and she stood watching.

Since most of the girls were in the pep band and would be playing until 5:00 or so that afternoon during the boys' game, they were having an early morning practice. It was another pregame for them, so it wasn't too intensive. Mainly, it was going over their plays, talking about how they had already beaten St. Labre, and a lot of shooting around the six hoops in the gym.

Halfway through the day, most of them loaded up on the bus to head back to Miles City. They staked a claim to the back of the bus and spent most of the ride laughing. Kennedy was getting a lot of flack— Austin had posted the photo of them that morning with the caption "She made the Terriers walk the plank last night." It was corny and mortifying but in an endearing way. And it made her feel a little special to be shown off that way.

She played with the band and sat with her team during the game, cheering for the boys. However, when Austin did something on the court, she would clap for him too.

The Pirates easily won the game. She tried to wait for Austin after, but their band director herded them out as soon as they had finished moving all their drums to the bus. She shot him a text letting him know she was sorry but that she would see him the next day, when they both would be playing again. "We're staying at a hotel," she wrote. "So, we should be able to catch your game."

The vibrancy of a semifinal game was unmatched—the pep bands playing, the extra fans in the audience cheering one way or another—it made what they were doing feel more real and alive. They came out with high expectations and managed to keep the game within ten points for the first half, but the Braves outran them on the court the following half with a lopsided score that was slightly cringe worthy. One elimination down: one more and their season would conclude.

Allen was disappointed, but he tried to hide it from the girls. However, he had been in this same position so many times and it worried him. His teams never could overcome that early morning game that they would be playing that Saturday morning. Hence, the over twenty years since they had made it out of conference play.

"Alright," he said in the locker room after the game. "It's okay, we're fine," he wasn't sure how convincing he sounded. "We just have to take on Ekalaka in the morning."

"Two upsets in one tournament?" Grace said, and he shot her a look.

"None of that," he snapped. "None of that attitude. I keep telling you girls: this is anyone's weekend." He sighed.

"Rest your legs tonight. I want you all in bed early, no swimming or anything." They all nodded back. "We'll watch the grab dinner, watch the boys, and then head back to the hotel. Seniors, where are we eating?"

Kennedy was stuffed. Austin had wandered up the bleachers to sit with her and her teammates, and she was leaning back onto the row behind her, making small talk with him as she watched the game before her younger brother's conclude. Soon, they would all make their way down to play pep band and sit in the cheering section.

Austin's team had had their own upset that morning against the Jordan boys' team, so he would be staying with his team at their own hotel and would be playing in the same game as her team would be, just in the boys' bracket and slightly later. Both their games would take place at the college instead of the high school, and she was hopeful she'd get to see at least part of his match since he would definitely catch part of hers.

"Are you ready for tomorrow?" he asked.

She shrugged. "I hope so," she answered. "We haven't made it to divisionals in twenty years. It would be nice to break that streak." Her phone buzzed in her lap, and she glanced at it but didn't turn it over, continuing her conversation with him instead.

A few minutes later, it buzzed again and then again. Assuming it was her mother, she flipped it over, and her stomach dropped at the contact name. Adam.

She grabbed Grace and pulled her out of the gym and to the bath-rooms. "Are you okay?" her friend asked.

Kennedy shook her head and held up her phone so she could see. Grace gave a low whistle. "Well, I told you. They always come back," she answered.

Kennedy shook her head. "Why though?"

Grace shrugged. "It's just how they are hardwired. They sense you're moving on and BOOM." Kennedy leaned back, surprised at her friend's volume. "They're back."

She glanced down at her phone once again. Three messages in just a few minutes. "Hey," said the first one. "Can we talk?" said the other. "Please?" finished out the third.

"Maybe he's drunk?" she said. Grace laughed.

"Well, yeah. Duh." She looked in the mirror, fixing her hair. "That's the prime time for them to come back. Then they can blame it on the alcohol later when you reject them." She looked at her friend and squinted. "You are going to reject him, right?"

Kennedy hesitated and Grace's eyes went wide. "No, no, no, no," she said. "I'm answering for you. Forget him. Austin is the nicest human I have ever met. Go out there and talk to him more," she said. She looked at Kennedy and then shot her hand out and swiped her friend's phone.

"Hey!" Kennedy said.

"You can have it back when I know you've thought this through," Grace answered, tucking it into her bag. "Now, go talk to Austin. He's a decent human and hasn't made you cry."

Grace finally gave her phone back as they got ready for bed that night. "I hope you've come to the right decision," she said.

Kennedy sighed. "I have to say something," she answered as she pulled on her pajamas.

Grace shook her head. "I can't stop you, so just please don't do anything dumb," she answered.

Kennedy slipped out of their room and sat on the floor. "Can I call?" she texted Adam. Moments later, her phone was ringing.

"Hi," his voice was deeper than she thought she remembered it being.

"Hi," she answered.

"How are your games?" he asked.

"Fine, I guess," she answered. "We will see how it goes after tomorrow morning."

"Yeah," he answered.

They sat in silence for a few moments. Finally, she spoke. "What did you want to talk about, Adam?"

He sighed. "I saw that guy who put up the photo with you," he said. "Is he your boyfriend?"

Her temper flared a little. "What does it matter to you?" she snapped. Hot tears sprung to her eyes, and she blinked them away quickly, putting her head back against the wall. Silence answered her.

"Is that all you wanted?" she asked.

"Yeah, I guess it was," he snapped back. "Good luck this weekend." The call ended with a beep.

She leaned forward, wrapping her arms around her knees and started to cry.

After a while, she went back into the room. Grace made eye contact and sighed. "Well?" she asked. Kennedy shook her head. "I can't," she murmured, climbing into bed with her friend. "I just can't."

They were up bright and early the next morning. Kennedy felt emotionally drained and didn't know how to proceed. She felt like she was going through the morning in a fog.

They made their way over to the community college game just after 7:00 a.m. Allen wanted plenty of time for them to get ready for the game that morning.

It was only the second time they would get to play the Bulldogs. They hadn't faced each other since the opening weekend of conference play, and a lot had changed between now and this game.

Kennedy was putting her hair up in a ponytail when Grace floated over to the sinks and the mirror her co-captain was using.

"Hey," she said. "I know... I know this is hard for you. Honestly, him calling you last night knowing that you're playing still was a dick move." Kennedy felt tears come to her eyes again and she looked up at the ceiling, blinking quickly.

Grace grabbed her arm. "Kenna. Look at me." Her friend looked over at her, clearly trying to keep her face from crumpling. "You are allowed to feel your feelings. You can cry and be pissed and scream for all I care—but wait until this game is over. This could be it. This could be the end for us. Take this energy, and lay it out there on the floor, okay? Leave it all out there." She pulled her friend in for a hug. "I love you," she whispered.

Kennedy put her arms around her as well for a moment before pulling away and wiping at her eyes.

Allen's blood pressure was through the roof, he was sure of it. He can't remember the last time a game had gone to overtime at districts, but here they were.

One of the Ekalaka girls had thrown up a "Hail Mary" shot in the dwindling seconds of regulation and made it, evening the score as the clock ran out. Grace, who had fouled out, had dropped to the ground beside him and the remaining starters plus Jo, one of the freshmen, had trotted off the floor looking dejected.

"Hey," he said, pulling them to a huddle off the bench. "It's fine, we're fine. Just keep doing what we're doing." But even as he said that, he was worried. He could feel the shift in energy between his players and the Lady Bulldogs as they had gone to their benches.

He took a deep breath, trying to calm his nerves. "Okay, ladies. We're going to go back out there and run 'Reba', okay? Man-on-man defense, full court press, force them to the sidelines and box them in. If they press back, we're going to drop into our press breaker, alright?" The clock was dwindling down. "Get a drink and catch your breath," he said.

He brought them back together as the clock counted down. "This isn't over," he said. "Dig deep. Dig the deepest you've ever dug. Put in another good few minutes. We've got this."

He raised his hand up. "Magic on three," he said.

He called a timeout with ten seconds left in the second half of overtime. The girls came to him. The energy in the gym was electrifying: both crowds were on their feet stopping and chanting. He imagined this is what it felt like when a state championship was on the line. He pulled the five girls on the court into him.

"This is it, ladies," he said. "This is really it. One shot and we go to another over time. One shot and we keep this up for another week." He glanced at the score 65-63 for the Bulldogs. He took a deep breath. "Here's what we're going to do." He pulled out his whiteboard. "Normal full court press break. I know Kyle Johnstone; he's going to press the hell out of us. But," he glanced around. "Rachel, in bound it to Kenna."

Kennedy blinked at him. "Me? Why?"

He grabbed her. "Because you are getting that ball passed into you and you are driving that thing up the court like you never have before and you are going to make that layup."

"Allen," she said, forgetting where they were. "I'm not a point guard I—"

"You can and you will." He looked at her hard, still holding on to her. "I believe in you."

She bit her lips and nodded. "Okay," she whispered.

"I can't hear you," he yelled.

"OKAY," she yelled back. He dropped her arm and raised his hand into the sky. "Pirates on three," he said.

She set herself up in the corner of half court. Sure enough, the Bulldogs came out ready to press. The O'Connell girl lined herself up so she was on Ellie, who had been bringing the ball up the court. The tall junior on Kenned placed herself ready for Kennedy to go set the screen, just as they had every other time.

The ref passed the ball to Rachel, who slapped it. Kennedy sprinted forward as she had done the last few times up and down the court, but as she hit the ten-foot line, suddenly changed direction and Rachel launched the ball down the court.

The Bulldogs post player couldn't keep up, and Kennedy grabbed the ball after a bounce and put it on the floor. She dribbled solidly up the court and made eye contact with the basket. This was it—her time to shine.

As she came up the right side of the hoop and brought her leg up for a layup, releasing the ball and the buzzer going off just after, something, or rather someone, collided with her and sent her flying through the air. She heard the yells and roars from the crowd as she landed on the floor and slid into the mats on the wall. The O'Connell girl, who must have grown wings to make it up the court in that amount of time, slid into her a moment later.

It seemed like time was passing in slow motion. Either that, or Kennedy just couldn't process what was happening at full speed. The ball was bouncing on the rim still as she looked up. Then, slowly, as it something had flicked it, it fell in.

As it did that, the ref, a younger guy with dark hair, was running up to them, his had making a fist and his whistle apparently being blown, though it was nearly impossible to hear over the sound of the crowd.

"33," he said. "You're shooting one."

The girl beside her slammed her hand in the floor, and the ref raised his eyebrows at her. She pulled herself off the ground and made her way to the bench, her head hanging low as she untucked her jersey. One of the other refs was signaling a five and telling her coach to put someone in, while the third ref was telling the two teams to go to their benches.

"KENNEDY," Allan's voice rose above the chaos. He was halfway out on the court. "Are you okay?" he asked making eye contact with her.

She nodded. She couldn't speak.

The ref led her to the line. He held up a one above his head and stepped back.

Scott watched his daughter from the top of the bleachers get up and make her way to the free throw line. He remembered her in the fifth grade, the first time he told her what he told all his kids, the same saying his friend now drove into the minds of the players in the girls' basketball program: Free throws win games. For a moment, that little girl was the one lining up. Just as suddenly, she was a young woman again.

Kennedy heard her father's voice echoing around her head. "Free throws win games, free throws win games, free throws win games" over and over again as she made her way to the line. She looked up, toward the top of the bleachers where she knew he'd be. There he was—he was standing. On his feet and clapping.

She put her feet on the line, lining her right foot up with the little nail on the line that marked the middle of the hoop.

The young ref bounced her the ball, and she caught it. Even though she had just made a shot with it, it felt foreign for some reason, different. She tried to ground herself and closed her eyes and took a breath.

Suddenly she was back in the shop and Jess, a seventh grader then, was telling her she needed to pick a routine for her free throw and stick to it. "Whatever you want it to be," she said. "Just do it every time. Clear your head with it and then do it every time once you've picked it.

Kennedy took a breath and opened her eyes. The Ekalaka crowd was so loud. She closed them again and forced herself to focus and then she opened them and put the ball to the floor. Three solid bounces, readjust foot line up, eye up the hoop, bend down, then shoot with an extended follow through.

The ball rolled off her fingers and into the air.

27

The sound was so loud it was deafening to all her senses. She didn't hear the screams of her teammates as they surrounded her as she made her way off the court. She didn't feel it when they knocked her to the ground and dog piled on her. She could barely process what she was seeing in front of her, as Grace put her face in hers.

It seemed like they were all moving in slow motion. As they climbed off Kennedy, she looked toward the entry door and saw a head of silky blonde hair dart out. She knew it wasn't who she thought it was, but maybe.

Now Kris was pulling her off the floor, yelling too. She couldn't hear him either. He was gesturing to her to line up, to shake the hands of the Bulldog girls. She nodded and stumbled into the line, shaking hands. The O'Connell girl was sobbing hysterically as she made her way down the line. They shook hands and parted ways.

Her team surrounded her again crying. Suddenly, all her senses hit her at one and she fell to the ground again.

Allen couldn't breathe. More than twenty years later and here they were. "I may be having a heart attack," he muttered to Kris as he leaned over trying to catch his breath. Kris smiled at him and clapped him on the back. "Come on, old man," he said, heading toward the locker room, stopping to grab the scorer's book from Allen's wife. She was crying hysterically.

"I can't believe it," she sobbed out to her husband as he walked past. Yeah, join the club.

He came into the locker room where the girls were all crying. How many times had he walked in here to give a speech about the end of the senior's careers and thanked them? Now, he seemed to be at a loss for words.

They were advancing to divisionals.

He stood in front of his team for what seemed like an eternity. Finally, he said the only words that were coming to mind, "Holy shit."

They all laughed through their tears and clapped.

It felt like it should be ten o'clock at night, so when the girls walked out and it was daylight it was a little jarring. Kennedy wasn't sure if the bus was running on gas or their energy as it drove them across town to the high school gym for the consolation game, where they would play Northern Cheyenne at 2:00 p.m. to see which team would go to the divisional tournament in 3rd and which team in 4th.

Marty Davidson and Kathy grabbed some sandwiches from Subway for the girls on their way back to the gym. They spread out on the bleachers and ate, watching the boys' game between Terry and North Cheyenne.

Grace slid down beside Kennedy as they finished eating. "Thank you," she said simply.

Kennedy looked at her friend. "For what?"

"For playing that game like you did," her friend started to tear up. "I know that wasn't easy."

Kennedy reached over and wrapped her arm around her. "You asked me to do something, and I knew it was important, so I did it," she answered. "And honestly, I feel a bit better."

Grace sniffed beside her. "I can't believe we're going," she said. "The curse is lifted."

Kennedy laughed. "Sure feels like it," she said.

"Have you heard how Custer's boys are doing?" her friend asked.

Kennedy shook her head. "I texted him after our game and asked him to let me know how they did," she said. "Hopefully, he gets back to me before we have to get ready."

The two continued eating in silence. Kennedy checked her phone one last time before they headed out on the court to see a "We lost" message from Austin. She looked at Grace and shook her head. Her friend shrugged. "Well, someone has to lose out," she answered.

With all the pressure off, the game against Northern Cheyenne was actually fun for the girls and their coaches.

They laughed on the court and shook off their errors. The more fun they had, the easier it was to score it seemed. To the surprise of everyone, including Allen (though he would never admit it), the girls easily handed the Eagles a loss and secured a minimum of third place going into the divisional tournament in Laurel the following weekend.

Austin showed up at some point during the half-time of their game and brought with him a slew of Custer players, both girls and boys, who cheered for the town they would be playing with the next year. Their band had also come over and played with the Hysham band during the halftime.

She went and sat next to Austin for the boys' game. The male Pirates had made it to the championship, so they were able to just stay in their general area through the next few games. At one point, they walked outside and around the school for a while.

He reached out and took her hand as they walked. It was so innocent and sweet—she had never had that with Adam. As they made it to the entrance again, he stopped her.

"I have a question," he admitted.

"Okay," she said slowly.

"I don't know what to call you, when people ask me what we are," he admitted.

She hesitated. How strange that this conversation was coming up now, after her conversation with Adam the night before. "I don't know what to call you either," she admitted.

"Well," he looked at the ground and kicked at it a bit. "Can I call you my girlfriend, then?" he asked her, still looking at the ground.

She hesitated a moment, not quite knowing what to say. For a moment, she was sitting on the floor of the hotel hallway again, not sure how to respond to Adam. Austin and she hadn't spent much time together outside of their messages, but there was just something about him and his sweet smiles that pulled her in. He looked up at her, a slightly look of panic on his face. She smiled at him. "Yes," she finally said.

A grin broke out across his face. She smiled back and pulled him back toward the door.

Grace was nearly giddy when she told her on the bus. "And to think, I set you two up," she said with a toss of her hair.

Kennedy rolled her eyes. "You set us up," she answered, "but he was the one who finally reached out." She sat pondering for a moment. "I still don't know how he got my number." It felt weird asking him, especially now.

Grace shrugged. "Does it really matter?"

"No," she answered. "I guess not."

The two busses met a line of lights, sirens, and cars as they hit the county line, as was tradition. Firetrucks, the ambulances, the sheriff's vehicles, and then a slew of personal cars would lead and follow them into the town where they would gather in front of the school and bask in the glory.

The girls plastered their faces to the window in the back of the bus, laughing and giddy. Allen turned in his seat and smiled at them. He was feeling a little giddy and giggly too.

"This still feels a bit like a dream," he admitted to Kris.

Kris shook his head, "I still can't believe this is the first time you've been on the bus for this."

"Way to rub it in," Allen said with a laugh.

Kris tried to backtrack. "I mean—well, you've had so many teams that had the potential to do this."

Allen nodded. They were coming up on the exit for town now. "I know what you mean," he said. "There were a lot of times we would be ranked in that top four category and something always seemed to go wrong." He turned in his seat to look at the girls again. He was starting to tear up a little. "That makes this so much sweeter. That we've come back from the bottom and now we're here." He looked at his assistant coach once more. "Anything that happens from here on out? It's the icing on the cake. This is enough for me."

His phone started buzzing in his lap. It was his older daughter, Courtney.

"Hey, honey," he said picking it up. "I know, I can't believe it either."

They gathered for speeches from the seniors under the tall, plaster Pirates that were outside the front door of the school. Paul spoke first for the boys, thanking everyone for their support, followed by the boys' coaches. They had finished out in second for the season and would be spending the next week practicing as Class C schools staggered their tournaments for the boys' and girls' teams.

"And of course," Martinson concluded, "we have to congratulate the girls on such a tremendous season. We're excited we will be able to cheer you on next week."

The community gathered around them clapped and cheered.

Grace was up next, and she spoke out about how proud she was to be on this team and how happy she was to have "broken the twenty-year dry spell of us making it out of the conference." Everyone around chuckled before Kennedy softly added a few of her own words about how they had come together to get here. Finally, Allen cleared his throat.

He was misty-eyed again as he began to speak. "I am so damn proud of this team," he began, suddenly getting choked up. He cleared his throat again. "It's our last time doing this as the Pirates, and it was no small feat to get here today. But we are here and next week we get to really show them what we are made of in Laurel." He rubbed at his eyes and turned so he was facing his team instead of the crowd. "I am so proud of each and every one of you," he began, but seeing that many of them had started to tear up as well, he quickly backtracked. "...maybe we will finish this up on Monday." The crowd laughed again. "Thank you to everyone who came out this week to cheer us on and for tonight. We really do appreciate it. And girls?" They all looked at him now. "I'll see you back in the gym next week."

29

Kennedy was walking out of practice on Monday when her phone started buzzing, showing her a number she didn't recognize. She glanced at it and tossed it into the back seat of her car. They would leave a voicemail if they really wanted to get ahold of her.

She drove Grace home and then started back out to the ranch. This was her only free night for the week, really, and she was looking forward to spending it alone. Tuesday they were going to have a small bonding night and take a trip to see a movie in Forsyth and then Wednesday they would have their team dinner and then Thursday they would be at divisonals.

She still couldn't really believe they were going. She had spent the last six years or so tagging along with the older girls when they went to watch the teams that beat them out proceed on. It was always a little disheartening to be there with the team, but not as a team. But not this year.

She wasn't planning on stopping at the memorial spot for her sister. But she found herself pulling off to the side of the road on her way home as she saw it coming up in the distance. She walked out alone, her hands tucked in the pockets of her jacket.

"Hey," she said. There was a little bit of a breeze here. She rarely stopped, this wasn't where she would feel her sister's spirit, but it felt like she needed to today in the dusk light.

"It should have been your senior year this happened," Kennedy said into the open space, looking down at the cross. "It's not fair that you never got to be a part of this."

"I know you were at the game that day. If I told anyone, they would say it was someone else I saw leaving the gym, but I know it was you. You were there watching." Kennedy wiped at her eyes. "Thank you for coming."

The breeze picked up slightly and Kennedy laughed, wiping at her eyes more. "Thank you," she whispered.

The rest of the drive home was uneventful. She pulled her bags and phone out of the backseat and was surprised to see that the caller from earlier had left her a message.

She wandered into the house and Otis trotted up. "Hey, buddy," she said, bending down to pet him and give him a kiss on his forehead.

She walked through the house and found her father watching a show about law enforcement in the living room. "Hey," she said, curling up on the couch. He looked away from the show and nodded at her. "How was practice?"

"Good," she answered. She pulled her phone out again. "Someone called me and left a voicemail—how much do you want to bet it's spam?" she asked.

"Probably," her father answered, turning back to the TV.

She pulled up the voicemail and clicked on it, quickly hitting the speaker phone button.

"Hi, Kennedy," the voice was kind of familiar. Her father looked back over and raised his eyebrows. So, it wasn't spam.

"My name is Neil Joseph, and I am the head women's basketball coach at the University of Billings. I'm calling to talk to you a bit about the games of yours I have gotten to see the last few weeks. If you could give me a call back...."

He was still talking, but Kennedy wasn't able to comprehend anything that he was saying at that point. She looked blankly at her father who was staring back at her, disbelief on his face as well.

Neil Joseph had been to quite a few of Jess's games starting her senior year, but she had never wanted to play ball in college. She was ready to let go of that part of her life and move forward; she had thanked him profusely for everything he had done for her over the last two years, but... "It's time for me to move on," she had said in their final conversation, just weeks before he read in the paper about her death.

He pushed to have Montana athletes on his team. They were a small program in the state, but bigger than the private schools. Grace Larkin from Hysham had reached out a few times, and she was a face and name he knew from her coming to his camps, but he had never felt like she could add to the team in the way he wanted her to.

The younger of the Helland girls was not a name he had been familiar with a few months ago, and he knew this was a gamble. She hadn't played her junior season of the sport—there were hardly any stats for her prior to this year. But after his junior captain, Samantha, had seen her play while she was watching some relatives' games, he had started digging.

She was solid on the volleyball court, so he knew she had some athletic ability. And looking back at her stats for the season, it was clear she had talent. "Just imagine if she hadn't gone through what she did, if she had played the last season," he lamented to his assistant coach in his office.

"Neil, are you seriously considering this?" his assistant coach had asked.

Neil had shot him a look. "These are promising numbers," he answered.

"She didn't even play last year!" he exclaimed. "For all we know, they could be a fluke."

Neil had leaned back in his chair. "Or not," he answered.

Neil had made the trek down to the Hysham gym a few weeks later with Samantha. Allen Davidson had come up and shook his hand before sitting down and chatting for a bit.

"I'm a little surprised you're here for Kennedy," he admitted. "She didn't play last year. To be honest I'm still a little shocked she's out on the court. She was adamant that she never would play again."

Neil had looked across the gym, finding her perched next to her family. "But she did go out," he said. "I don't know if I would be able to do that after going through what she went through."

Allen had been quiet for a moment. "That's fair," he said, finally. "What do you want to know about her?"

The two had talked for a while before Samantha and Neil left. She looked on him on the way back to the car in the parking lot. "Well?" she asked.

"Yeah," he said. "I see it too."

There were some loose ends that needed to be tied up first with girls he had already been talking to for the next year. But now that that had all been handled, there was a spot for her. Now to convince her to take it.

Her hands were shaking. She had listened to the voicemail another four times and still hadn't gotten the courage to call him back. She glanced at the clock. It had been nearly two hours since he called. She really needed to do it now.

She sighed and opened her phone. She knew what she should say—"No." She had never wanted to play college ball. So, why was she so nervous?

She had memorized the number the last time she listened to his voicemail. Now, she slowly dialed it back.

It rang once. Halfway through the second ring, he answered. "This is Neil," he said.

She took a breath. "Coach Joseph," she said. "Hi, it's Kennedy Helland returning your call."

She made a beeline for her coach's room at lunch. He was sitting at his desk grading papers when she came in.

He looked up and then looked back down. "Hi, Kennedy," he said.

"Were you just not going to tell me about all of this?" she asked.

He sighed. "I'm sorry," he said, setting his materials aside. He had spoken to the college coach the night before as well and knew why she was upset. He gestured to the chair at the front of the room. "Let's talk about it."

"I don't want to talk about it," she answered, though she did sit down with her bag. "What the hell am I supposed to say to Grace?" she asked.

He raised his eyebrows. "What did you say to Neil?"

She looked at the floor. The plan was to tell him no. "I told him I would get back to him after tournaments," she admitted.

"But you're going to say 'Yes,'" he said.

She looked up at him and sighed. "I don't know."

He looked at the young woman that he had known since she was born. The first time he met her, he never would have predicted that they would be having this conversation.

"Kenna," he began, then he stopped. "Kennedy, I have known you since pretty much day one. I know how you work and how you think. You have a hard time making up your mind and you like to ask those around you how you should make decisions. Don't do that this time." She covered her face, but he kept going. "You look to others for advice and there is nothing wrong with that. But this needs to be a decision that you make for yourself by yourself. I can't answer it for you, but you also can't let others—like Grace—sway your opinion. When's the last time you did that?"

She looked at him now. She was crying. "I don't know," she admitted.

"Yes, you do," he answered. He stood up and pulled his jacket off his chair. "You were the one who finally decided to go out for basketball. That decision came from you and look where you are now. How many people have college coaches looking at them after essentially one season?" He opened his mouth again to say, "You have someone looking out for you," but stopped himself before it came out. He paused instead and collected himself as he went to leave. Just before stepping out the door, he said one final thing to her: "Whatever you decide is going to be the right decision for you. And I can tell you've already made up your mind, even if you don't want to admit it. But let this be your decision and no one else's."

He pulled the door shut behind him as he left the room. She sat alone in there until the bell rang.

Soon, they were all gathered around the table at Allen's once again, laughing and eating. Kennedy was trying to be present, but she was struggling to stay a part of the conversation. She had spent her lunch that day filling out an application for admittance to the University of Billings. "It's just good to have options," she told herself as she went through the boxes. "This doesn't mean anything."

Grace passed her the pasta and she smiled at her friend. She was going to lose it when she told her, even if she said no. She already knew that.

When they pulled into the driveway, Kris turned off the pickup and looked at her. "Well?" he asked.

She had looked out the window, not sure if it was wrong of her to just get out or not.

"Kennedy." She turned and looked at him now.

"Yes?" she asked.

"I know Neil Joseph called you earlier this week. What did you say?"

She didn't answer and looked back out the window. "I told him I'd reach back out after tournaments," she said finally.

Kris sighed. "Kennedy, you can't not do this."

"You think I don't know that?" she snapped, turning to look at him. He recoiled slightly and she tried to soften her voice for this next part. "It's just... it's hard, okay?" she said.

Kris nodded at her. "Okay," he answered. "Well, I'm here for you if you do want to talk about it."

Now she felt like she could open the door. "I'll drive myself in the morning since I have to go to class first," she said. "Thanks for the ride."

They were matched with the second-place team from their neighboring conference for the opening game of the tournament. It was the Bridger Scouts, a team they had not gotten a chance to see yet that season.

There were a few key players based on the information that Allen had been able to pick up from other coaches, and he spent a long time talking to the girls about who they would be guarding on the way up to Laurel.

Now, in the locker room, he looked over them again nodding slowly.

"I'll be honest," he finally said. "I didn't think we would be here today. I kind of thought we would all be driving up in our separate vehicles and watching from the stands."

He extended his arms. "But here we are."

He had finally stopped crying over the fact that they had advanced, that they had done it, twenty years later. Now, however, they were in uncharted waters and he wasn't sure how to guide them.

"Whatever happens this game, hell, this weekend," he made eye contact with each of them before continuing on. "I'm proud of you all. Damn proud. Everything from here on out? It's icing on the cake. It's those rainbow sprinkles that get everywhere for absolutely no reason. It's the cherry. So," he nodded again, "get out there and have fun. The ball in in our court now."

He watched the final seconds of the clock tick down and let out the air he had been holding in his chest for what seemed like the entire quarter. He looked at Kris who was smiling and shaking his head. The screams behind his bench were deafening.

What kind of coach was he, not believing his team could do this?

He blindly followed them through the hand-shaking line at the end of the game. The Scouts' coach, much younger than he was, shook his head at his colleague as they shook hands. "What's you secret to turning a season around like that?"

Allen didn't have an answer. "Magic," he finally said. For all he knew, it could be.

They stayed to watch the following games on the other side of the bracket. They already knew that they would be facing Reed Point-Rapelje again the next day, but Allen was curious to see how the other games went. St. Labre and Absarokee won their games, with the 6C Absarokee team winning over their 4C counterpart in an upset.

"I can't believe Wibaux lost," Grace lamented.

Kennedy looked at her friend as they walked to the bus that night. "Anything can happen at tournaments," she answered. "Look at us."

They continued on in silence and were nearly to their ride when Grace spoke again, saying something both of them had been thinking—something the entire team had been thinking but no one had said out loud yet, for fear they would jinx it: "If we win tomorrow—" she began.

Kennedy cut her off. "—we go to state," she concluded.

Grace shook her head. "How the hell did we get here?" she asked.

Kennedy shrugged. "Magic," she answered.

Tournament games were always close, and the semifinal on Thursday evening was no exception. Except, based on the beginning of the season, it should have been.

Kennedy had trotted over to the Renegades' head coach after hearing her name called out and went to shake his hand. Suddenly, it was like they were back in Lavina, that first game of the weekend.

"Good luck," he had said, "and welcome back."

This time, though, there was something different about it when he shook her hand. She couldn't quite place it though, as he gripped her for a moment longer than she felt he should. "We meet again," he said, looking at her hard. "Good luck."

She remembered the bundle of nerves she had carried onto the court that day. How little and how much changed in just two and a half months.

"We do," she answered. "Good luck to you too."

Like she had done in December, she fist bumped each of the refs on the way to her team's huddle. Now, however, something inside of her seemed to awaken. It was strange, how different she felt now, looking at the faces of her teammates and peers. There was a fire in her that was telling her that now was the time to make it count. "Let's do this," she said, breaking up their chants. "Pirates on three."

It was down to the last few moments. They were down by two and had no timeouts left. Grace had brought the ball up the court, snaking around and avoiding being fouled, but she passed the ball to Ellie, who caught it. She was open.

She looked to pass it to Kennedy, but the senior shook her head. Allen's stomach was somewhere under the floor. Ellie was not the best at converting. "PASS IT IN," he bellowed. "ELLIE, PASS IT TO KENNEDY."

The sophomore looked to pass again, and Kennedy shook her head. "Shoot!" she called out.

Allen looked at the clock. He swore that time had slowed down. 1.2 seconds. 1.1 seconds. He looked back at Ellie, his clipboard in a death grip. She shot.

Kennedy yelled, "Shoot!" again. Ellie looked terrified but she made eye contact with the basket and launched it.

It bounced once as the timer ran out, the motion around her stopped. Her opponent stopped pushing her back in a box out and they both turned and watched. It hit the backboard next, then the front of the hoop before bouncing once to the side and then back.

It seemed to suspend itself on the edge of the hoop for a moment. She felt the girl beside her tense up.

Grace was just past half court, watching it all unfold in front of her. The ball seemed to be defying gravity. She was silently watching, yet something inside of her was screaming "JUST FALL IN."

Allen's arms had gone straight up into the air with the clipboard in hand. Kris was half raised from the bench. The team on the bench had a death grip on each other in the unknown.

The ball fell through the hoop.

Pandemonium was the word for what happened next. The Renegade coach was yelling that she had shot after the buzzer. Kris had his hand on Allen's shoulder in a death grip. Grace was still at half court; she couldn't quite bring herself to move. Kennedy was still staring at the basket while her opponent pulled her jersey out of her shorts and brought it to her face. Both sides of the court were yelling: the Pirate fans were screaming it was fair and the Renegade fans were shrieking back that it wasn't.

The refs were huddled in the middle of the court, talking.

Allen finally found his voice. "Girls, come here," he cried out hoarsely. "Come here."

They gathered around him on the court, his five starters. He started talking, though he wasn't even sure what was coming out of his mouth. He looked at each of them in a daze, finally landing on the sophomore who had shot.

She looked like she may cry. "I shot too late," she whispered.

"No." He grabbed her shoulder hard. "No, you did exactly what you needed to, that was a good shot." Still, he found his eyes being drawn to center court where the refs were still conversing.

He looked back at his team, trying to keep his breathing even. Whatever was taking that long was not a good sign. Even the crowd was resigned and sitting in silence, waiting. He turned and looked at his wife and noticed his daughters sitting behind her for the first time; they were holding hands, staring intently at the refs.

The whistle brought him out of it.

He looked at the man in the center of the court who raised his hands into the air above his head.

Basket good.

Kennedy looked at her best friend and made eye contact. Neither one seemed to be able to move for a moment even knowing what they knew. The rest of the team mauled Ellie, screaming and pulling her in. But the two seniors found each other on the court, finally. Their screams echoed around the gym with their teammates and their friends and family in the stands.

Somehow, they made it into the line to shake hands with the Reed Point-Rapelje team, who seemed to be in disbelief. Quite a few of them were crying as they made their way down the line.

Their coach stopped Kennedy again at the end. "Good luck at State," he said.

She had smiled back at him. She was crying now too. "Thank you," she said.

Her mother pulled her in for a hug and so did her father. A real hug, even. Not his normal side hug.

She was still on an adrenaline high, and nothing they were saying was really making sense to her right now, though. She was smiling at them and laughing and crying at the same time. Hunter was calling and she was on the phone with him, not knowing how to process what he was saying either.

And then suddenly Austin was there. Her heart was thumping as she pulled him in for a hug before realizing what she was doing and quickly stepping back. Her eyes were tearing up again, and she rubbed at them and sniffed. "You made it," she said. He smiled at her. "I wouldn't miss this, that was amazing. You were amazing."

She laughed again and pulled him in for another hug, giggling and sniffing. "I like hearing that," she thought to herself.

30

Kennedy clipped the small microphone to her uniform jersey at practice on Wednesday. The young blonde woman was smiling at her when she looked up.

"That looks perfect, Kennedy," she said. "Now, I'm just going to ask you a few questions about how we got here and where you're going next."

Kennedy nodded. "Okay," she said. It was barely a whisper.

The reporter had first reached out to Allen on Saturday night after they lost the championship to St. Labre. The girls had been on the bus home, uncertain about what was to come. He had told her to reach out to him again after their game on Monday.

They had finished in second, which meant they had a ticket to state. However, thanks to the challenge game rule, they didn't actually have it punched yet.

Wibaux had beaten Reed Point-Rapelje in the consolation game, and they had jumped at the chance to play again against the Pirates.

The girls had found themselves back in the Laurel locker room on Monday evening, preparing to play again.

Their nerves were through the roof as they gathered together and Allen talked. Kennedy had processed maybe a tenth of everything that came out of his mouth and finally he seemed to realize they were all lost in their thoughts.

"Hey," he said sharply. They had all turned to look at him. "You are all acting like you lost already. You haven't lost. I don't know what this is," he extended his arms out to all of them, "but knock it off. We haven't even stepped on the court yet. And if we are going to win this—I need you all to believe we are going to win this."

Kennedy knew he was right. But why was it so hard to believe him?

No one had said anything, and suddenly his temper flared. "No," he said. "Nope." They all blinked at him. "No. You all aren't lying down and letting them walk all over you. Are they older, more experienced? Sure. Have they been playing together since they were in elementary? Yes. But that doesn't mean anything. Because I know they do not have the heart that you all have. I cannot even explain everything that has happened to this team in the last month, but it's something bigger than us. Do you want to look back on this game in five years and think 'Oh, well, I could have tried harder?' or "What if?'" Kennedy made eye contact with her coach here. She was haunted by "What if?"s enough already. "No, you don't want that," he said. "So, let's leave whatever this," he gestured wildly at the group again, "and leave it in here. And leave everything out on the court, okay?"

He was looking at Kennedy now. She nodded. "Okay," she had said.

It still felt like magic when they won; none of them seemed to be able to believe it when they came off the court, but they just kept doing it. The disbelief of an underdog doing so well was a story that the media liked, according to Hunter, when Kennedy had called to tell him they were running a piece, and it was now their turn to talk about it.

The blonde reporter was named Abigail. She was beautiful and dressed professionally, minus her shoes. She was wearing sneakers, something Kennedy found comical. She found herself fixated on her Nikes.

"I like your shoes," she said. The reporter flashed her a white smile. "Thanks," she answered. "You have to pick comfort over style when you're on your feet all day."

"Are you ready?" she asked.

Kennedy glanced behind her. The team was running drills. Grace and Allen had rejoined them after they finished talking to her. She was on her own. She looked at the reporter. "Sure," she said.

"And now," the sports anchor was saying on the screen, "we go to Hysham, where it seems like, according to them, magic is happening."

Grace giggled as they showed the larger-than-life Pirate statues at the front of the school and her voice began to fill the TV speakers. "I don't really know how we got here," the co-captain said. "But here we are."

Abigail, the female reporter, had her voice come on next. "The town of Hysham is the county seat of Treasure County and the home of the only school in the district: Hysham Public Schools. With an enrollment of just under seventy from kindergarten to twelfth grade, the small town is close knit and homey. A small school, even for Class C, the town has struggled to send its girls' basketball team out of conference play for more than two decades." The B-roll of the segment showed the school, some of the classrooms, and finally the girls practicing the day before. Abigail's face suddenly filled the screen again. "Until now, that is."

Allen was there now. "I don't know," he said. "Statistically, we shouldn't be getting on that bus on Wednesday afternoon to head to Missoula, but we are."

"Yes," Abigail said. "The more than twenty-year dry spell has ended, and the Lady Pirates made it to divisionals... but that wasn't the end of that. They are now, for the first time since the 1980s, state bound."

Kennedy was on the screen now. "We kind of came up with this phrase," she said, laughing a little, "magic is happening... I guess you could say our season, especially the last few weeks, has been kind of like magic."

"You could say that," Abigail answered in a voice-over as some footage from the divisional tournament rolled. "A sixth-place team in the conference that has somehow turned everything around and is now one of eight teams remaining in the state for Class C girls basketball."

More footage from the weekend before. Back to Grace. "We just... something clicked for us," she said. "We can't really explain it. And now it's like... the pressure is off now and we are just having fun."

"I've been coaching here since I started teaching here," Allen said. "And honestly, this is the last year of us being the Pirates. We don't have the numbers to sustain a program in the future, so this is it. We're co-oping with Custer next year. I don't know if that's what pushed us to this success or what or if there is something else out there that's on our side, but this is probably the most fun I've had coaching in these last two decades." He laughed. "Maybe don't air that, I coached my daughters," he said.

Now a shot of the lobby filled the screen, and Kennedy's heart hurt a little. "This season highlights the fun, but it comes on the coattails of tragedy."

Jessica Helland's face filled the screen next, in the hotel room the team was gathered in. Abigail continued on; her voice was now somber. "Two years ago, the Pirates were on a roll and preparing for a post-season run. One night, though, that all came to a crashing halt."

"Waking up to a phone call like that," Allen was barely holding it together on the screen. "It's life-altering. She was my daughter's best friend. I had to take on a role of coach and dad that week that I never would wish on anyone else," he said, shaking his head. "How do you come back from that? How do you play in the gym where you said 'goodbye' to your teammate just days before?"

Suddenly, old footage of Jess was on the screen and they all gasped. A picture of her clapping hands with Kennedy came on the screen to finish out the reel. "In the early mornings of January 27, 2013, after coming home from a basketball game, Jessica Helland was in an auto accident on the two-lane road leaving her parents' house. It shattered a team and left a younger sister and teammate who didn't know how to move forward."

"You didn't play last year," Abigail said from off screen. It was a clear statement despite her not being on the mic.

Kennedy was on the screen now. She shook her head now. "I didn't think I would ever play again," she said. "It just hurt too much."

"What changed?" The reporter asked off camera still.

Kennedy had looked away, tears coming to her eyes. "I don't know," she answered. "I honestly do not know what made me come through those doors this year."

Kris was on the screen now. "She thought we didn't know that she had spent the last two years shooting in the shop," he said with a laugh. "We all knew."

"I'm still surprised she's out here," Grace said with a laugh as well. "She was adamant that she would not pick up a ball again, but here we are."

"She was late that first day," Allen said. "I gave her one pass and told her she had better be there on time the next day." Abigail laughed in the background.

"You really don't know what made you go out again?"

"No," Kennedy said, more photos of her and her siblings filling the screen. "Kris coaching, I think was part of it—he told me it helped him feel connected to her again, and I was missing that connection."

A shot of Jessica's memorial now. "Not knowing where she was going that night... it leaves so many unanswered questions. I just didn't want this and basketball to be another one of those for me," Kennedy's voice said in a voice over. "I felt like I needed to finish what we started."

"Did you expect this season to go this way?" Abigail asked.

Kennedy shook her head, back on screen again. "Are you kidding?" she laughed. "No, never. I'm glad I came out, though," she said. "I wish she was here with me, but I think she is in her own way."

Grace chimed in now as more footage of them celebrating on Monday night with their win over Wibaux playing. "I don't think any of us really expected to have this magical season that we are having," she explained. "And maybe that's why we have found this success. Because we just... we just accepted what happens happens and that's helped us get here."

Allen filled the screen once more. "I can't explain it," he said. "I really can't. But there's something about this group of girls. It's really been something."

"Are you ready for it to be over?" Abigail asked.

Grace came on first. She laughed. "I mean, can you ever be truly ready for it to be over?" she answered. Another shot of her. "I'm lucky, I get to play next year at Yellowstone."

Another shot of Kennedy. "And what about you?" she asked Kennedy. "What are your plans after this season?"

Kennedy gave a small smile. "I guess I'm not quite as ready to hang up my shoes yet after all," she answered. "I'll be playing in Billings next year as well, but for the Rimrockers."

Abigail was walking in front of the school now in the last clips. "The Pirates are on their way to Missoula now," she was saying. "And we look forward to seeing what magic they have left up their sleeves this season. Back to you, Steve."

The anchor's face was smiling. "A little extra magic for those Pirates, this weekend," he said. Now, as Kennedy Helland and Grace Larkin mentioned, they have both signed to continue to play at the collegiate level here in the Magic City with Grace heading to Yellowstone College to become a Moose and Kennedy, surprisingly, heading to the University of Billings after taking her junior year off from the game." He looked over at the anchors. "Crazy, and maybe a little bit of magic indeed, right?"

Grace had taken the news better than Kennedy expected when she told her on Sunday about her campus visit she was going on the next day, quickly thrown together after she had called the college coach back after they won their first game on Thursday. "I mean," she said. "You have to do what you have to do." She was clearly upset and trying to hide her tears, but she had put on a brave face for Kennedy. "Maybe we will get to guard each other someday," she said, wagging her eye brows at her friend.

She hesitated slightly. "I am glad you'll be around if it ends up working out," she said. "You'll just be up the road from me instead of across the state."

Growing pains came in every friendship, yet the two were trying to work through theirs. That meant supporting each other even when the other one hurt. They had hugged for a long time after that, and a few days later, as Kennedy signed her papers declaring where she would be going, finally, Grace and she had taken a photo in their respective school's swag and posted it to their respective social media accounts. This time, Kennedy had no issue captioning it.

"Basketball & Besties" she wrote.

They had been paraded out of town again, and the pep rally had tunneled them out. Their teachers had cheered them on, as had the community as they boarded the bus and headed out.

Ten hours later, they made it to their hotel and got checked in for the night. They had stopped and practiced lightly in Bozeman that afternoon, shooting around for a bit to loosen up and run through plays.

They went to dinner together, an Italian place that Hunter had recommended to Kris from his many travels through the area. Kennedy found herself looking around the table and thinking about the piece that had aired that night. It was a little crazy how they had gotten here, how they had found themselves at the state tournament that weekend. It was a bit like magic.

"Pirates on three," Allen said at the end of the first game. "One, two, three—"

"—Pirates," they chanted back.

They had easily overcome the first-place team from the western division. Even with it being the boy's divisional weekend as well, the fans had come out in full force.

His daughters were in the stands again, as was Hunter Helland. He was sitting next to his older child, Courtney. The two of them dated off and on throughout high school and most major holidays in college, but it seemed like this time they had both accepted that it was time to move on, at least based on a conversation he had had with Courtney a few weeks prior.

"Dad," she had said. "I just... I can't with him anymore. I can't keep doing the same thing and hoping it will change this time."

"That's very mature, honey," he had said. He was working on drawing out a new play and was a bit removed from the conversation.

"Honestly," she said, "we hold each other back and we both know it."

"Mhmmmm," he answered.

"Dad, are you even listening to me?" she said.

"Sure am," he absentmindedly answered.

"Coach."

That got his attention. "Yes?"

She sighed. "How much longer are you going to do this?"

"Do what?" he answered. It was the week before tournaments: he had things to do.

"This," he could feel her exasperation through the phone. "Coach."

He sat in silence for a moment. "I don't know," he finally admitted.

Now, seeing his kids in the stands—no longer the little girls he helped raise, but beautiful, strong women... the conversation echoed in his mind.

When would their kids be out on the court? When would they bring new men home for him to meet and size up? When would his games start colliding in the moments he never wanted to miss of theirs?

They had played the latest game in the evening and got to rest their legs for nearly a full twenty-four hours the next day. They were playing Scobey, a powerhouse in the northeastern division.

They got to the U's gym early to watch the game before theirs. Either they would take on the winner of the St. Labre-Roy-Winifred game or the winner of the loser out Manhattan Christian-Westby-Grenora game to go to the consolation game on Saturday. It was a bit surreal to be there after Kennedy had decided to attend the school in Billings instead. It was another "What if?" but a less scary one. One that she wasn't sure she would regret.

The game started with Scobey going on a few runs and driving up the score quickly, taking a nearly twenty-point lead. Kennedy felt as if something was off, but she couldn't quite place what it was.

The third quarter, the lead of the Spartans started dwindling as Grace suddenly got hot again after an ass-chewing from Allen on the bench from a few turnovers she shouldn't have had. She came off the bench with a fire again and ran headfirst into the game. Kennedy came out as her friend subbed in for her along with Maddy in for Rachel. As she passed her friend, though, Kennedy suddenly felt a sense of dread. Something didn't feel right.

She sat down on the padded chairs. She could see her parents across the gym, sitting next to Grace's parents. They were all smiling and chatting. Why was she the only one who could feel something was wrong.

"Allen?" she said as he was yelling something to Grace as she brought the ball up the court and didn't acknowledge her.

"Coach!" there was suddenly a sense of panic in her. He waved at her. "Not now, Kennedy," he said.

"Coach!" she repeated. He looked at her now as Grace drove in.

The scream echoed across the gym.

Allen watched the color drain from the senior's face, and he whipped around. "Can I go out?" he asked the ref beside him. The young woman supervising the game held a hand out to him, clearly indicating "wait."

Two of the refs were standing around Grace, who was writhing on the floor in pain, sobbing hysterically and holding her knee to her chest. One waved at Allen and immediately he was on the court.

His heart was pounding in his chest. "Grace?" he murmured as he got to her. "Grace what's wrong?" she kept crying in response.

"Grace," he said again. "Grace, I need you to talk to me, okay?"

"My knee," she got out finally. The athletic trainer was suddenly on the floor next to Allen. "Coach, can you move over, please?" She asked as she bent over his player.

Allen stood up and ran his fingers through his hair and looked out to the crowd. Her father was standing up, looking at his daughter on the floor. Allen looked at the trainer. He wasn't sure what to do. "Should I get her dad?" he asked.

The trainer didn't answer him. Class C didn't have trainers at their game, and he wasn't really sure how to interact with this person. He looked back out at the crowd and waved. Immediately, his senior's dad was on his way down the bleachers. Kris was out on the court with him now. "Let me help," he murmured. "Go talk to the girls."

The ref was still standing next to his bench when he got back. "Coach, we will need a sub," she said. Grace had been helped to her feet by the trainer and Kris, and there was light clapping echoing around the arena.

He blinked at her. "Right," he said. He was numb.

"Uh," he looked at Kennedy. She was staring at her best friend, still white. "Uh, Jo," he said to the freshman. "Go in. Ellie, you're point."

He wasn't exactly surprised they lost. It took a long time for Kris to come back out of the area they had taken Grace to. When Allen looked at him, he felt a moment of hope until he saw his assistant coach's face. He didn't say anything, just shook his head and sat down.

The girls shook the hands of their opponents, who were screaming on their own. Allen quickly shuffled off, looking for his starting point as Kris ushered the other girls to the locker room.

He found Grace and her father in the university's training room. The athletic trainer had strapped her leg into the thick brace that would define her for the next few months.

Her father looked at Allen and came over before he could get to Grace.

"It's—" he began, but Allen shook his head. He already knew.

"Can I talk to her for a bit?" Allen asked. Her dad nodded.

"I need to go call her mom and update my wife," he said. He looked back at his daughter. "Honey?" She didn't respond. "I'll be back in a few."

Allen went and sat next to Grace. Her tears had dried to her face. She was staring at the ceiling.

"Did we win?" she asked. He leaned forward on his elbows and looked at the floor before turning to look at her.

"No," he answered.

Her face crumpled again and she looked away.

"Grace," he began, but she stopped him.

"Please, don't," she gasped out.

He sat another moment and leaned back in his chair. They sat in silence for a moment before he spoke again.

"I won't say too much," he said. She sat in silence, so he continued on. "I knew that sometime this weekend, we would have this conversation. I'm sorry it has to be now, before the very end.

Do you remember what I said you when we were eating, after our first game?" She didn't respond. "Well, I do. I told you that I had high expectations for you. That I wasn't going to hold back and you needed to step up and handle it or step aside for the betterment of this team." He could tell she was crying still, but she was also listening.

"You did it. You stepped up when we—when I—needed you to the most. I know it wasn't easy, you know. And I knew there were a lot of days that you didn't want to do what I asked, but you did."

He was crying now. "I am so excited to see you continue to grow on the court in the years to come. Your coaches are getting a hell of a young woman and player, but this is just the beginning of all the memories that are yet to come."

He paused to take a shaky breath and she went to speak, but he held his hand up. "Let me finish." She fell quiet again.

"Thank you for the last four years and for always giving it your best," he said. "I am so thankful and proud of you and everything that you have done as a Pirate. It's been magic to see you learn and grow."

She cut him off now. "I can't stay and watch," she sobbed. "I can't. It's going to hurt too much."

He nodded a bit. "The next day is going to be hard—I know that and you know that. But I hope you and your energy shows up over the next day, because they are going to need it, even if you aren't on the court." He looked at her. "That's what it means to be part of a team. Plus," he paused here and she turned toward him slightly, tears running down her face, "there's someone you owe a bit to stay out even when it's hard."

He fell silent. She didn't try to speak again. They sat in silence until her father came back. Allen stood up and shook his hand. "You've raised a hell of a woman," he said. He looked at Grace. "I'll come find you when we're ready to leave," he said.

She nodded weakly. "Okay," she whispered.

Kris wasn't saying anything while they waited. Finally, Allen came in. Kennedy waited for Grace to bounce in too, but nothing.

She looked at her head coach and he pulled his lips into a thin line. She felt her heart break a little.

"No," she whispered.

Allen sat down heavily on the bench. "Girls," he said. "I have some news...."

Grace was already on the bus when the rest of them go on. Kennedy rushed back to her friend and put her arms around her.

"I'm so sorry," she whispered.

"Me too," answered Kennedy.

The other came up and hugged her as well, one-by-one. As they found their seats, they started off to the hotel, sitting in silence.

She looked down at her phone. Jack had lost out of divisionals that afternoon in an upset. He was going to start the drive to Missoula with her grandparents that night. They were hoping to make it there by morning.

She left him know she loved him, and he told her he loved her too. She turned her phone over as it went off again. She flipped it over and glanced.

"Grabbing Austin now," it said.

"You're grabbing Austin?" she typed back. "How did you even get his number?"

"I've had it all summer," he typed back a few moments later. "From some scrimmages we did in Custer."

The little typing bubbles remerged. "Who do you think gave him your number?" he asked.

Kennedy stared at it for a little while before locking her phone again.

She knocked on Kris's door later that night. Her brother came and opened it, and she wandered in. Allen had Marty staying with him this trip, so they were in their own room.

She went and flopped down on the second bed that he clearly wasn't using.

"Hi," he said.

"Hi," she answered, rolling over. "Can we talk now?"

He sat on his own bed. "It seems we already are," he said.

"Kris," she began, "do you think everything happens for a reason?"

He sat for a moment, not sure how to proceed. Finally, he spoke. "What do you mean, a reason?"

"Like, Grace tearing her ACL right now... do you think that is something that had to happen?"

Kris nodded for a moment, chewing on his lip. "I think we all have choices to make and things to do and we control ourselves and those choices," he answered.

"So, you don't believe in fate?" she asked.

"You're getting very philosophical tonight," he said.

She sighed. "I'm sorry. I'm just trying to process this," she answered.

"We don't always get to understand what has happened to us, Kenna," he said.

She sat in silence for a moment. "But why not?" she asked.

"Character development?" he said with a chuckle, but she didn't laugh. Now it was his turn to sigh.

"I don't think we get to know why things happen to us that change us," he said. "I don't know why we sometimes face things that are difficult or hard to understand. None of us do; but I do believe that good things happen to good people and that we grow from the things that challenge us."

"You know what my next question is going to be," she said.

"Why did she get in the pickup that night," he said. He got up and went to sit next to Kennedy instead. "I ask myself that every day. But I can never get an answer. For a while I tried to find it at the bottom of a bottle; then I would scream it at God. Now, I ask myself that question every time I drive by that curve in the road."

"It would just be so much easier if we—" she began but Kris cut her off.

"—but we don't." He said sharply. She looked at him and he composed himself for a moment. "It would be easier," he conceded, "but we are never going to know. But do you know what we do know?" he asked.

"What?" she answered.

His voice was softer now. "We know how much she loved us and how much we love her. We know she loved to dance and to be in the city. We know we had eighteen wonderful years with her." He looked hard at his sister now. "And we know that Grace is going to come out the other side of this. And we know that she will be okay. There was nothing we could have done to stop that play from happening, just as there was nothing we could have done to stop the truck from rolling two years ago. We weren't there.

"We never know when our time is up. We aren't given a signal or a sign. But we do know when we need to move forward and move on.

And we look back and see this tremendous growth, even if we don't know it at first."

He nodded at his door. "You better get to bed," he said. "Big day tomorrow."

She pushed herself out of his bed and moved toward the door. Her hand was on the handle when she turned back. "Kris?" she asked.

"Yeah?" he answered.

"Do you feel her, though?" she was looking at him now.

He smiled at her. "Of course, I do," he answered. "Don't you?"

They were playing Westby-Grenora the next morning. It was odd for Kennedy to go to the captain's meeting by herself, but she shook the hands of the other two girls.

She felt the emptiness of the bench with Grace not next to her that morning, even though her friend was just a few feet away, clapping along with the girls. Kennedy was brought to her feet as her name was called out. Now she was in motion.

Allen watched as Ellie brought the ball up the court one more time as the time dwindled down. They were winning regardless now and would play in the consolation that afternoon for hardware.

He looked at Kris and sighed. "Well, guess our number is up now," he said as the buzzer went off.

"One more this season," answered his assistant.

He looked at his coach sadly. "Yeah," he answered. "One more this season."

One more in his career.

31

He had told his wife, Marty, the night before that this was it. She had gone into shock. "What do you mean, this is it?" she asked him.

"We all reach our time, Mar," he answered from the bed in the hotel room. She was talking to him from the bathroom where she had just gotten out of the shower. "This is mine."

"Why?" she asked. She was in disbelief.

"The co-op is a fresh start," he answered. "They deserve a fresh coaching staff and new beginnings on the court. And it's a fresh start for us too."

His wife had laughed. "A fresh start for us?" she said. "What does that mean?"

He sighed. "It means our daughters have grown up and we're empty nesters, but it sure doesn't feel like it. It's time we focus on us and our future together and we get to explore and travel a bit before our babies start having babies."

She looked at him hard now. "You're serious," she said.

He nodded. "I am."

"Have you told them yet? The girls?"

"No," he answered, as she crawled into bed next to him. "I'm waiting for the right time for that."

The right time came before their final game the next day. He asked them to be ready early, so he could tell them before they played. He had gone back and forth about telling them and when, but something said he needed to do it now. He was standing in front of them when it seemed to sink in, and he confessed to them what he was planning.

There was a lot of disbelief at first. Then anger. He fielded questions left and right. But finally, Kennedy stepped up and spoke. "Thank you, Coach," she said. She looked at her teammates and then sat down.

Slowly, the mood changed. One-by-one, they stood and spoke. "Thank you, Coach" (with a couple of German phrases thrown in by the exchange students). He laughed until his laughter turned into tears.

They talked for a while in the locker room about it all. About the team they were going to face. About the teams they had faced. About the season as a whole. Everything spilled out, at the cusp of the last game and the final buzzer.

Finally, their coaches went out and left the girls alone. Normally now they would dance and laugh, but the mood was different today.

"I can't believe this is it," Ellie said. Kennedy smiled at her.

"For now," she answered. "You have two more years," she said.

"Yeah," answered Ellie. "But there are a lot of endings right now. This is your last game..." she looked at Grace and smiled sadly. "...and Grace's too. And Coach's. And our last one as Pirates." She looked around the room. "There's a lot of endings happening today."

Kennedy looked at Grace, who smiled softly and reached out and took her friend's hand. Kennedy looked out over her teammates.

"There are a lot of endings," she said, "but there are a lot of beginnings right now too. New beginnings for Grace and me, new beginnings for Coach, new beginnings for you all. We shouldn't have to be sad at every ending, because at the end there is always a new start." She squeezed her friend's hand hard. "We've all been playing games for people all season," she said. "Grace was playing for her future, you all were playing for that last run of being Pirates, I was playing for Jess...." She took a shaky breath. "But today, let's not do that. Let's not play for someone else. Let's just play for ourselves."

At a consolation and championship game, it was tradition for all the members of a team to be announced and walk out and shake their opponents' hands. It started with the coaches, then the managers, if there were any. Then the nonstarters, starting with the youngest and working their way up. Then, finally, the starters would go and meet their opponent in the middle and then jog over to shake the hand of the opposing head coach. It was a fun dance to watch.

Kennedy watched her non-starting teammates step forward and wave their hands at their families in the crowd and around the gym. The excitement in their eyes made her heart flutter a bit.

When her name was called, she looked up at the small crowd gathered for her. Her grandparents, her parents, her brothers, and Austin were all cheering. She smiled at them and waved and then waved at the rest of the crowd before trotting out to shake the hand of the Westby-Grenora player.

"Good luck," they said simultaneously. Kennedy jogged over to the opposing coach and shook her hand as well before going and fist bumping the refs.

The lineup was finished and they gathered together, swaying back and forth and yelling until she brought her hand up in the huddle and the rest of the girls did too.

"Pirates on three," she chanted. "One, two three—"

32

Epilogue

She was adjusting her cap in the mirror they had set up in Ms. O'Brien's room. She had finally done what all the other senior girls did and cut off all her hair; it barely brushed her shoulders today.

Her valedictorian speech was typed neatly and sitting on a desk. She went over and started flipping through it while Jack sat next to her and played on his phone.

"Life stories are graded," Ms. O'Brien said, handing Kennedy hers. She wandered over to Grace, who was trying heels for the first time since her surgery (though Kennedy wasn't sure she was really supposed to be doing that) and passed her own stack of papers to her.

"Good timing," Kennedy said. She flipped to the back page: 99%. "Because a 100% means there was nothing you could have changed," she thought with a laugh. She looked at the note in red underneath it. "Thank you for sharing," it said. "This is only the beginning."

She looked at her epilogue. They had been tasked with rewriting a poem about reliving their lives to fit their own life at this point, as they left high school.

Every word in Kenna's rang true.

Soon they were lining up and walking out, carrying the "candles of knowledge" through the dark gym in their black graduation gowns. She handed her candle to her brother and hugged him at the end of the aisle. She had never gotten to do this with Jessica, but she was excited to do it with Jack.

"Love you," she whispered as she made her way up the stage. Their new "Third Place State Finishers" banner hanged prominently behind the makeshift stage.

The receiving line was long. She hugged the people of the community one-by-one, thanking them for being involved in her life as they congratulated her. It was a lot like that funeral day, more than two years ago now. When she saw him, her heart stopped a bit.

Adam smiled at her. "Hey," he said.

"Hey," she answered.

"Congratulations," he told her with a smile.

"Thank you," she answered, smiling back. She noticed the girl beside him and he looked at her. "Oh," he said. "Uh, this is Zoey."

Kennedy's heart seized a little in her chest—just a pang. But she smiled. "Hi," she said. "It's so nice to meet you."

They wandered off a few moments later, and Jackson leaned forward as she waited for the next group to come up. "Thank God," he muttered. "Now maybe he'll leave you alone."

Kennedy turned and looked at him. "What?" she said.

He winked. "I like Austin better for you."

Kennedy laughed a little and looked at the next group of people. "Hi," she said. "Thank you for coming."

She was walking around the lawn the night, a beer in her hand. She didn't care if others saw her with it right now. Adam appeared, just as she knew he would. They stared at the stars in silence before she spoke.

"She's really pretty," she said.

"She is," he agreed.

She looked at him. "I'm happy for you," she said.

"Kenna," he began, but she stopped him.

"That was exactly what I needed it to be when I needed it," she answered. "And I hope it was what you needed too."

He nodded. "It was."

She smiled at him. "Then it is what it is." She reached down and squeezed his hand once last time. "Coming to spend time with us this summer?"

He nodded a little, his own beer in his hand. "Here and there," he answered.

"Then I'll see you around, Adam," she said, turning and walking away.

The next morning, she took the four-wheeler out to her sister's grave. Austin, a town kid, was hanging on for dear life on the back. "Are you sure we should be going this fast?" he asked. She laughed in response. Finally, they made it up the hill to where she was.

They walked in silence, each carrying something. He had a bouquet of roses. She had a basketball. He laid her flowers down on her gravestone and stepped back to stand next to her. This was the first time she had brought him here—the basketball hoop off to the side was a new touch her brothers had just installed at her request. A cement pad would go in later that summer so she could shoot around with her sister again.

She didn't know what the next day would bring for her or for anyone else, but in this moment, standing in front of her sister's grave, with the arms of someone who made her laugh around her, looking out over her valley, she, for once in her life, felt real and true peace.